IMAGES
of America

SILVERTON

On the Cover: Pond Monkeys, 1905. A couple of "pond monkeys" from the Roaring Twenties wrestle fresh logs into the intake of the Silver Falls Timber Company. Operating between 1912 and 1947, the mill was the economic backbone of Silverton, Oregon, for over 40 years. (Drake Brothers photograph.)

IMAGES
of America

SILVERTON

Gus Frederick

ARCADIA
PUBLISHING

ISBN 978-0-7385-7533-9

Published by Arcadia Publishing
Charleston, South Carolina

Printed in the United States of America

Library of Congress Control Number: 2011920133

For all general information, please contact Arcadia Publishing:
Telephone 843-853-2070
Fax 843-853-0044
E-mail sales@arcadiapublishing.com
For customer service and orders:
Toll-Free 1-888-313-2665

Visit us on the Internet at www.arcadiapublishing.com

This work is dedicated to my daughter, Genevieve Frederick, the first native Silvertonian of the clan, and my mother, Dorothy Janet Munson Frederick, who has been here longer than either of us!

Contents

Acknowledgments		6
Introduction		7
1.	Silverton Overview	9
2.	Civic Infrastructure	17
3.	Farm and Industry	27
4.	Schools and Education	47
5.	The Business Community	55
6.	Transportation Changes	73
7.	Music, Sports, and Theater	87
8.	Celebrations and Events	99
9.	History and the Future	117
Bibliography		126
Index		127

Acknowledgments

The citizens of Silverton do not need to be reminded of our uniqueness. We know that already. Unlike many small communities, we have maintained and celebrated our history, warts and all. Besides an active and professional volunteer historical society, many members of the founding families still live in the area and have kept our history alive.

The problem with a work like this is not a lack of material but trying to decide which images and anecdotes to use. Over the years, we have been blessed with numerous photographers—without whose work this book would not be possible. So, I would first and foremost like this book to honor the many photographers of Silverton over the years.

From the Silverton Country Historical Society (SCHS), I'd like to thank Kathy Hunter for recommending me for this project; Chris Schwab; Larry Thomas; and, especially, Carolyn Hutton for opening the doors and getting me pointed in the right direction. And, I'd like to thank Jack Hande for his encouragement by example in his *Stories of Silverton* series. Jack had gotten his old school friends and others to recount their experiences growing up in Silverton during the 1920s, 30s, and 40s. This encouraged me to hit up members of my generation for a similar endeavor.

I am indebted to the family of the late Quentin Estell, especially Mylrea, who allowed me into the piles of historical Silverton ephemera her father had collected over the years. And to my Navy buddy, the late Rick Ernst, of the multigenerational Cooley and Morley clans. Rick knew where all the town's skeletons from most any era are closeted. And, of course, I am thankful for Curt Almquist, my former roommate from the North Water Street Boardinghouse and current town photographer, for access to the Bill Hanson collection, as well as his own family's material.

A special thanks goes to Barb Lokting of the Geer family. Her genealogical background covering this unique Oregon family was invaluable in helping piece things together. Additionally, Dave Hegeman and the crew at the Oregon State Library photograph archives, City Manager Bryan Cosgrove, and Silverton mayor Stu Rasmussen were all helpful when it came to filling a few photograph gaps. And I am grateful for Paul and Sue Nida, my next-door neighbors, for last-minute proofs and encouragement.

I would also like to thank my editors at Arcadia, new mom Donna Libert and Tiffany Frary, who picked up the messy ball after Donna left for maternity leave. Finally, I wish to acknowledge and thank the citizens of Silverton—past, present and future—for their part in making history!

Introduction

Unlike most small communities in Western Oregon in the 19th century, Silverton was laid out pretty much around its local environment. Instead of the rigid north-south grid of the township and range system, in 1854, Silverton's founding mother, Polly Crandall Coon, decided to plan the town around a large old Oregon white oak tree. She named the new town Silverton after Silver Creek, which flowed by the old oak several hundred yards to the south. The tree had been a meeting place along the Santiam trail for the local Native Americans of the area. Indeed, they continued to use it as such, even after the town grew up around it.

An earlier community known as Milford had previously been started several miles upstream from the current downtown. Milford was not platted and was soon abandoned. Ai Coolidge, who later joined with Jake McClaine to create Silverton's first bank, had a store in Milford at the time. Coolidge physically moved his store from Milford to the newly platted community of Silverton. The move took several months, and during this time, the store remained open, even while its location changed.

As the town grew, so did its influence and importance. One year before statehood, Silverton hosted the first convention of the then-new Republican Party of Oregon. And through the influence of many of its citizens, they ensured that the new state of Oregon would enter the Union as a free state without slavery, albeit with some ugly compromises, including black exclusion laws.

After the Civil War and the arrival of the railroad, Silverton was literally connected to the world. The economy of those times was, for the most part, localized. As a whole, the community was self-sufficient for the majority of life's necessities—and the rest could be ordered from the Montgomery Ward's catalog for later arrival by rail.

During the latter part of the 19th century, Silverton became a major exporter of processed grain products. The Fischer Flouring Mill on South Water Street provided local farmers with a ready outlet to the world. As more and more rail lines appeared elsewhere, Silverton's usefulness in that arena waned.

Meanwhile, a new industry took hold: timber. Silverton had long been home to sawmills over the years, but the turn of the 20th century ushered in an era of industrial timber operations, including Silverton Lumber Company in 1906 and then the much larger Silver Falls Timber Company. These mills kept the town humming for half a century until the big logs ran out. The year 1947 saw the closing of Silver Falls Timber Company and another shift in Silverton's economics.

The postwar boom saw cheap petroleum, improved roads, and a growing society. The ease of transport coupled with cheap fuel caused another economic shift in Silverton. Most of its traditional self-sufficiency gave way to more imported goods and services. With meager employment options, the demographics shifted to that of a bedroom community, or commuter town, for nearby Salem and, to a lesser extent, Portland.

Like many small communities, Silverton saw its historic downtown area fade in importance as more fringe-belt businesses sprang up along the edge of town, such as shopping centers and various industrial operations. In spite of this, Silvertonians remain a proud and independent lot. Downtown, while diminished, has not gone away. Indeed, a visitor from 100 years ago would have no problem recognizing the Silverton from their era.

This community of just under 10,000 souls is actually quite diverse as small rural towns go, stemming from a unique community background that not only tolerated different beliefs and ideas but also embraced them. One indicator of this is the Silverton Kiwanis Club's church directory sign at the entrance to town that lists two dozen different Christian denominations.

Probably most important in regard to this particular book is the fact that Silverton has also been blessed with a number of fine photographers over the years—both professional and amateur. This includes James A. Balch, who started a daguerreotype gallery in 1857, operating it for several years after. He later relocated to Brownsville and then up to Lyle, Washington, in the Columbia River Gorge. His son Frederic Homer Balch was the author of one of Oregon's first published historical novels, *The Bridge of the Gods*.

Next on the scene was William "Bill" Jones, who opened a gallery on Main Street in the 1880s. He was also instrumental in the initial publication of the *Silverton Appeal*, allegedly catching the first issue as it flew off the press. He relocated to Aberdeen, Washington, in 1904, selling his business to June and Emory Drake. Many of the images in this edition are from Bill Jones. Members of the Jones family are still involved in the field of photography.

The Drake brothers quickly filled the vacuum created when Jones left. In particular, June Drake took it upon himself to document his world. This world was Silverton from the first half of the 20th century. Many of the images not from Bill Jones are those of June Drake. Emory Drake left the business in 1908, after the first studio burned down. June kept the moniker, however.

June Drake's legacy extends beyond photographs of Silverton, as he mounted a one-man lobbying effort to have the area surrounding Silver Falls protected and declared a park. Through his personal intervention, coupled with his dynamic images of the Silver Falls group, he convinced a Depression-era Oregon state legislature to name Silver Falls as Oregon's largest state park.

In the 1950s, another Bill came on the scene. Bill Hanson filled the shoes left by the aging June Drake. His *Silverton Appeal* "Business of the Week" portrait series captured the citizens of the day in their element. He also shot many of the aerial photographs in this book, as well as most of the Silverton and Oregon centennial celebration images.

Over the years, many other photographers have also contributed to our memories. The Almquist family, in particular, has spawned generations of images. Curtis Almquist currently manages Almquist Studios in the tradition of Hanson, Drake, and Jones.

Curt's uncle Paul Almquist also was an advanced amateur and an old friend of the author of this book. Several of Paul's images from Silverton's centennial and various shots taken by Curt's grandfather T.P. "Trix" Heidenstrom are included here.

And, of course, there are many images of photographers who were not identified, but I felt that they would fit with the theme of this work.

Silverton, like many other communities, is going through yet another transition in economic structure. One of the key manifestations of this phenomenon is a greater emphasis on re-localization and sustainability. The ever-growing selection of local organic produce at our supermarkets and the birth, or rather rebirth, of the Silverton farmers' market drives this point home.

Change is inevitable. And change will come to Silverton, as it has before. What that change will entail is for the future to tell. But no matter what changes occur, or what happens in the world, Silverton will remain Silverton. As Homer Davenport wrote in the preface to his autobiography, "That's why I love it so dearly and that's why it's yet home to me."

—Gus Frederick
Silverton, Oregon

One

Silverton Overview

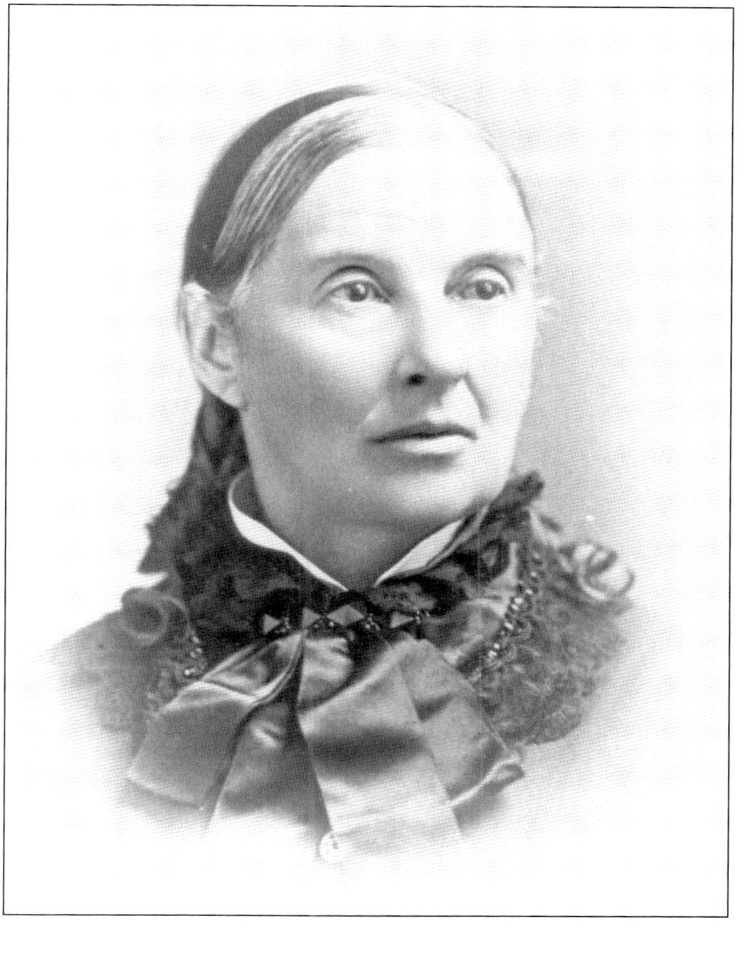

Silverton's Founding Mother, Polly Crandall Coon Price. In the early 1850s, Beaford Smith built a sawmill on Silver Creek, about where city hall is today. Next to this new mill was the Donation Land Claim of Polly Coon, widow of Thomas L. Coon, who created and registered the first town plat for Silverton, Oregon, with the Marion County surveyor's office in 1854. She started selling lots, and the rest is history. The following year, in 1855, she married Steven Price, a local sawmill owner. (Courtesy of SCHS.)

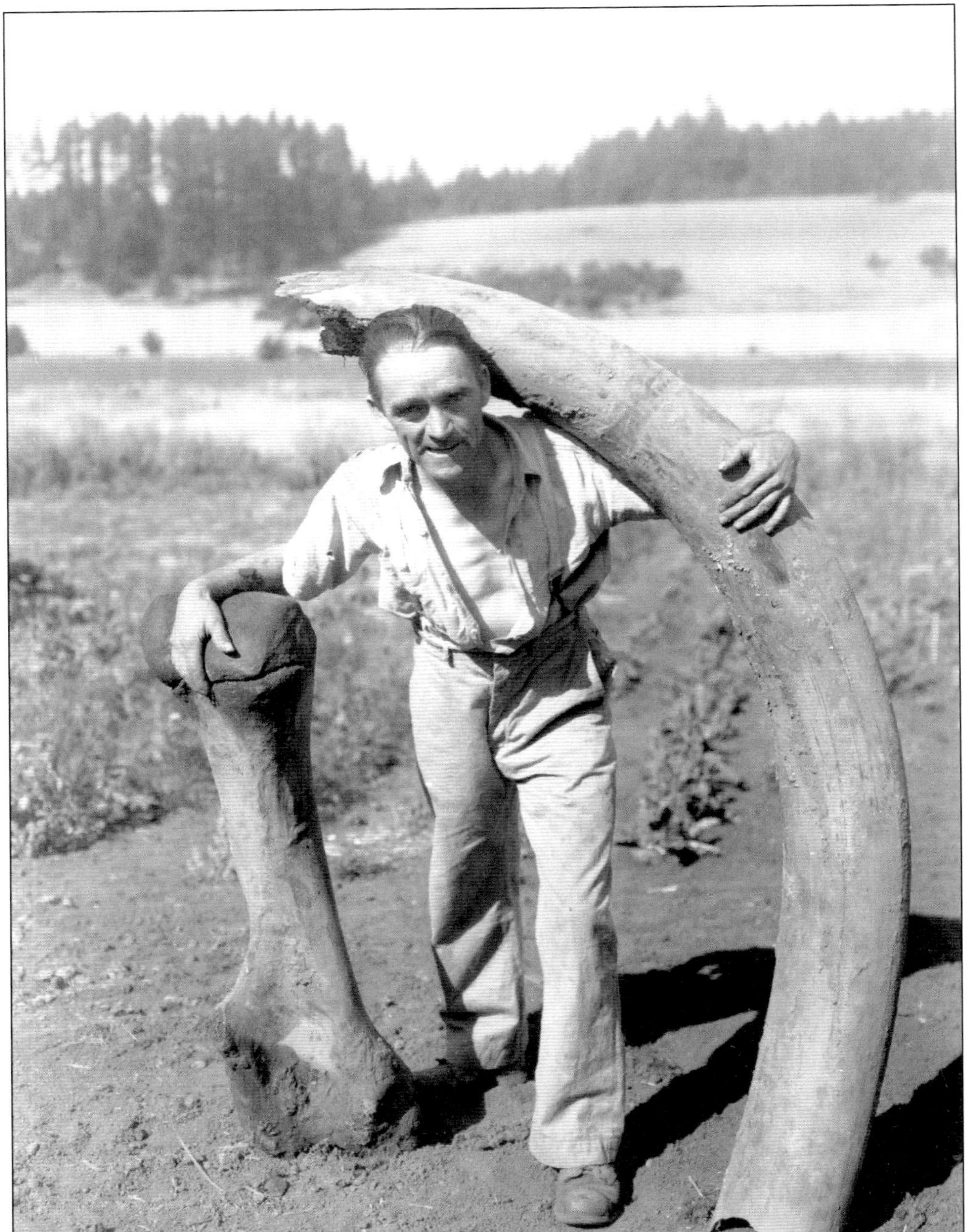

MAMMOTH BONES IN EVANS VALLEY. In 1940, Evans Valley farmer Paul Pinson was digging an irrigation pond in a swamp for his flower farm west of town when he uncovered a huge ivory mammoth tusk. Eventually, Pinson dug up the bones of numerous other prehistoric creatures, most likely from the end of the last Ice Age. It is possible that the large number of bones found in Evans Valley may have been washed in by one or more of the Ice Age floods, which inundated the area under hundreds of feet of water and built up the soil of the Willamette Valley from the erosion of Central Washington. (Drake Brothers photograph; courtesy of SCHS.)

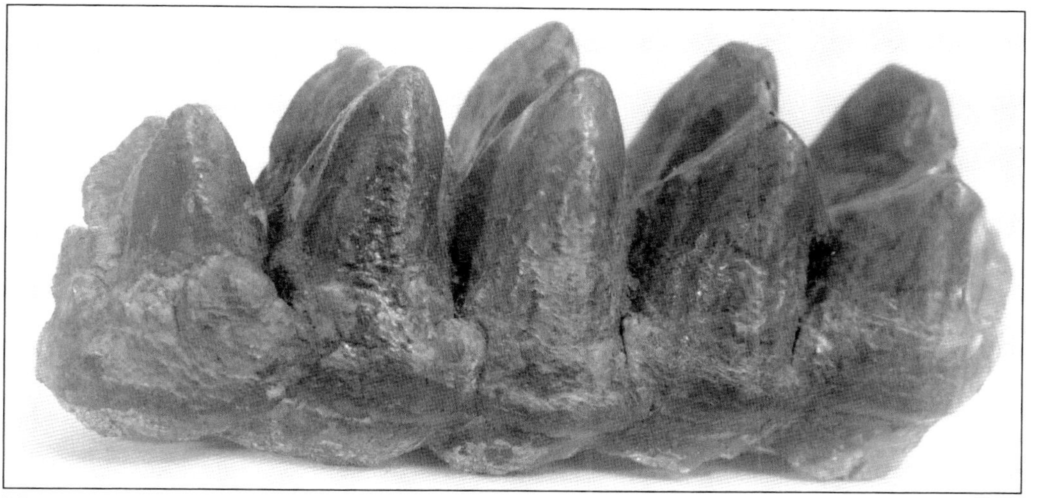

Mastodon Teeth, 1946. Pinson displayed the items, for 50¢ a peek, until the remains apparently crumbled to dust over time because they were not properly preserved. Soon the onset of World War II focused attention elsewhere, and further excavations were not undertaken. Ice Age remains had been found previously in 1905 on the same farm by then owner Bernt Storlie. He kept it a secret for years until a young June Drake discovered portions of an ivory tusk while hiking nearby. Storlie told Drake that he kept it a secret so that his farm would not be disturbed. A similar find in nearby Woodburn has become quite a scientific and educational endeavor. (Drake Brothers photograph; courtesy of SCHS.)

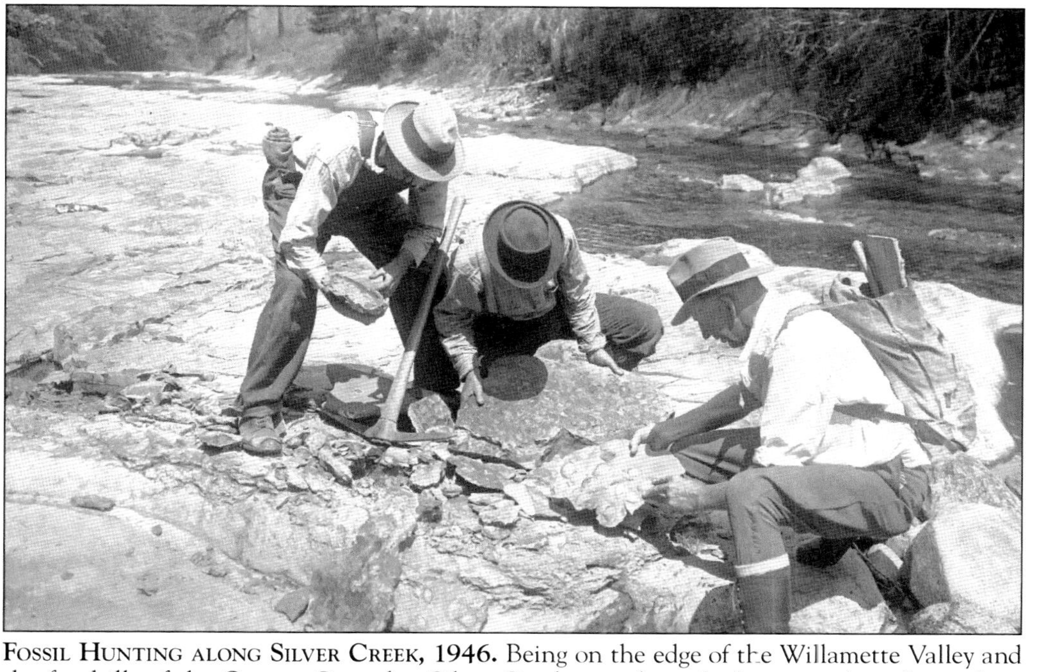

Fossil Hunting along Silver Creek, 1946. Being on the edge of the Willamette Valley and the foothills of the Oregon Cascades, Silver Creek cuts through the young lava flows, deep into the much older sedimentary layers that were formed when the Silverton Country was under an ocean over 50 million years ago. It is quite easy to uncover fossil shells from this area. (Drake Brothers photograph; courtesy of SCHS.)

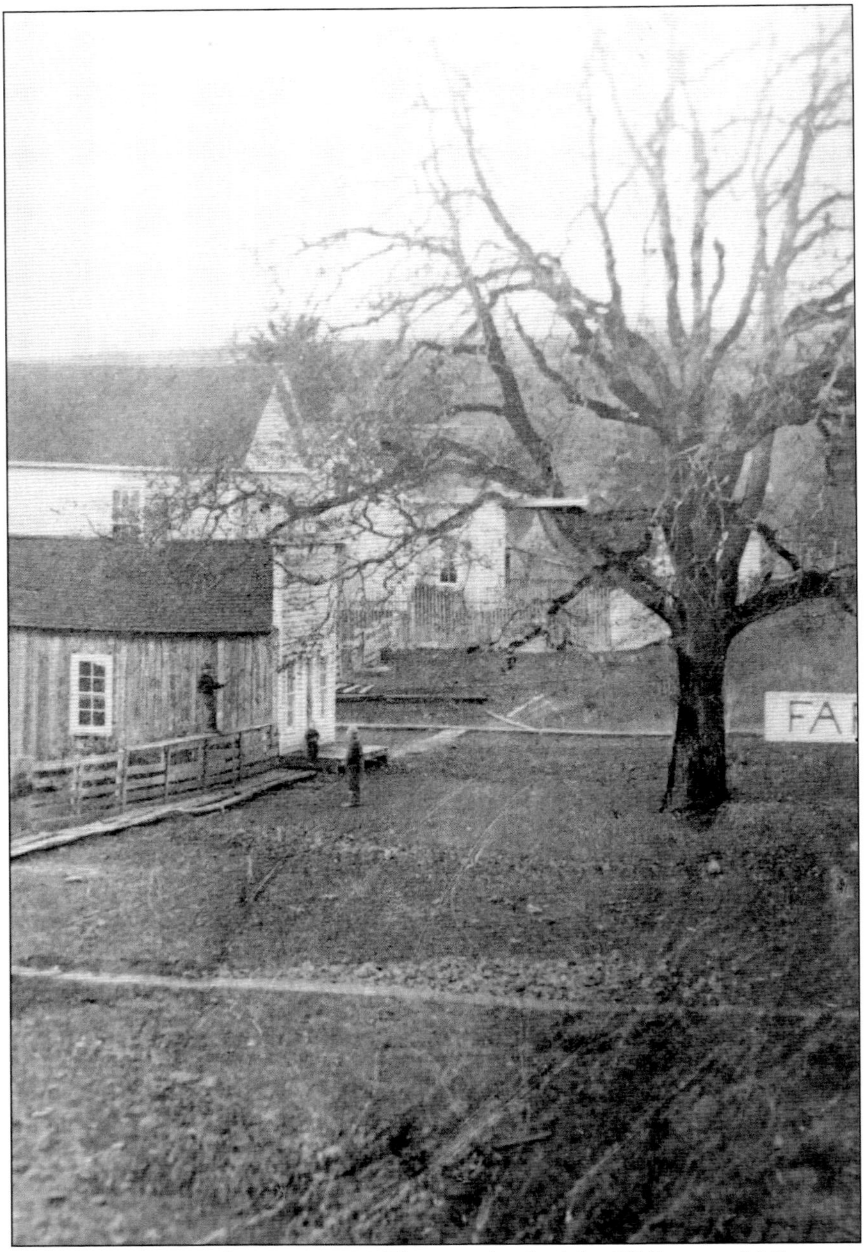

OLD OAK TREE AND MAIN STREET, 1866. The grassland of the Willamette Valley gave way to open Oregon white oak savannas, which in turn transitioned to dense forests of Douglas fir, cedar, and hemlock on the lower sloops of the Cascade foothills. The city of Silverton was intentionally platted around one of these large white oak trees. Prior to the arrival of Europeans, the Santiam clan of the Kalapooian peoples had used it as a longtime meeting place and continued to do so as the town grew up around it. The original pioneers appreciated that fact. Sadly, not much is known of the customs and beliefs of these ancient peoples. Those few that survived the pandemics of small pox and other diseases were forcibly relocated elsewhere and stripped of their land and culture. (Courtesy of SCHS.)

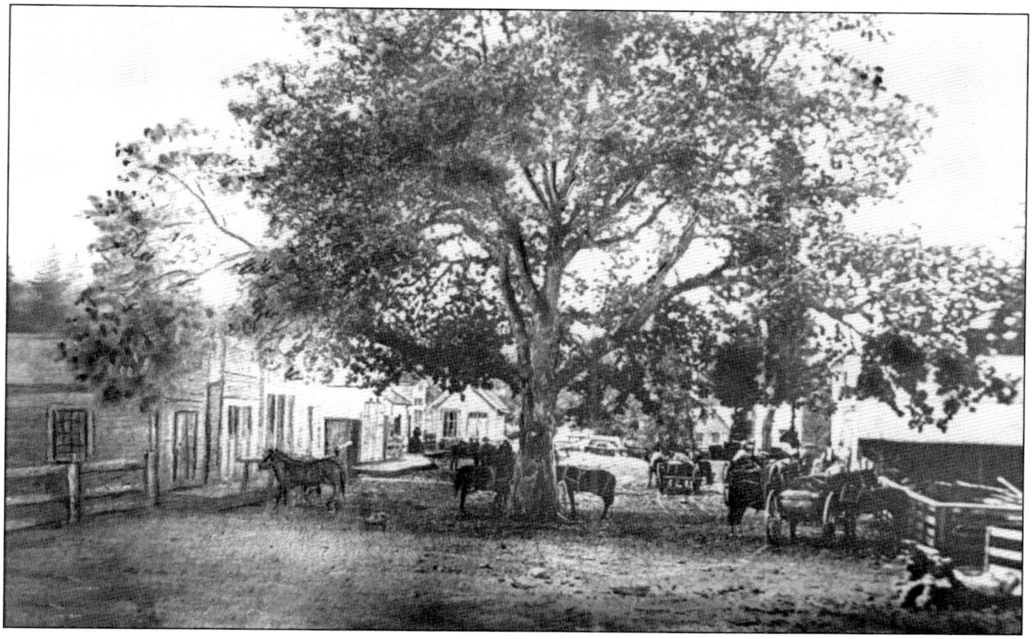

The Old Oak Tree, 1868 and 1890. Homer C. Davenport stated the following in the preface to *The Country Boy*: "The giant oak, the tree that had the beautiful stories to tell, was voted 'guilty' and was slain. That evening, as its huge branches were divided among the town's people, a small party of big men gathered at the stump of the tree. They were mad men and sad men as they realized that Silverton had to change, that a newer element with higher collars and smaller hats was in command. Many of their best and bravest citizens had already gone beyond the call of human voice, others would soon follow, and the tree, being one of them, had also, made obeisance to the demand of society, fashion, and wealth." (Both, courtesy of SCHS.)

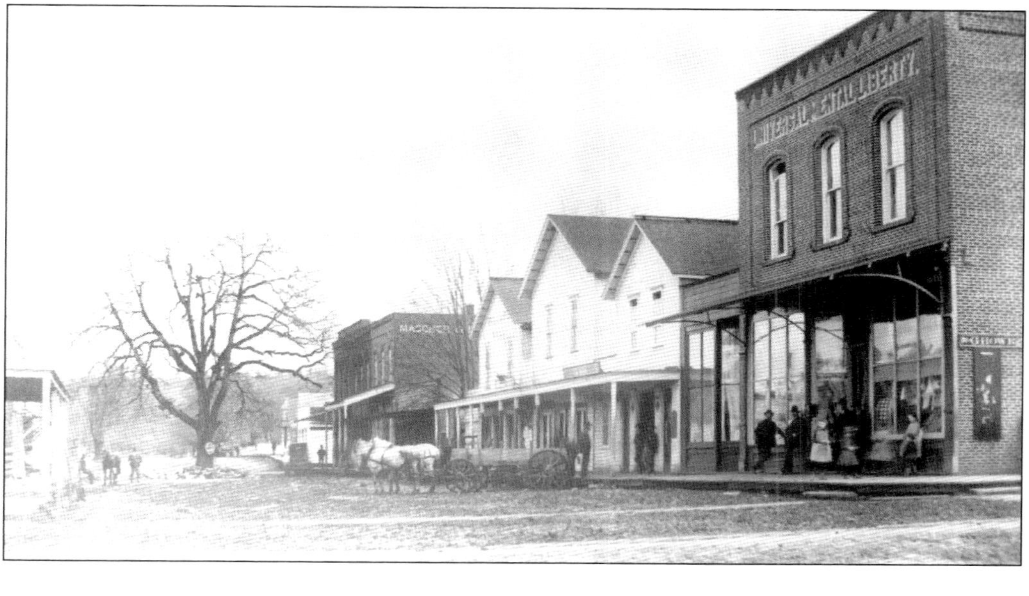

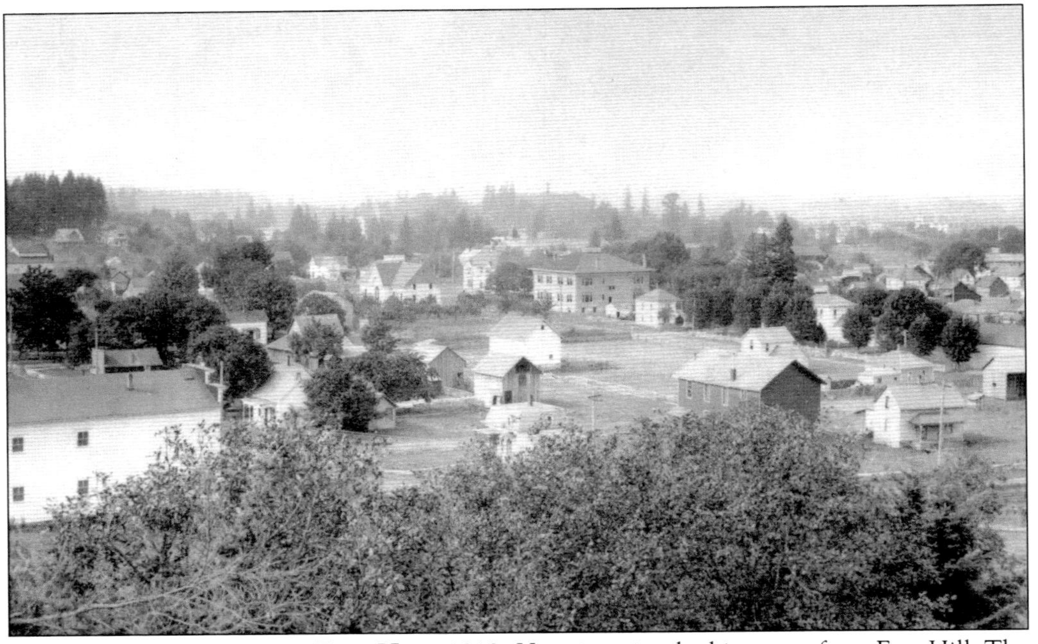

Looking Downtown from East Hill, 1912. Here is a view looking west from East Hill. The large building on the left is the American Legion Hall, now Oak Street Church. The large building to its right is the original Silverton schoolhouse built in 1866. It remains today as the oldest surviving structure in Silverton. It was rotated 90 degrees to its current orientation several years after this image was taken. (Drake Brothers photograph; courtesy of SCHS.)

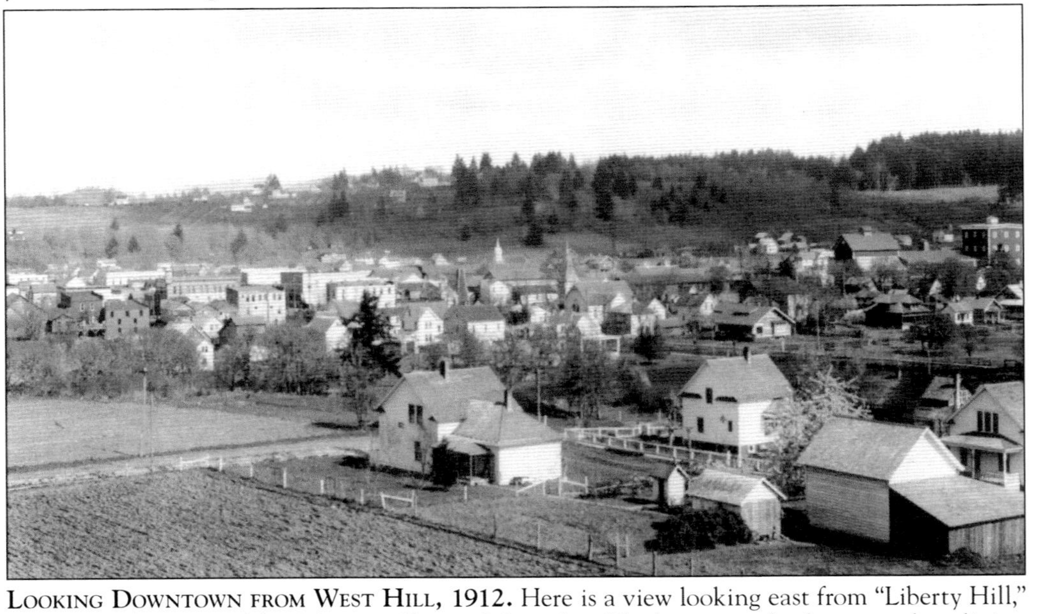

Looking Downtown from West Hill, 1912. Here is a view looking east from "Liberty Hill," the current location of the Silverton Hospital Complex. The houses in the foreground are lining Welsh Street. The downtown business core is in the middle of the left-hand side of the photograph. Look closely to make out the pointed top of the Wolf Building's water tank. (Drake Brothers photograph; courtesy of SCHS.)

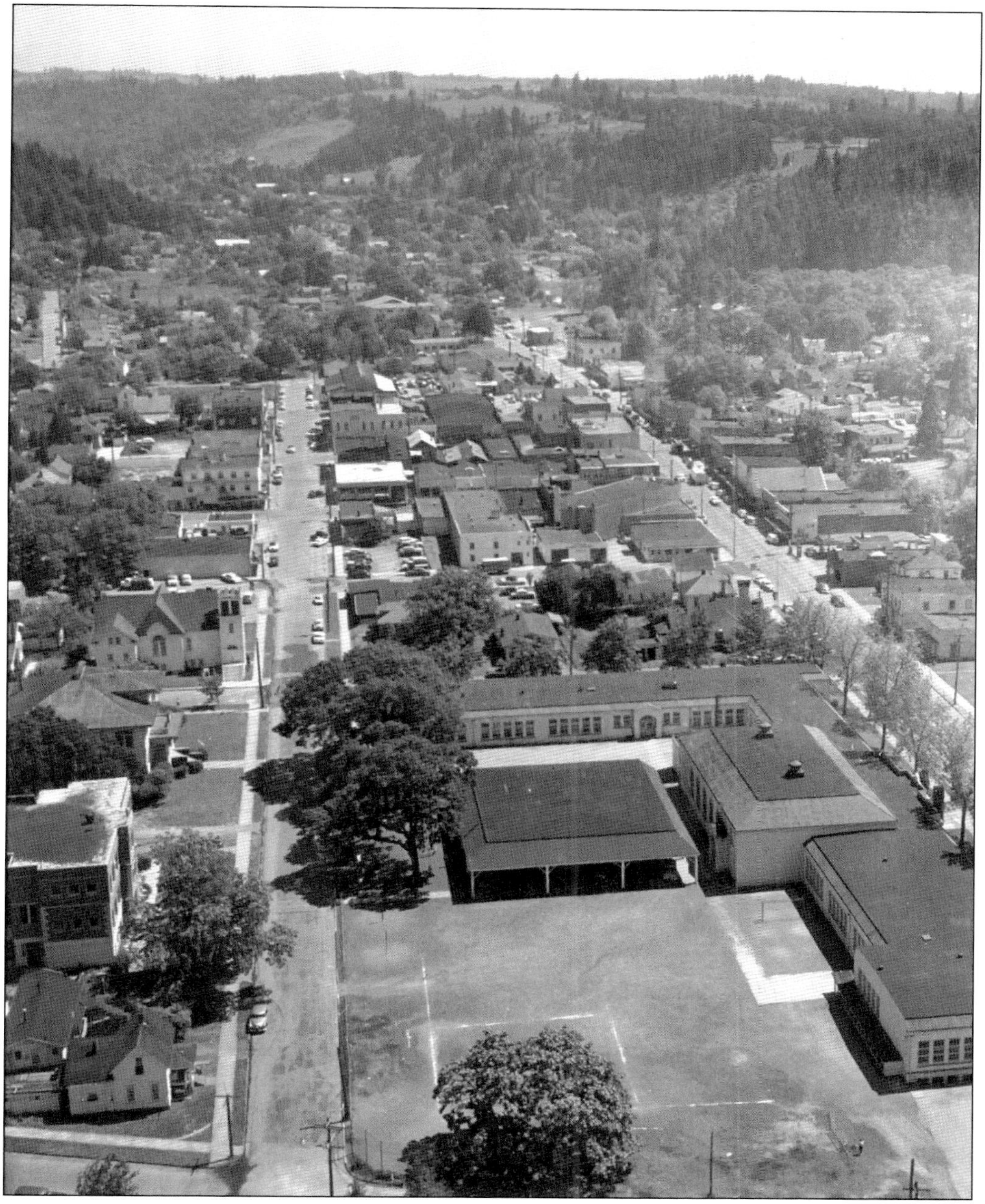

LOOKING SOUTH, 1957. With Eugene Field School in the foreground, this low oblique aerial view looking south shows the Silver Creek Canyon. The school, built in 1922, sits between First and North Water Streets. The school, which is still in use, now boasts a high-speed Internet connection to the Silver Falls School District's wide-area network. (Madelyn Studios photograph; courtesy of SCHS.)

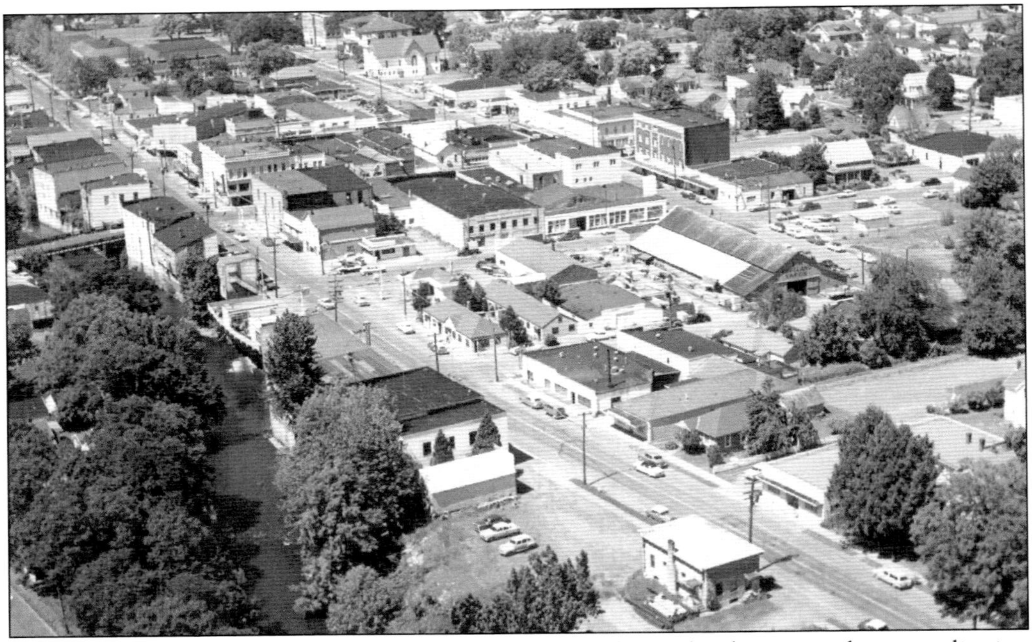

LOOKING NORTH, 1957. This low oblique aerial view shows the downtown business district. The small block building in the immediate foreground is the only remaining structure from the Fischer Flouring Mill. Now known as the Fischer Building, it is available to rent from the city for special events. City hall is next door, and Silver Creek is to the left. (Madelyn Studios photograph; courtesy of SCHS.)

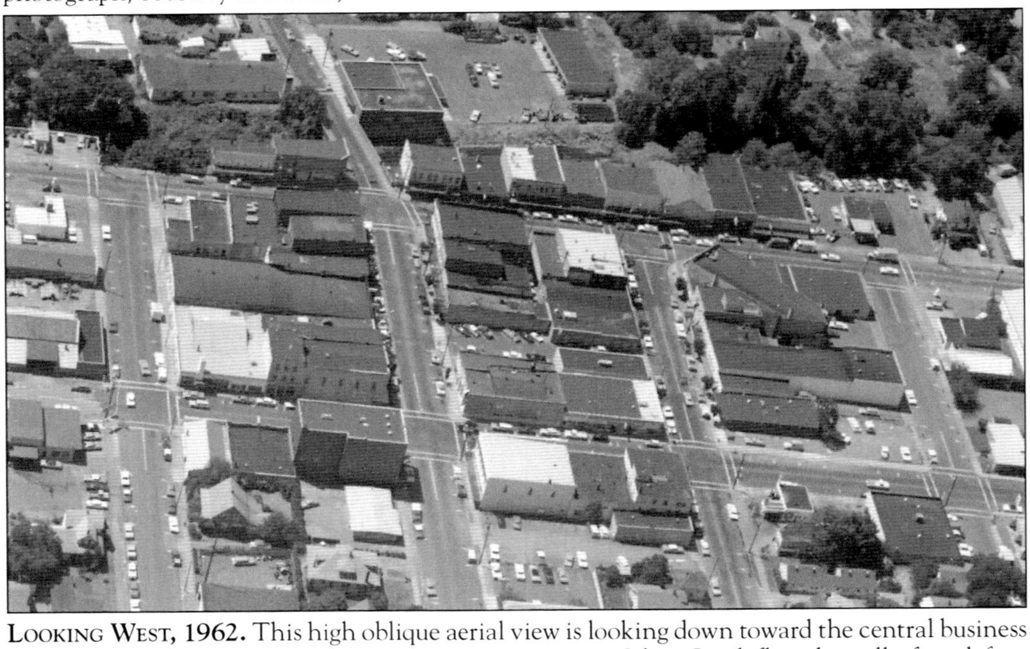

LOOKING WEST, 1962. This high oblique aerial view is looking down toward the central business district. The road running down the center is Main Street. Silver Creek flows laterally, from left to right, behind Water Street. The old oak tree was in the middle of East Main Street, just above the intersection of Main and First Streets. (Bill Hanson photograph; courtesy of Almquist Studios.)

Two

Civic Infrastructure

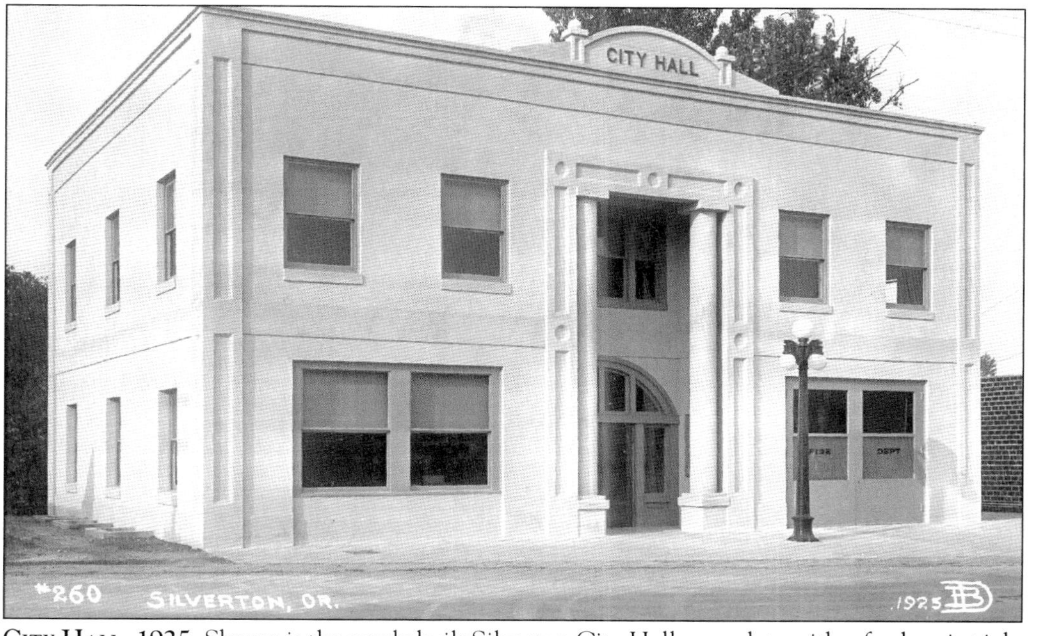

City Hall, 1925. Shown is the newly built Silverton City Hall, complete with a fresh paint job. The structure was expanded years later, and the fire department relocated to its own building in the 1980s. (Drake Brothers photograph; courtesy of SCHS.)

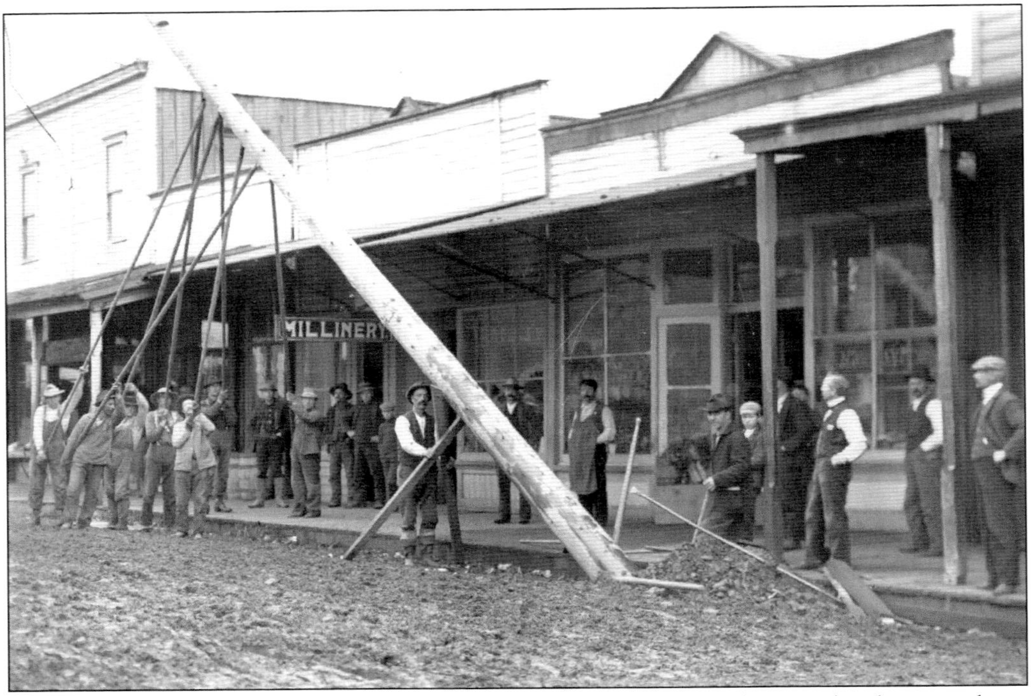

Installing Utility Poles, 1890s. Silverton was an early adopter of new technologies and was finally wired to the outside world via the original binary telecommunications media, the telegraph. Electricity from a local hydropower plant and an interurban telephone network soon followed. (Courtesy of SCHS.)

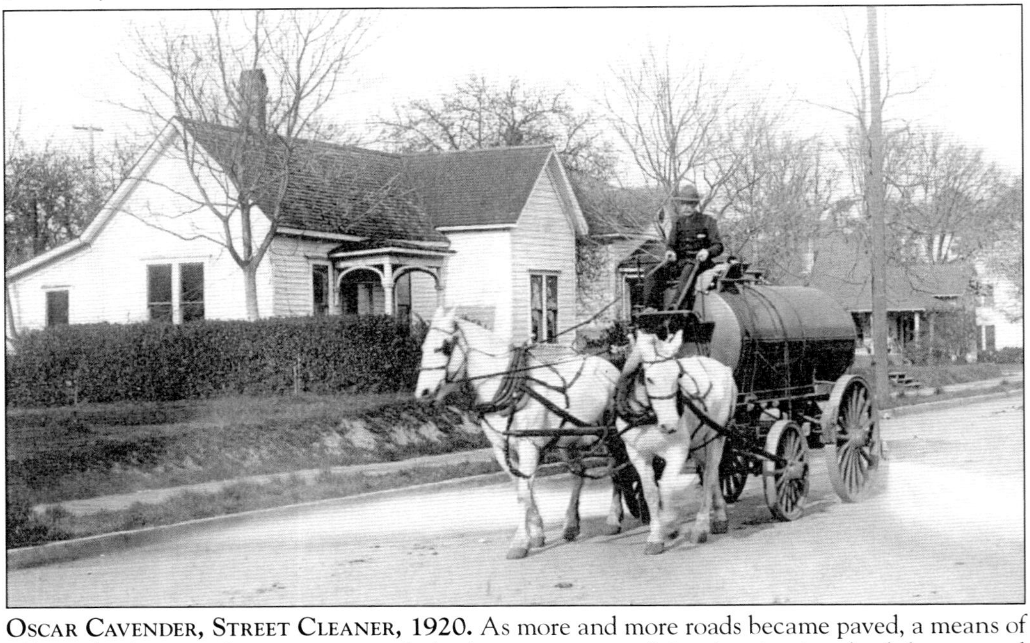

Oscar Cavender, Street Cleaner, 1920. As more and more roads became paved, a means of efficiently cleaning them was required. At this point, most of the cleaning involved the removal of "horse exhaust." (Courtesy of SCHS.)

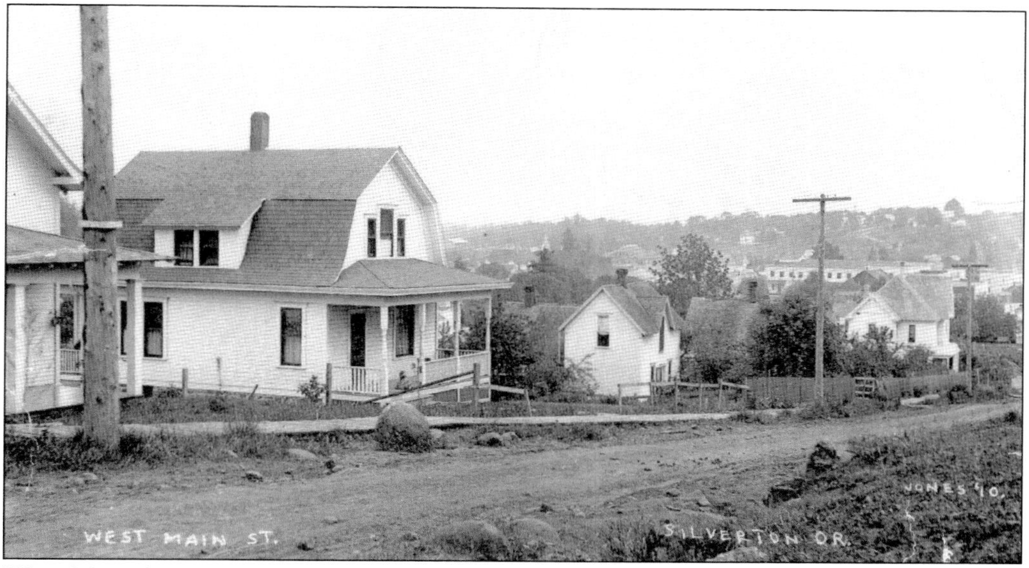

WEST MAIN STREET, LOOKING EAST, 1910. As Silverton expanded and more homes were built, the city recognized a need for careful planning of future development. This view on West Main Street was taken close to the corner of Center Street. Over 100 years later, these houses are still here, but the street is now paved. (Drake Brothers photograph; courtesy of SCHS.)

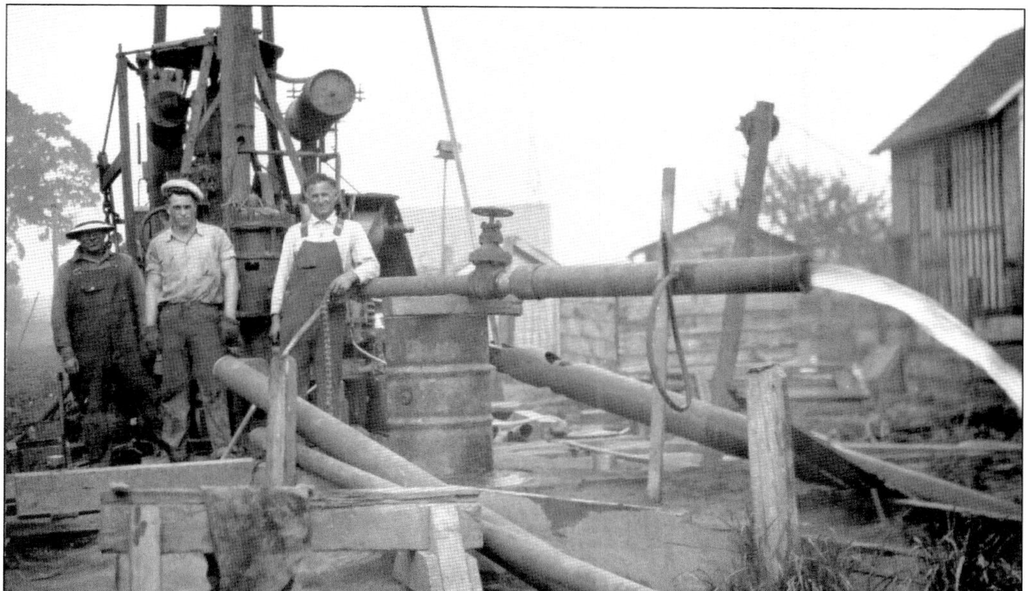

SILVERTON'S FIRST WATER WELL, 1936. By 1910, pollution had made Silver Creek's water undrinkable. Over the next several decades, the city and the Silver Falls Timber Company pursued various ways to bring cleaner water to a growing town. In the 1930s, the city drilled at a site chosen by a geologic consulting firm, but it was a dry hole. Next, a local water witch was hired and picked a spot near the end of Norway Street. This new location provided close to half a million gallons per day. However, the water required extensive treatment to remove dissolved minerals. It was capped for use in emergencies only. (Courtesy of SCHS.)

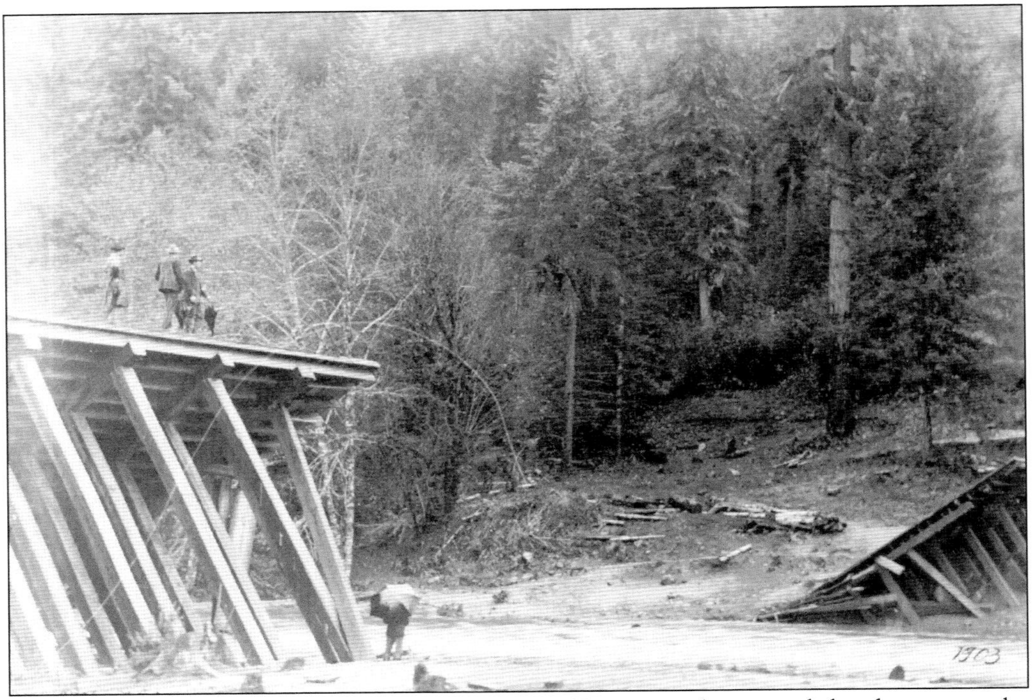

POWER PLANT DAM UNDER CONSTRUCTION, 1903. To create a big enough head to power the hydroelectric generator, a wooden dam was constructed across Silver Creek. With the then-plentiful timber, everything was made of wood. (Courtesy of SCHS.)

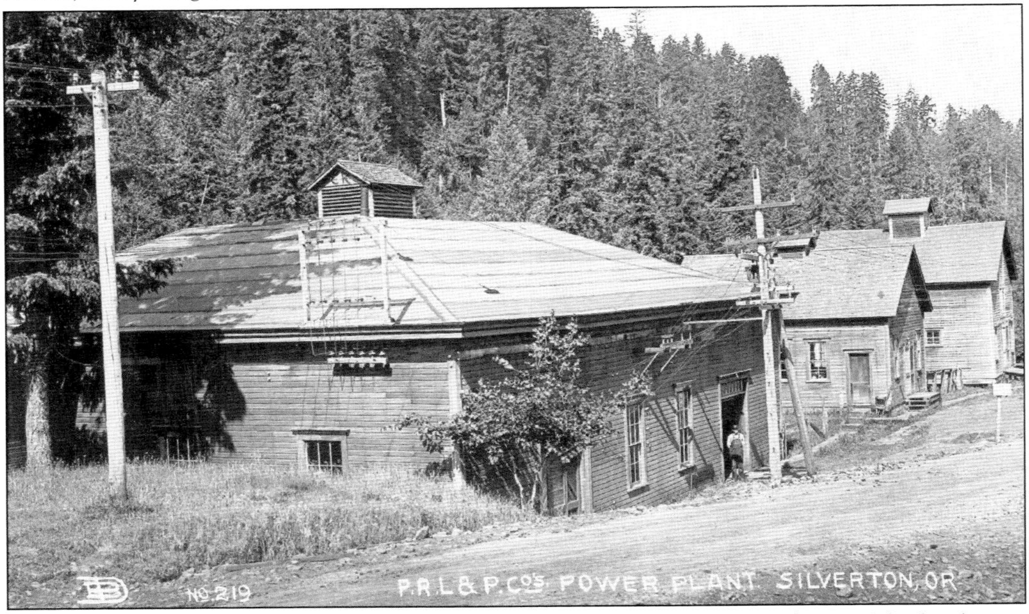

PRL&PC POWER PLANT, 1914. Clyde Ramsey stands in the doorway to Silverton's hydroelectric plant. Started by Percy Brown, it was sold to the Portland Railroad Light and Power Company. Brown then went on to build and run Silverton's first interurban telephone network. (Drake Brothers photograph; courtesy of SCHS.)

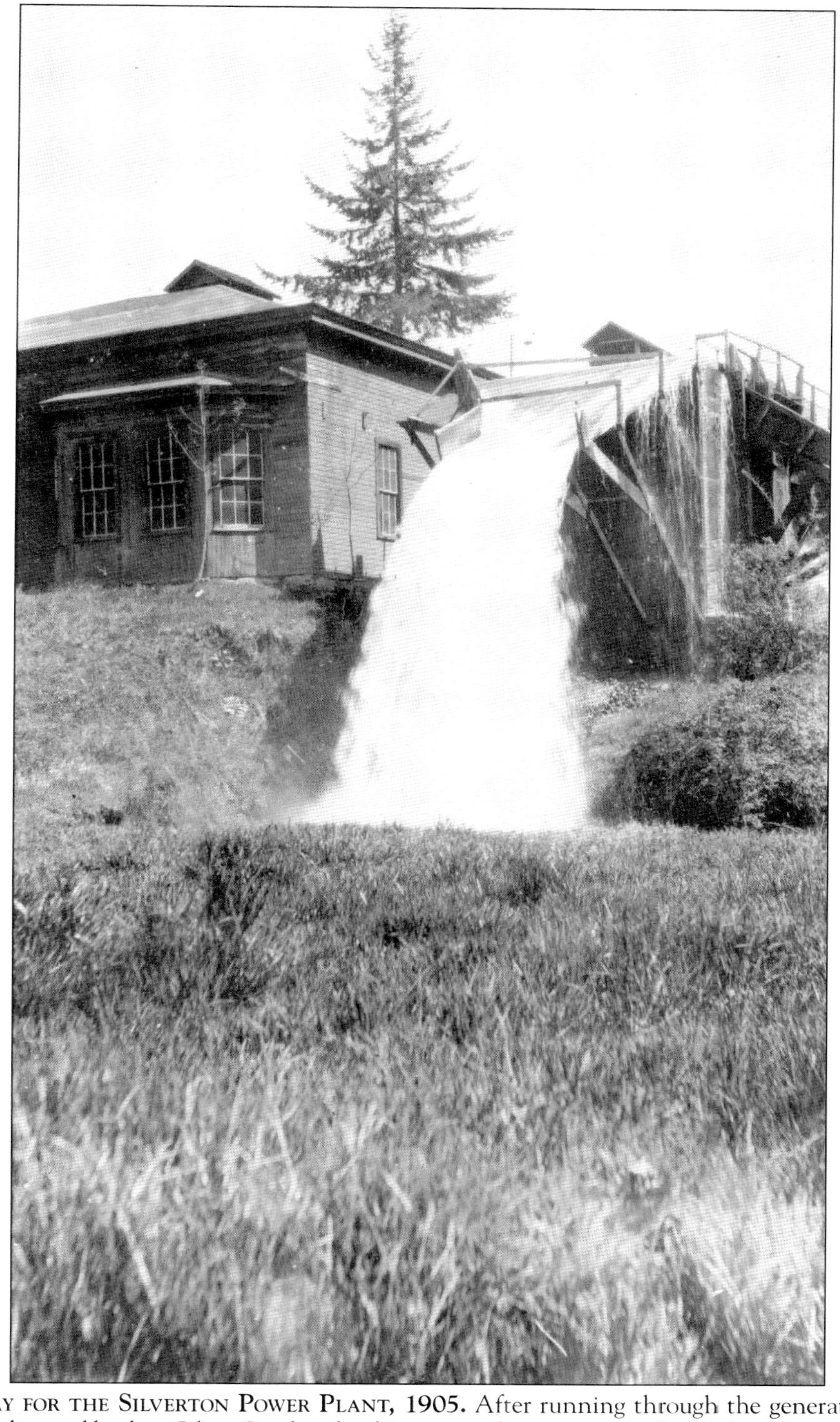

SPILLWAY FOR THE SILVERTON POWER PLANT, 1905. After running through the generator, the water is diverted back to Silver Creek to lend its energy downstream to the Fischer Flouring Mill. (Courtesy of SCHS.)

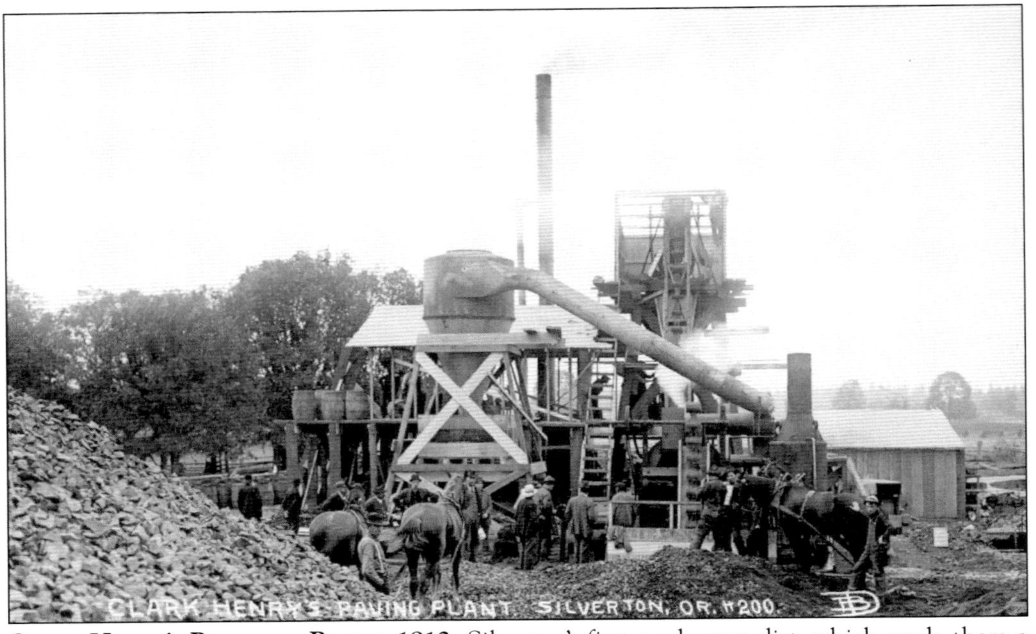

CLARK HENRY'S PAVEMENT PLANT, 1912. Silverton's first roads were dirt, which made them a bit tricky to deal with in the winter. In the early part of the 20th century, macadam streets were becoming popular. Macadam involved mixing layers of rock with tar or asphalt. This appears to be such an operation. (Drake Brothers photograph; courtesy of SCHS.)

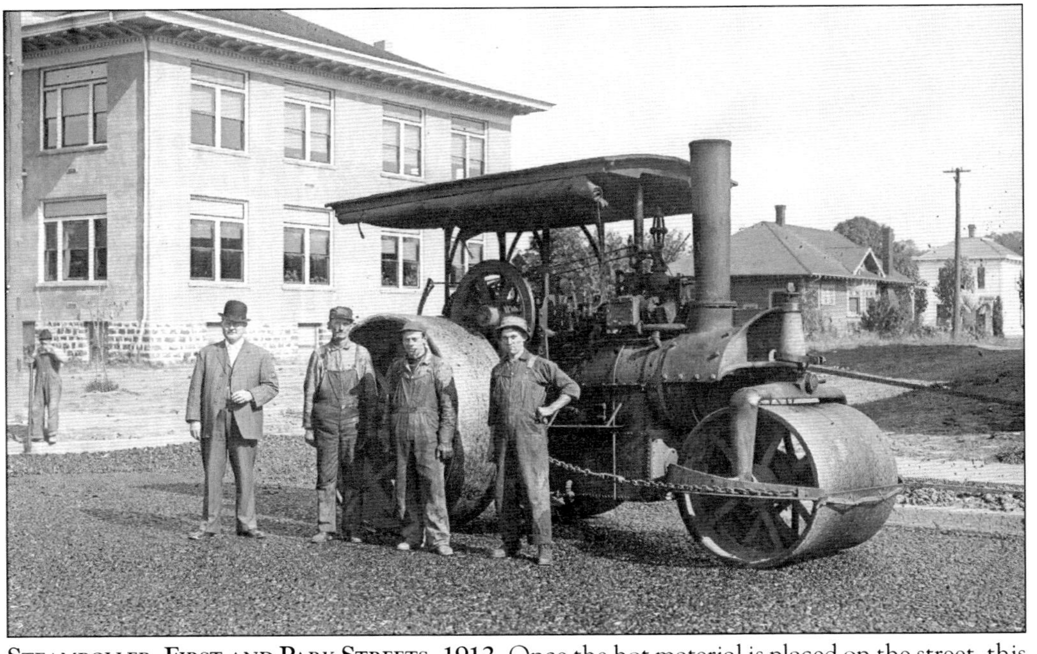

STEAMROLLER, FIRST AND PARK STREETS, 1912. Once the hot material is placed on the street, this large steamroller would compress the mixture. It would cool and harden into a smooth surface. (Drake Brothers photograph; courtesy of SCHS.)

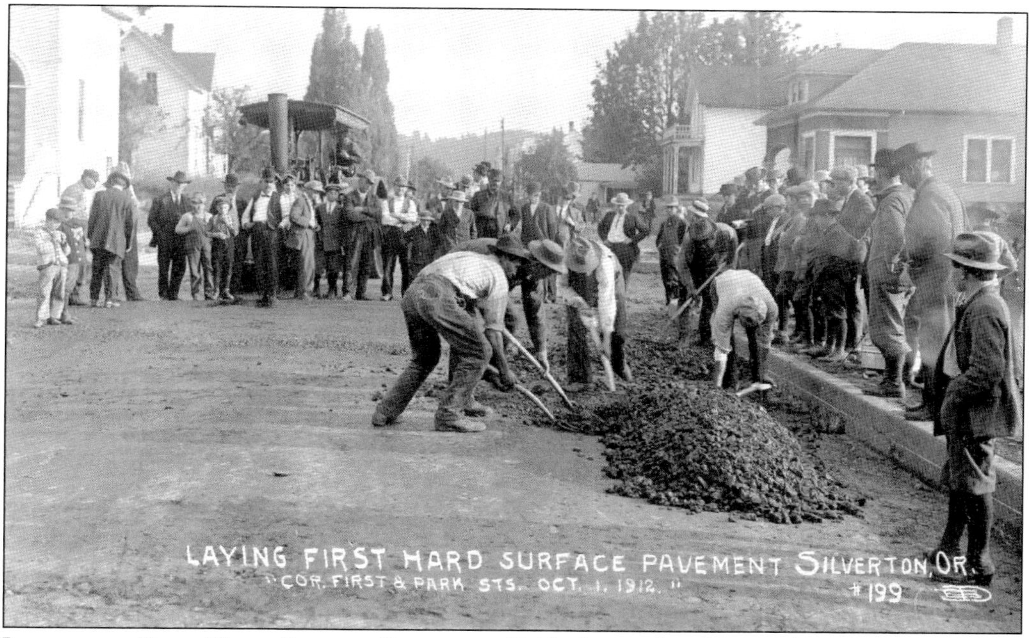

LAYING THE FIRST HARD SURFACE PAVEMENT, 1912. A crowd gathers at the corner of First and Park Streets to watch the laying of the first hard, durable pavement. (Drake Brothers photograph; courtesy of SCHS.)

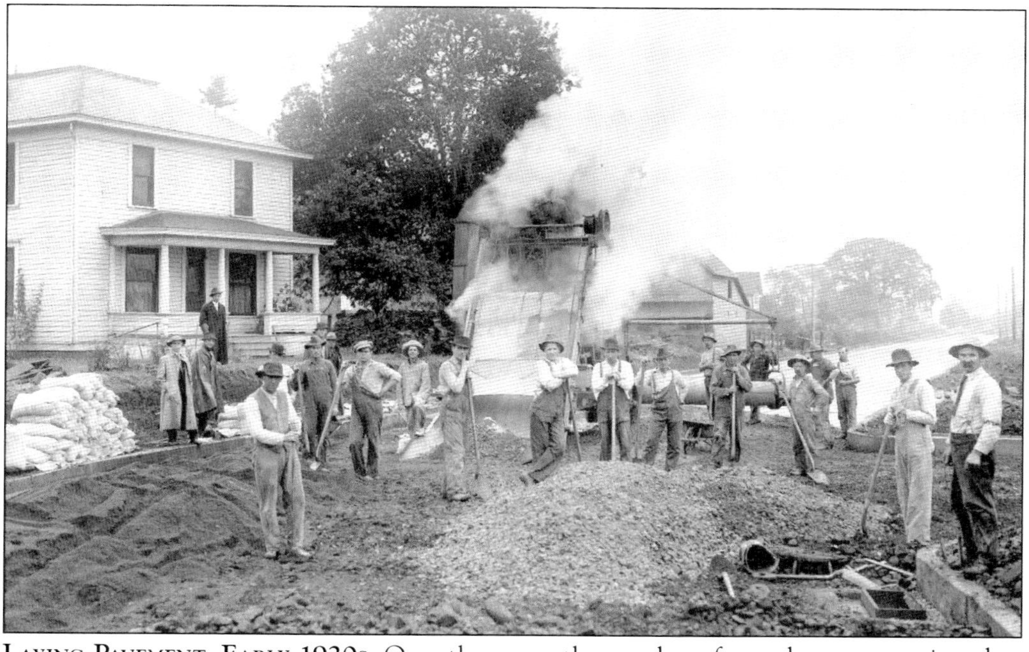

LAYING PAVEMENT, EARLY 1920S. Over the years, the number of paved streets continued to increase. Here is the intersection of McClaine and James Streets. The house on the left now has a large tree in front of it, and a car wash is across the street. Standing second from the right is George Almquist. To the left of the dumper is T.P. Trix Heidenstrom. (Drake Brothers photograph; courtesy of SCHS.)

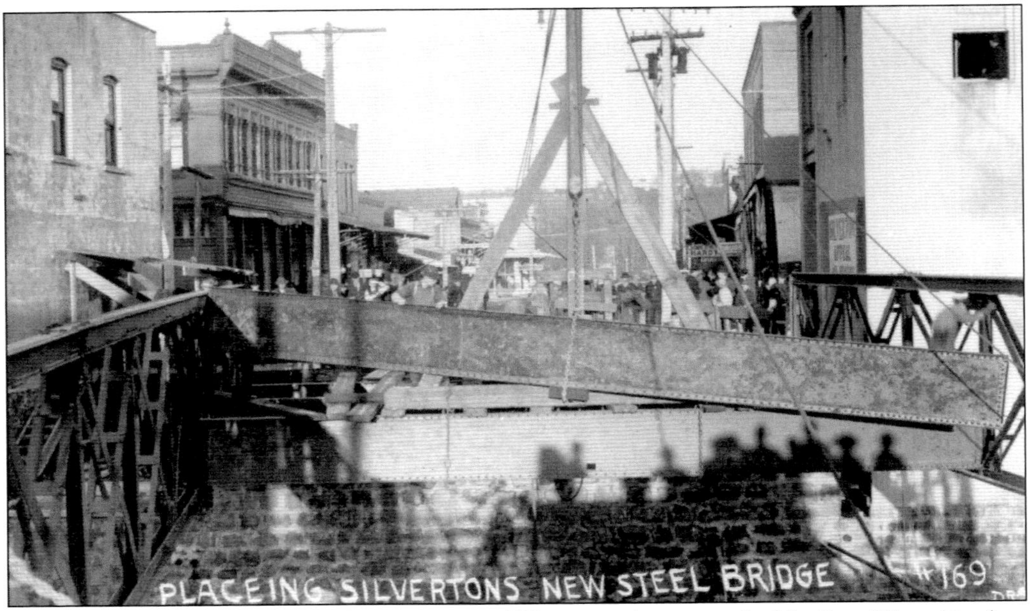

PLACING BEAMS FOR THE NEW BRIDGE, 1910. When people got tired of fording Silver Creek, a covered bridge was built to extend Main Street across the creek. At the time, this was the most efficient type of bridge, as the covering somewhat protected the structure from the elements. By 1910, the old Main Street Bridge was beginning to show its age. Other construction materials were now available via rail, so it was decided to replace the bridge with a modern steel-truss structure. (Drake Brothers photograph; courtesy of SCHS.)

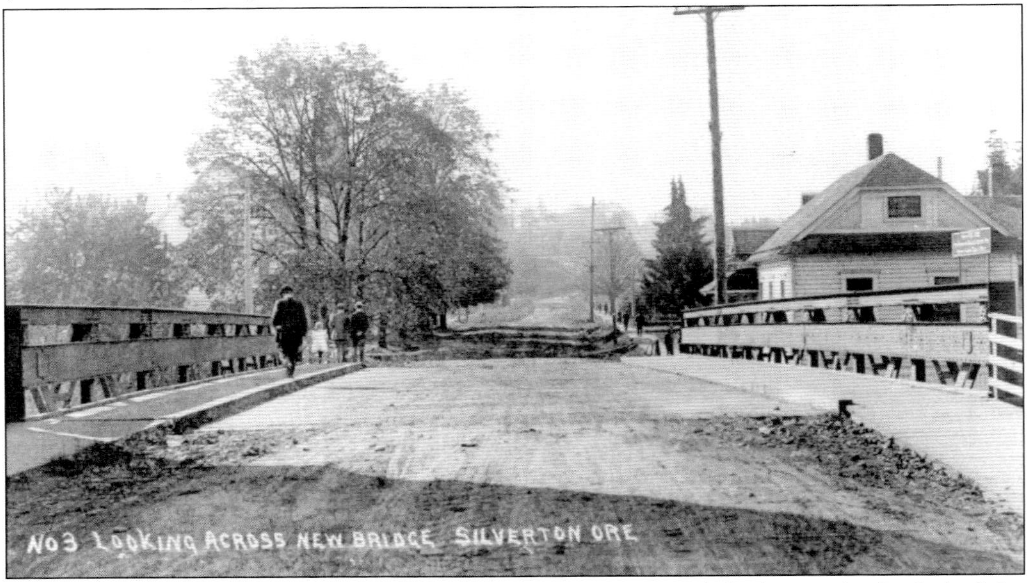

THE NEW BRIDGE OVER SILVER CREEK AT MAIN STREET, 1910. While the new bridge lacked the charm of the old, it provided a very utilitarian role in the continued growth of the community. Across the bridge, on the right, is the future site of Percy Brown's Interurban Telephone Company, with dentist J.W. Welch's current office on the top floor of the building. (Drake Brothers photograph; courtesy of SCHS.)

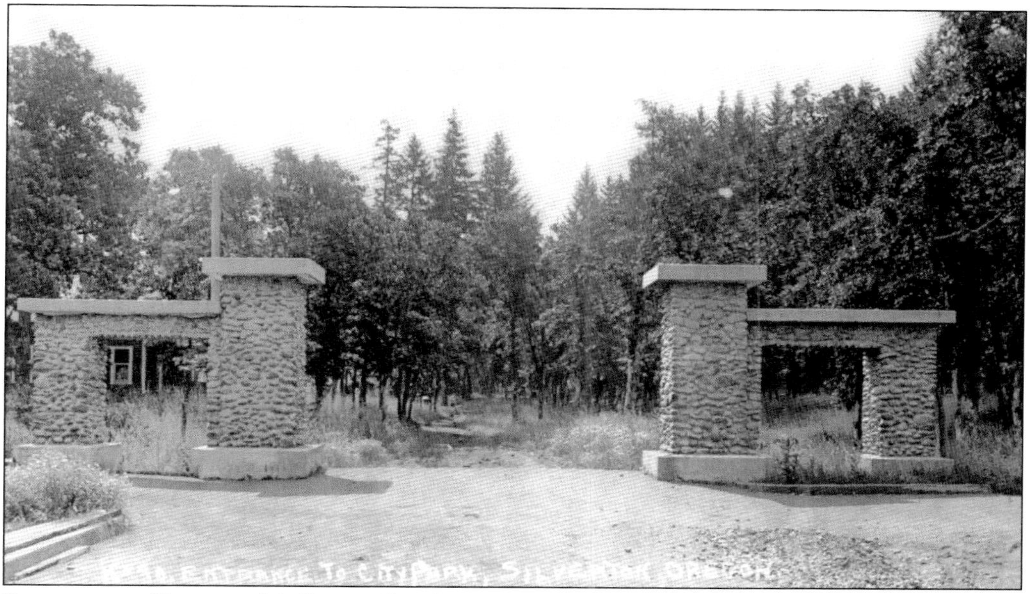

Entrance to Coolidge-McClaine City Park, Early 1920s. With its original stonework entryway made by local mason Harry Desart, the Coolidge-McClaine City Park beckons visitors. The dirt path is now a parking area, and the trees have been thinned out. It is the center of Silverton's summer social life, celebrating strawberries, Davenport, and fine art, though not necessarily in that order. Silverton's pioneer bankers, Ai Coolidge and Jake McClaine, donated the land. (Drake Brothers photograph; courtesy of SCHS.)

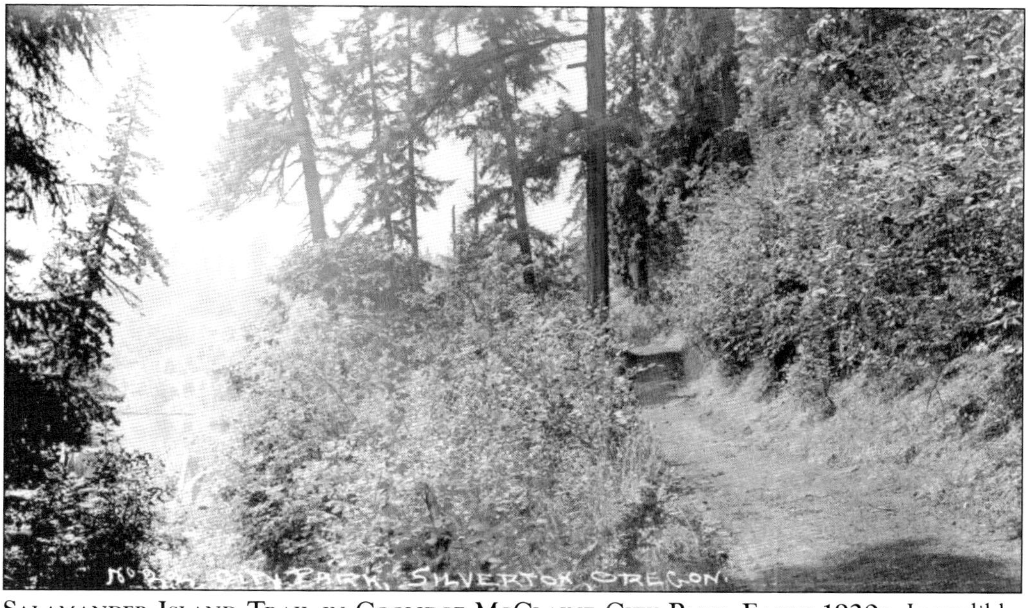

Salamander Island Trail in Coolidge-McClaine City Park, Early 1920s. Incredibly, this scene remains much the same today. The Salamander Island area is the site of the old Fischer Flouring Mill's water intake. The holding pond is visible to the left in this photograph. Its ruins are still visible to those souls who brave the steep trail down the bank. (Drake Brothers photograph; courtesy of SCHS.)

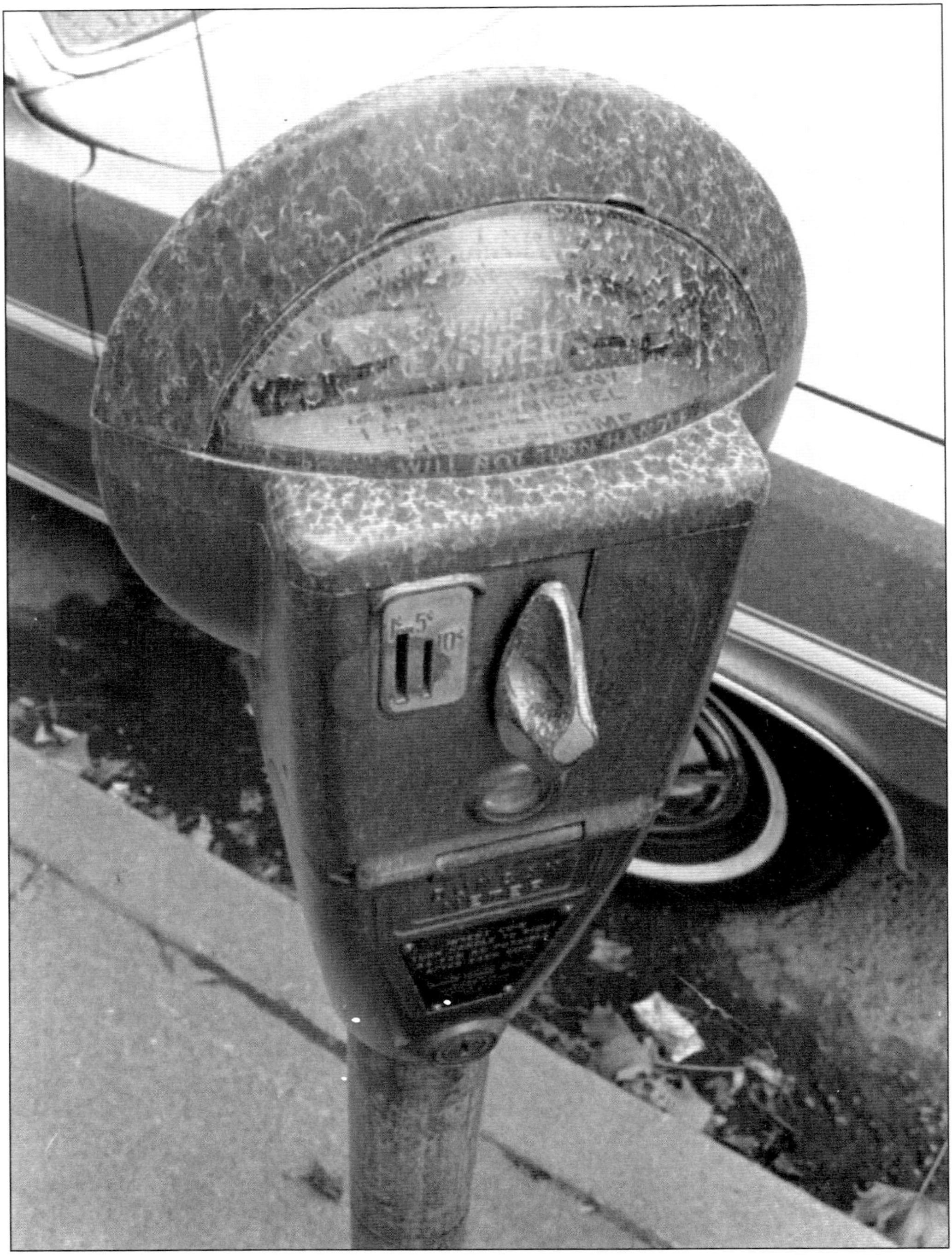

Ash from Mount St. Helens on Parking Meter, April 1980. Sometimes, the world comes to Silverton, as it did several times when the town found itself downwind of a volcano. Mount St. Helens, known as Loowit to the natives, came to life. The town was coated with a thin layer of a gritty ash and water mixture, as seen here on an old-style penny parking meter (less than 20 remain). (Gus Frederick photograph.)

Three

FARM AND INDUSTRY

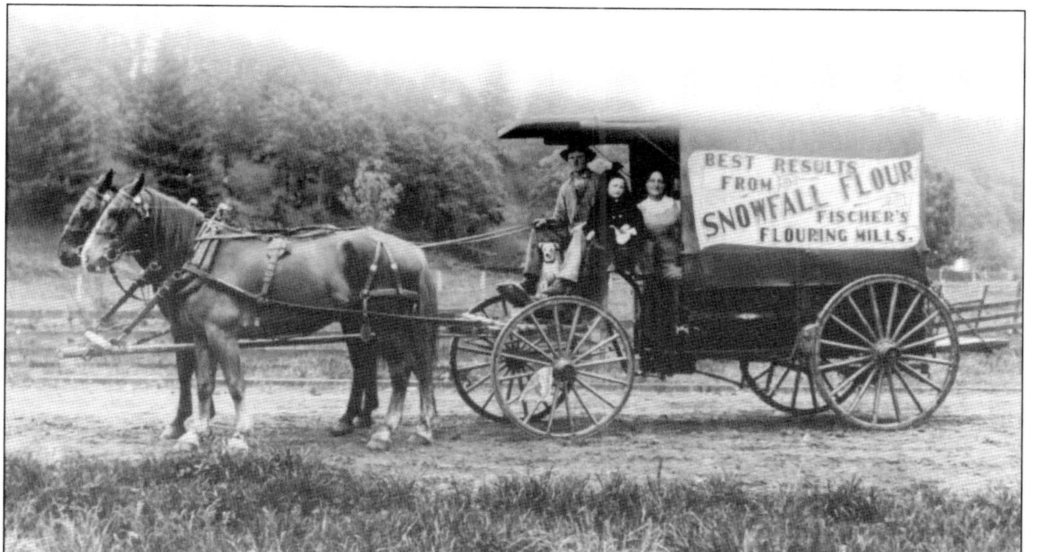

FISCHER FLOURING MILL WAGON, 1903. Initially, all of Silverton's industrial base was processed agricultural and timber products. As transportation networks changed and availability of local resources dwindled, Silverton's economic base fluctuated. Local sustainability eventually gave way to centralized, long-distance distribution networks. (Courtesy of SCHS.)

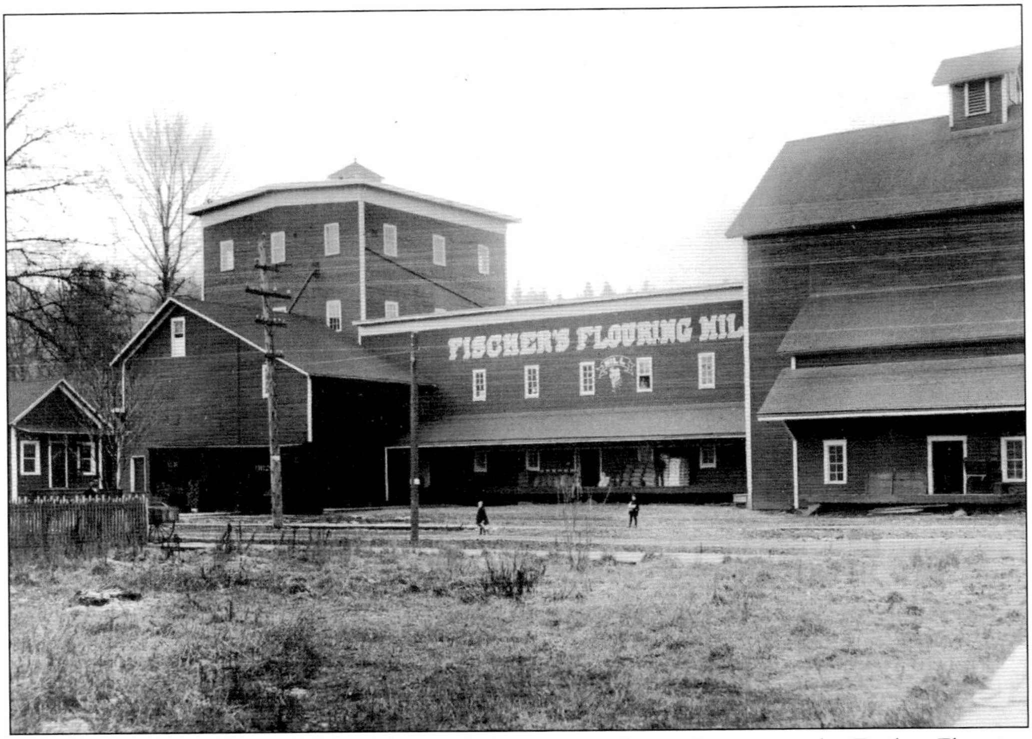

Fischer Flouring Mill, 1900. Silverton's first non-timber industry was the Fischer Flouring Mill. Making use of the plentiful grain grown in the Willamette Valley, this mill soon expanded to include a huge complex and its own dedicated rail spur. (Courtesy of SCHS.)

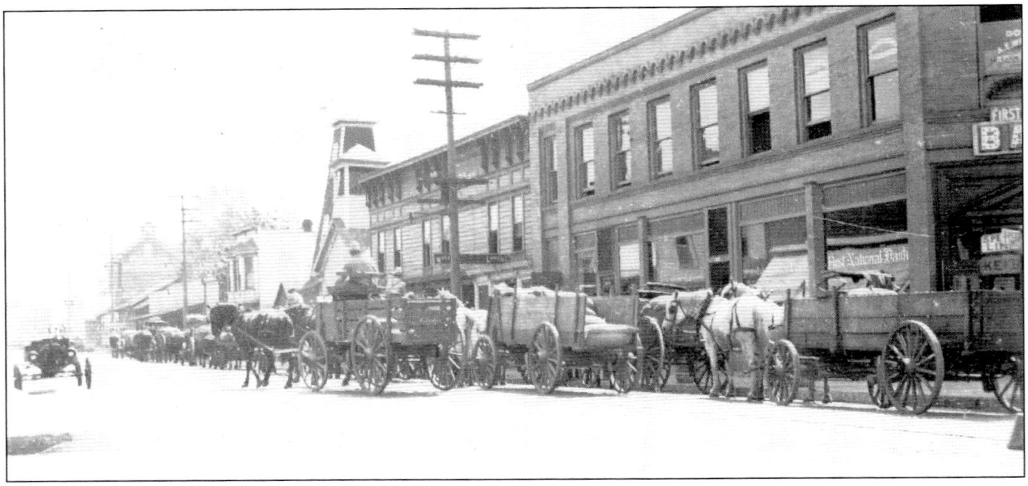

Wagons on Water Street, Early 1900s. Waiting to unload grain, these horse-drawn wagons queue up along South Water Street. An early automobile is visible on the left, which could have been Percy Brown's two-seater Maxwell (see page 114). (Courtesy of SCHS.)

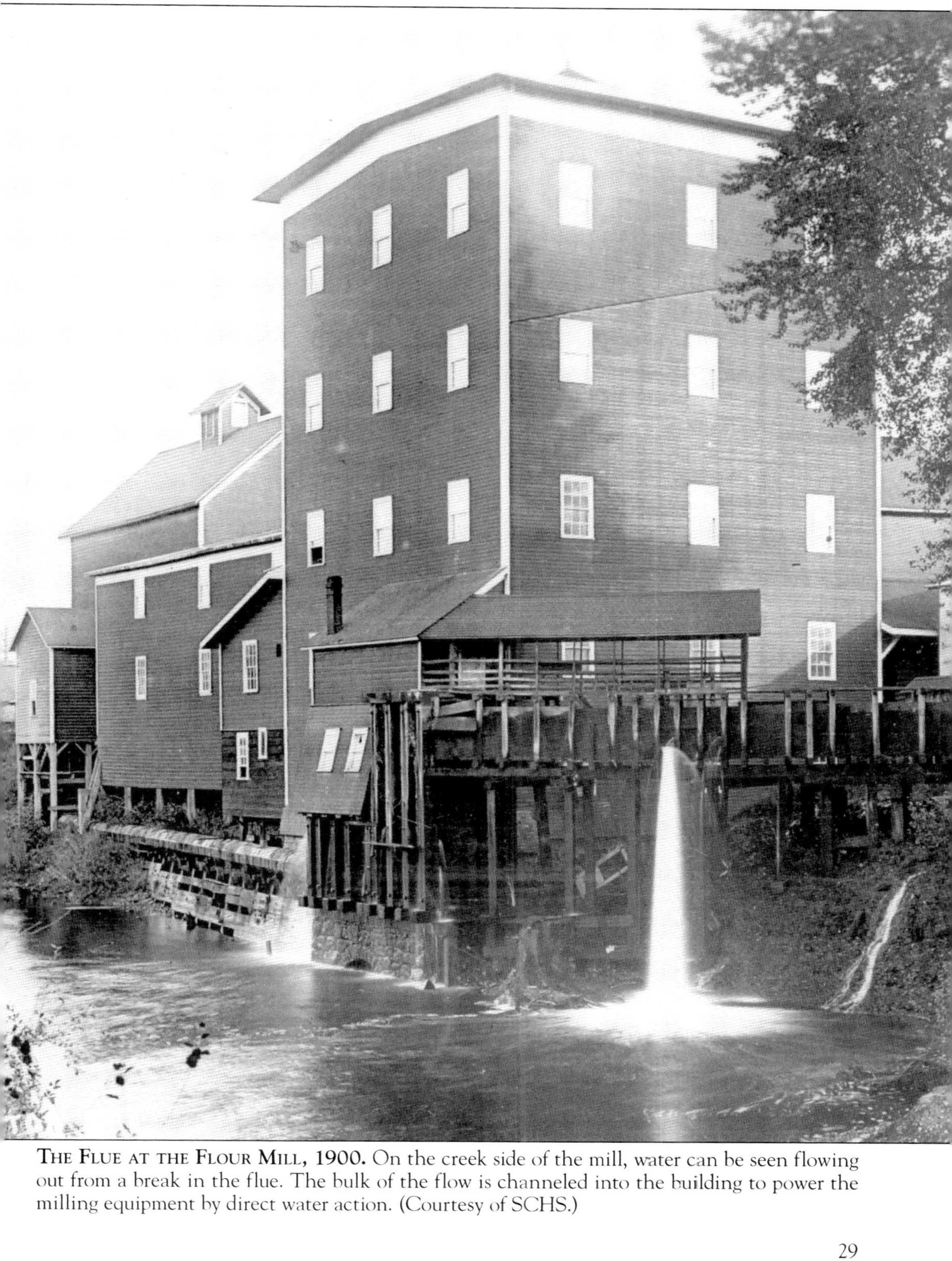

The Flue at the Flour Mill, 1900. On the creek side of the mill, water can be seen flowing out from a break in the flue. The bulk of the flow is channeled into the building to power the milling equipment by direct water action. (Courtesy of SCHS.)

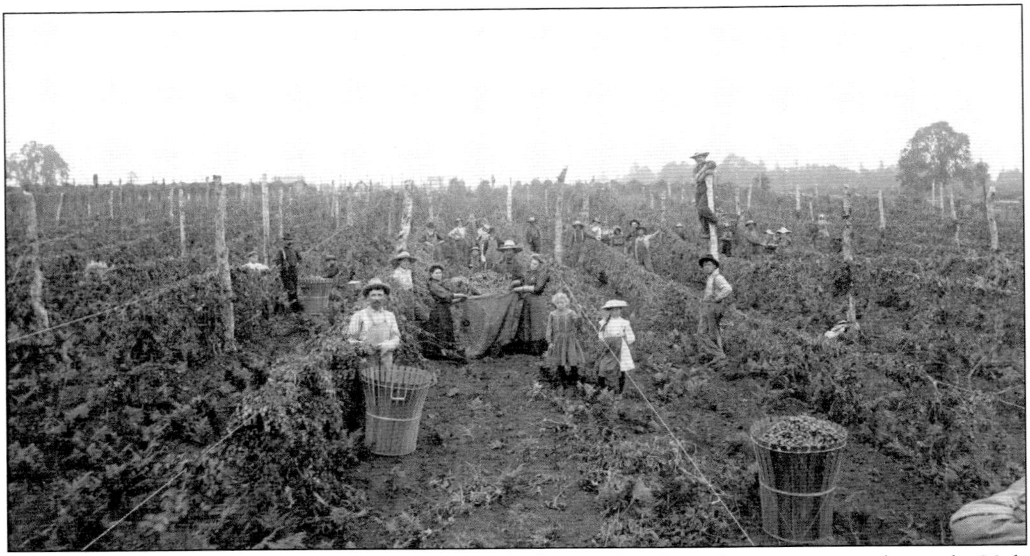

Hops Pickers, Early 1900s. A bit more work than today, hops harvesting in the early 20th century required agile young boys to scramble up the poles to lower the lines that the vines were hanging from. Once lowered, the pickers would pull the blossoms off the vines and place them in wooden baskets. (Courtesy of SCHS.)

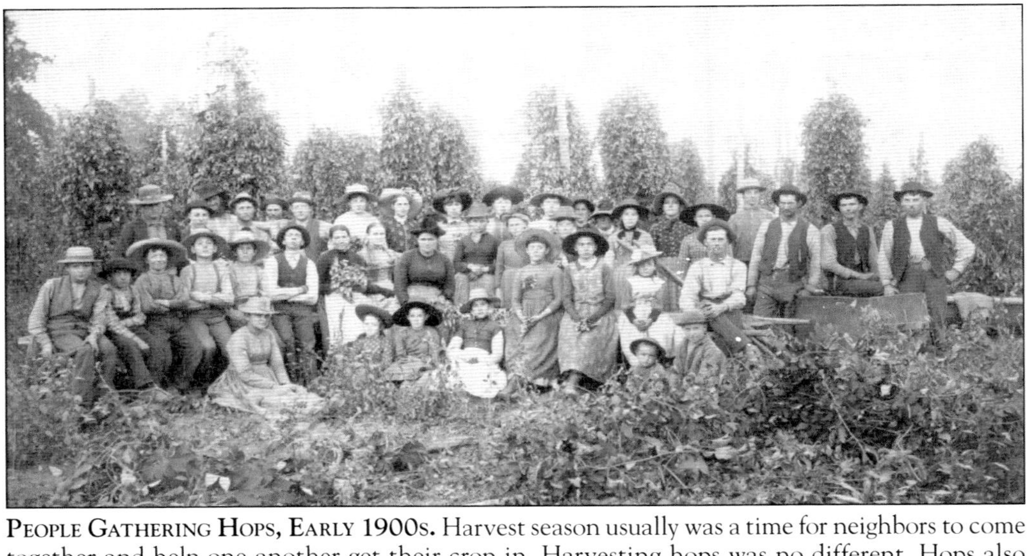

People Gathering Hops, Early 1900s. Harvest season usually was a time for neighbors to come together and help one another get their crop in. Harvesting hops was no different. Hops also provided a source of income for young men and women who were out of school for the summer. (Courtesy of SCHS.)

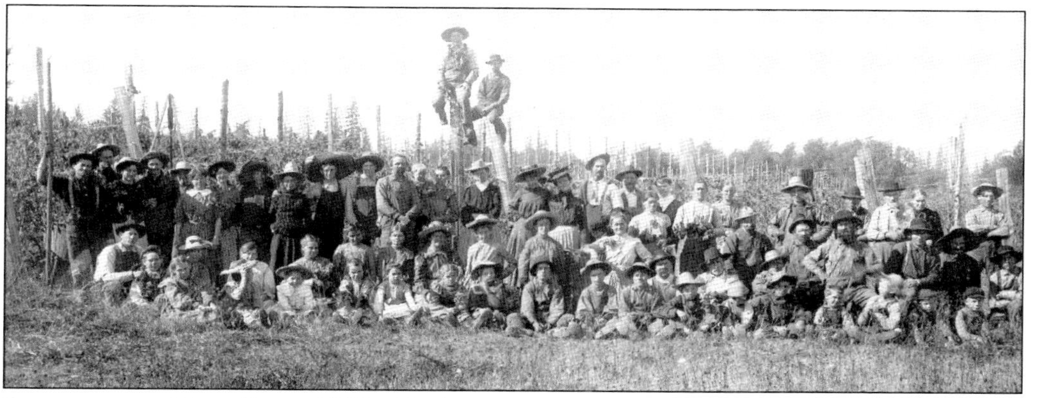

Chipping in to Help, Early 1900s. The harvesting process for hops was a multigenerational and cross-gender activity. Every able-bodied individual joined in. It is believed that the pole climbers probably had a pretty fun time during the harvesting season. (Courtesy of SCHS.)

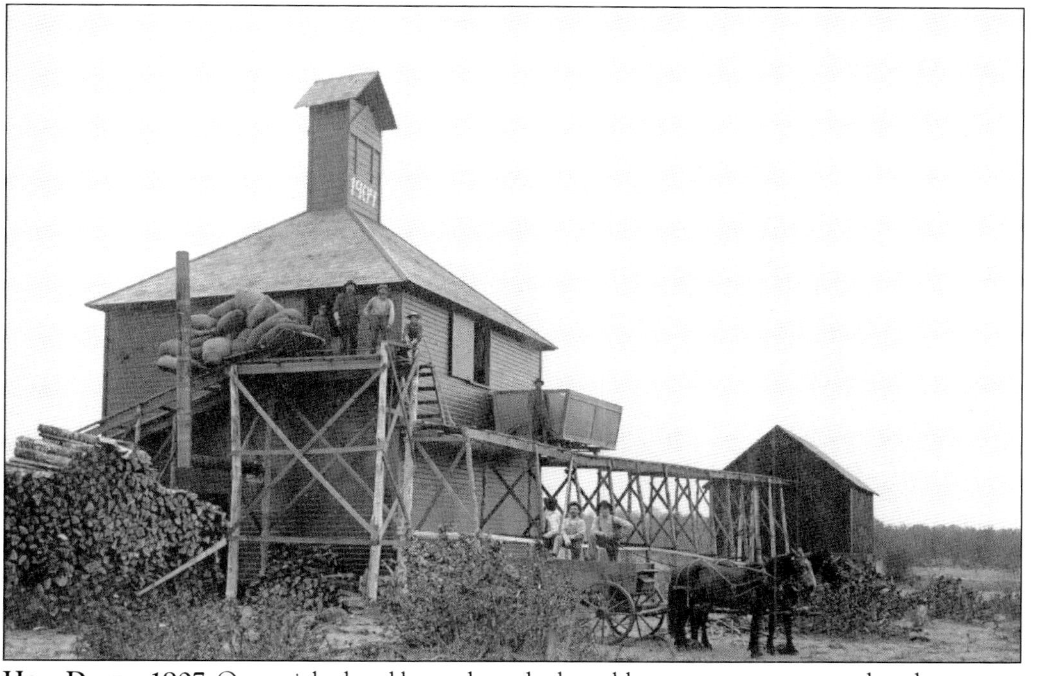

Hops Dryer, 1907. Once picked and bagged up, the hops blossoms are transported to the nearest hops dryer for packaging. These old-style hops dryers used to dot the landscape, but over the years, more efficient ways of drying have been employed by modern "hoperations" in the area, which remains a major commodity. (Courtesy of SCHS.)

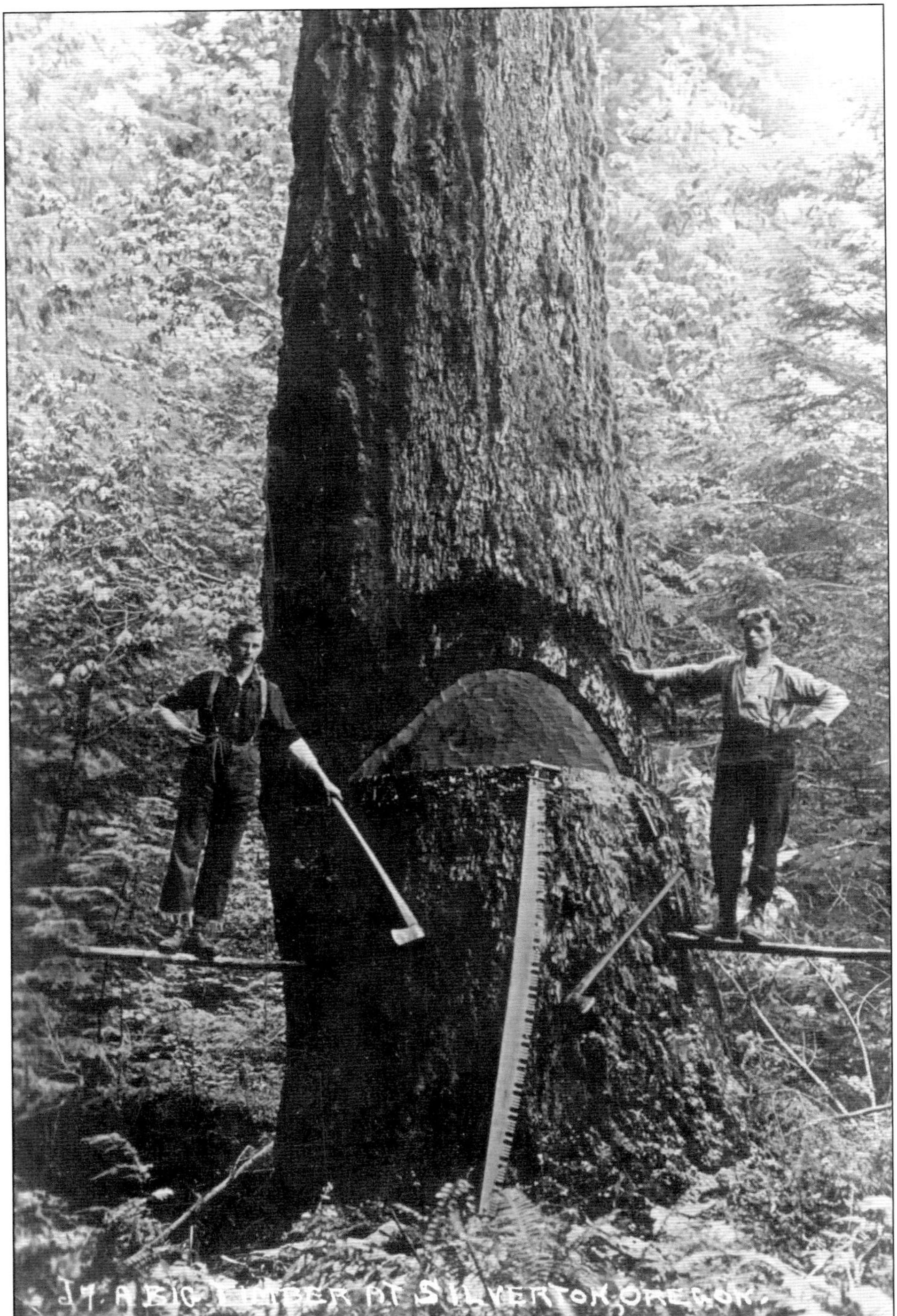

BIG LUMBER IN SILVERTON, 1914. With an old-growth Douglas fir, two fellers are taking a photograph break. The large crosscut saw was called a misery whip. It was kept lubricated by dripping kerosene on the blade from a special hooked bottle that hung above it. (Courtesy of SCHS.)

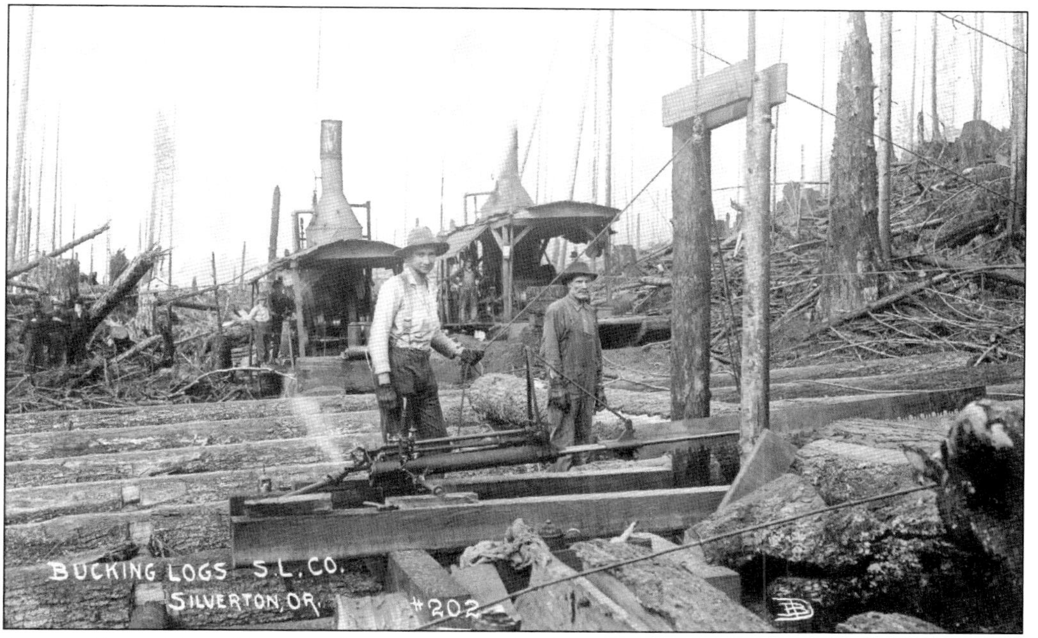

ABIQUA BASIN CAMP BUCKING LOGS, AROUND 1915. Prior to being transported to the mill, logs were hauled by steam-powered "donkeys" to a staging area. Silver Falls Timber Company ran several of these remote camps. Bucking involved sawing the logs into uniform lengths so that they would fit neatly on the flatbed railcar. (Drake Brothers photograph; courtesy of SCHS.)

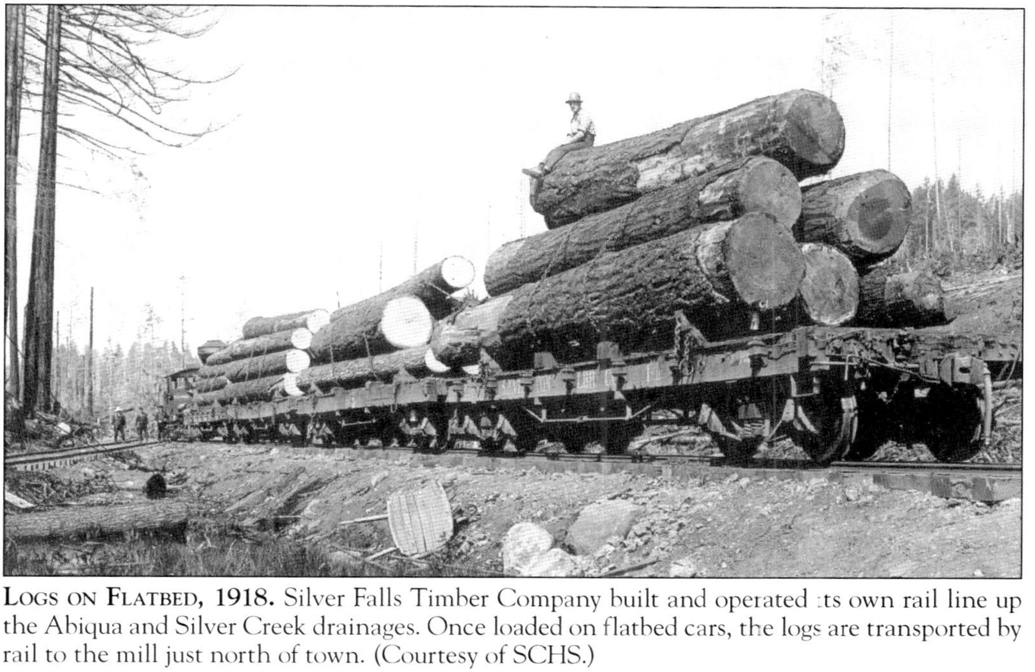

LOGS ON FLATBED, 1918. Silver Falls Timber Company built and operated its own rail line up the Abiqua and Silver Creek drainages. Once loaded on flatbed cars, the logs are transported by rail to the mill just north of town. (Courtesy of SCHS.)

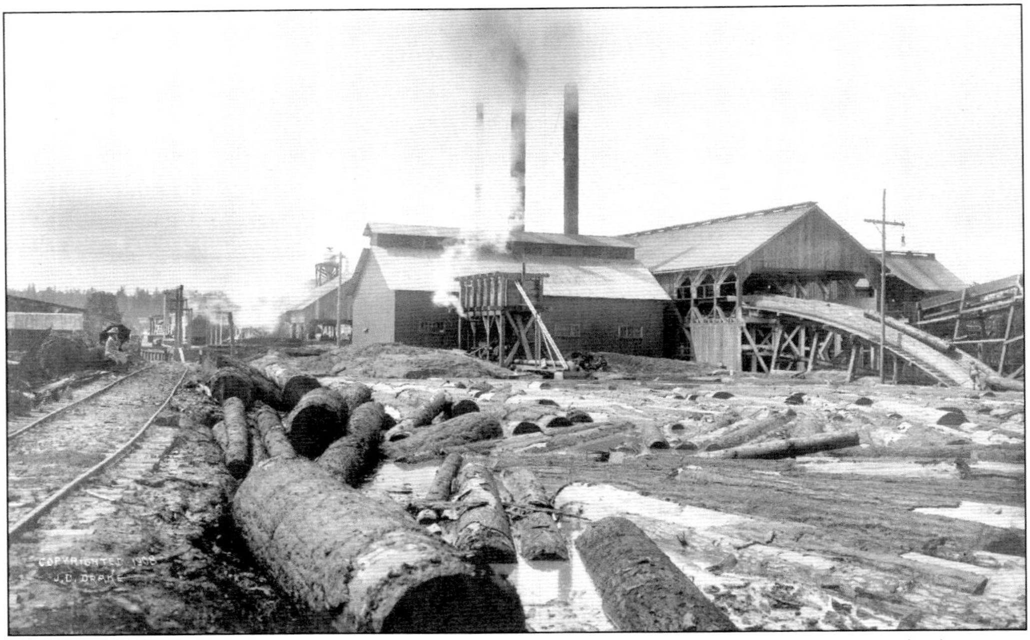

Silverton Lumber Company Log Pond, 1908. Once at the mill, the flatcars dump the logs into a large artificial pond created by diverting the Abiqua Creek. The "pond monkeys" direct the logs to the conveyor ramp, which pulls the logs into the mill by a chain. Silverton Lumber Company was in business from 1906 to 1925. (Drake Brothers photograph; courtesy of SCHS.)

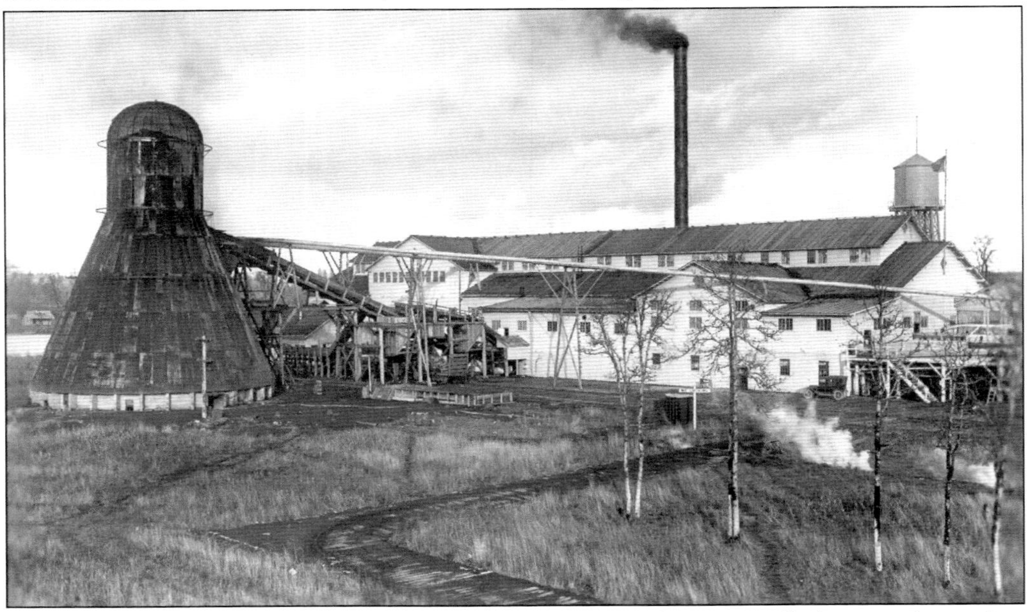

Silver Falls Timber Company Wigwam Burner, 1920s. With any sawmill, the major by-product was sawdust. Today, all that waste is considered valuable, but back in the day, it was something to dispose of. The easiest way was to burn it. The "wigwam burner" (named for its shape like a wigwam) was designed specifically for burning mill wastes. The unique structure on top helped prevent stray sparks. (Courtesy of SCHS.)

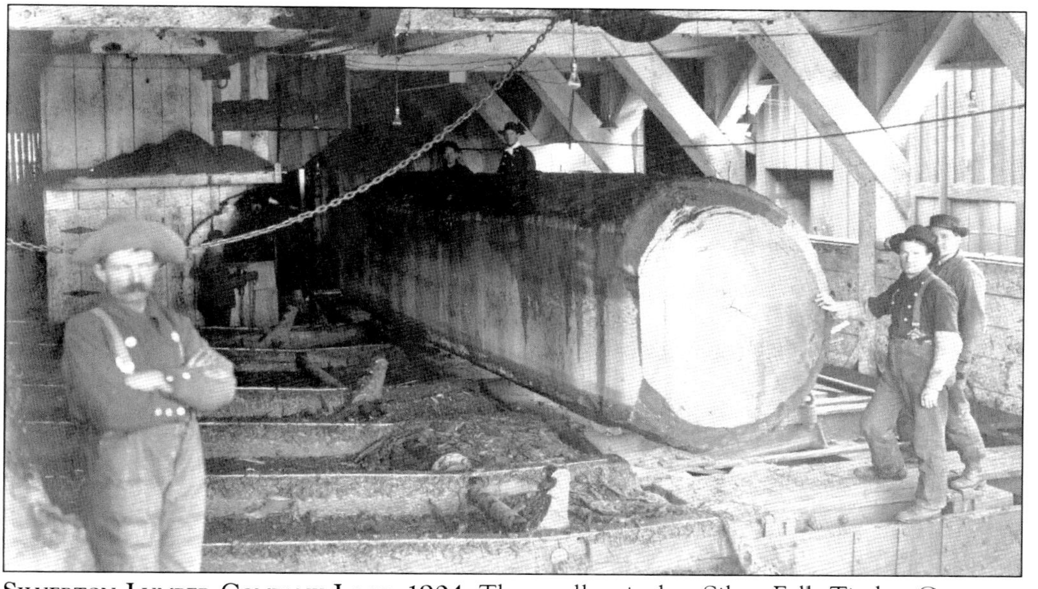

SILVERTON LUMBER COMPANY LOGS, 1904. The smaller rival to Silver Falls Timber Company was the Silverton Lumber Company. It started several years earlier but never equaled the size of its future rival. It went out of business in 1925. Here is a large Douglas fir log getting sliced into huge planks. (Courtesy of SCHS.)

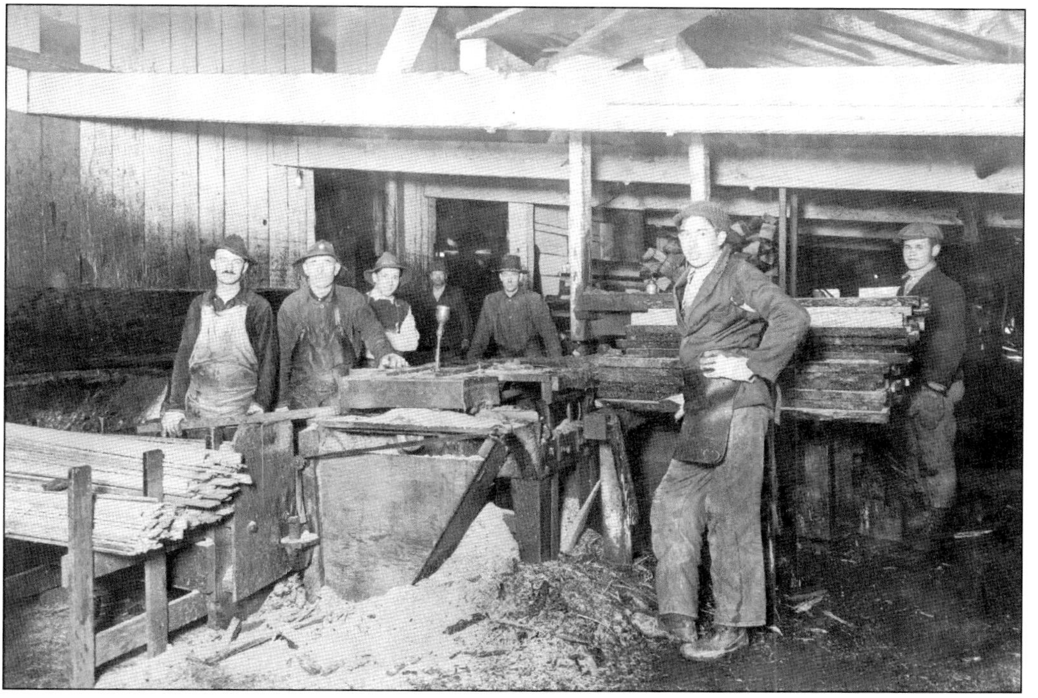

SILVER FALLS TIMBER COMPANY LATH MILL CREW, 1920. Within the mill, different areas created different wood products. Here is a lath mill, which is where strips of wood were cut into laths. Laths were mainly used in home building. A lath covered with plaster was a common material used for walls. (Courtesy of SCHS.)

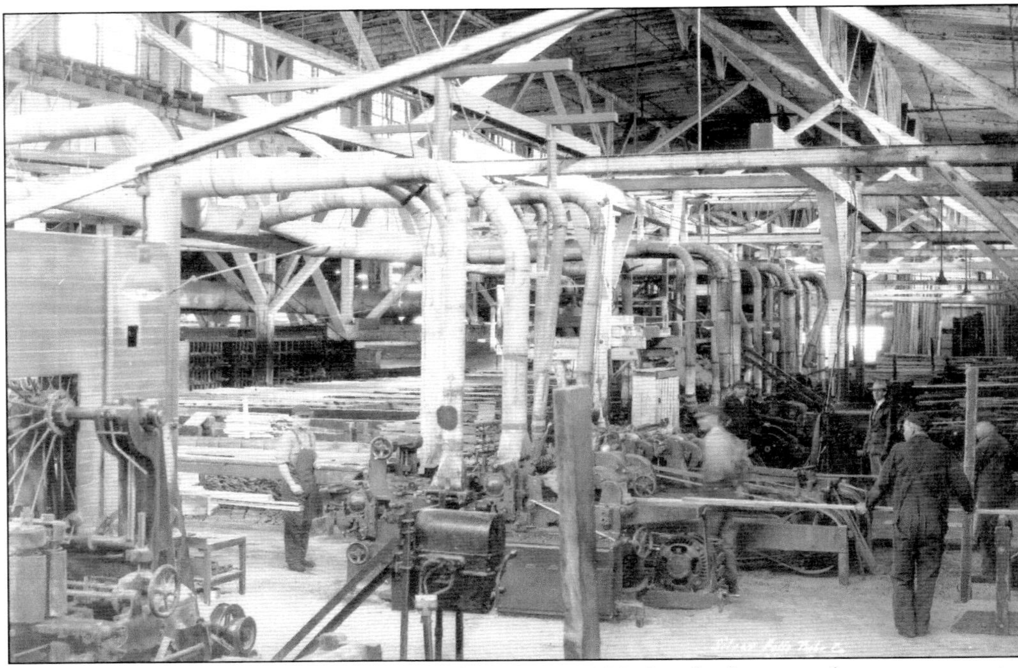

The Interior of Silver Falls Timber Company, 1923. Inside the vast plant, an extensive network of locally manufactured ductwork channeled sawdust out and away from the operation. (Courtesy of SCHS.)

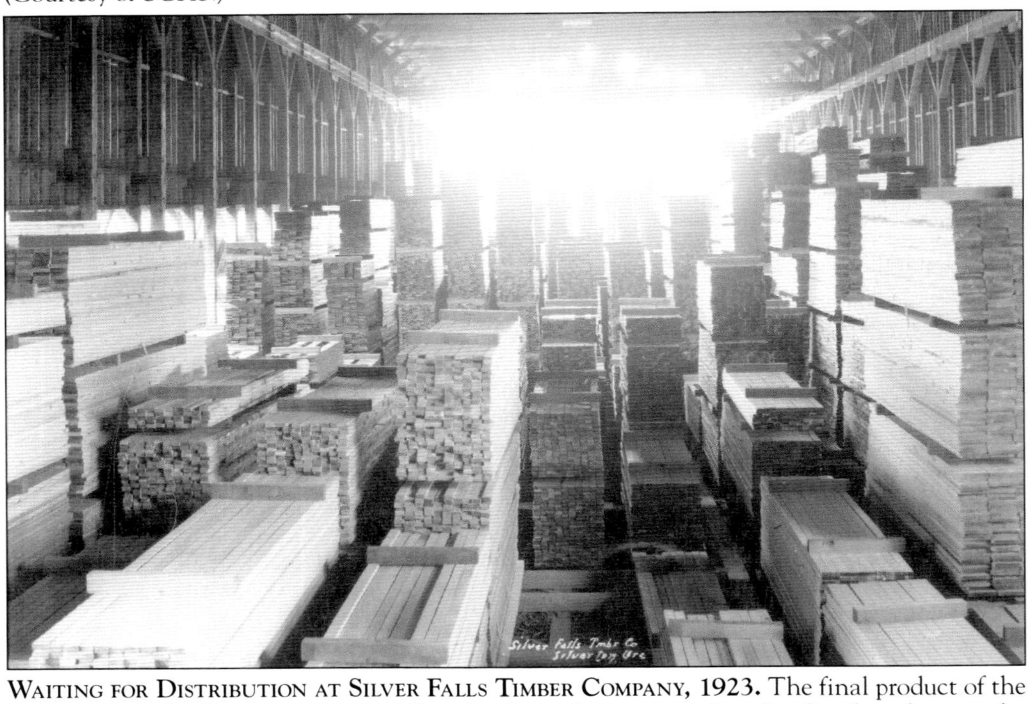

Waiting for Distribution at Silver Falls Timber Company, 1923. The final product of the mill sits ready for shipment. Finished Douglas fir products are ready to be distributed across the nation. (Courtesy of SCHS.)

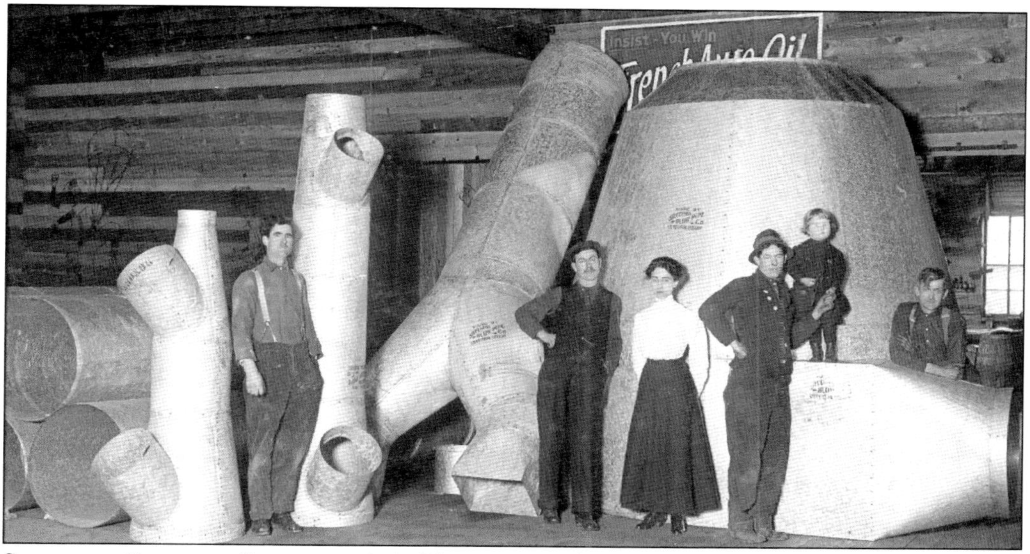

SILVERTON BLOWPIPE FACTORY, 1913. Those pictured are, from left to right, two unidentified workers, Sylvia McGinnis, Allen Smith, Erwin "Smitty" Smith, and unidentified. All the exotic ductwork at the Silver Falls Mill came from here, the Silverton Blowpipe Factory, or from Eastman Brothers. Note the cartoons drawn on the wall to the left. Drawing cartoons on any available flat surface was a longtime habit of Silverton youth. The artist is unidentified, but semiprofessional cartoonist Knute Digerness, who was active at this time, could have been the creator. (Courtesy of SCHS.)

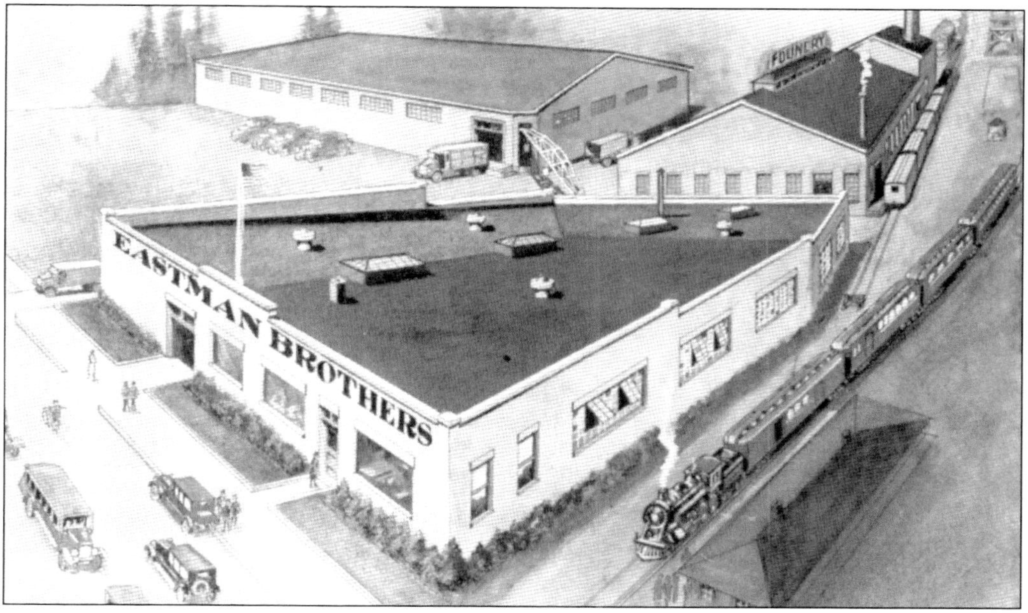

EASTMAN BROTHERS FACTORY, 1929. Here is an artist's rendering from *Oregon Magazine*. The Eastman Brothers manufactured furnaces and heating systems. The company is still in operation and is now located near the old Silverton Airport. The foundry, shown in the upper right, is the only industrial operation at the same location. (Murray Wade illustration; courtesy of the Estell family.)

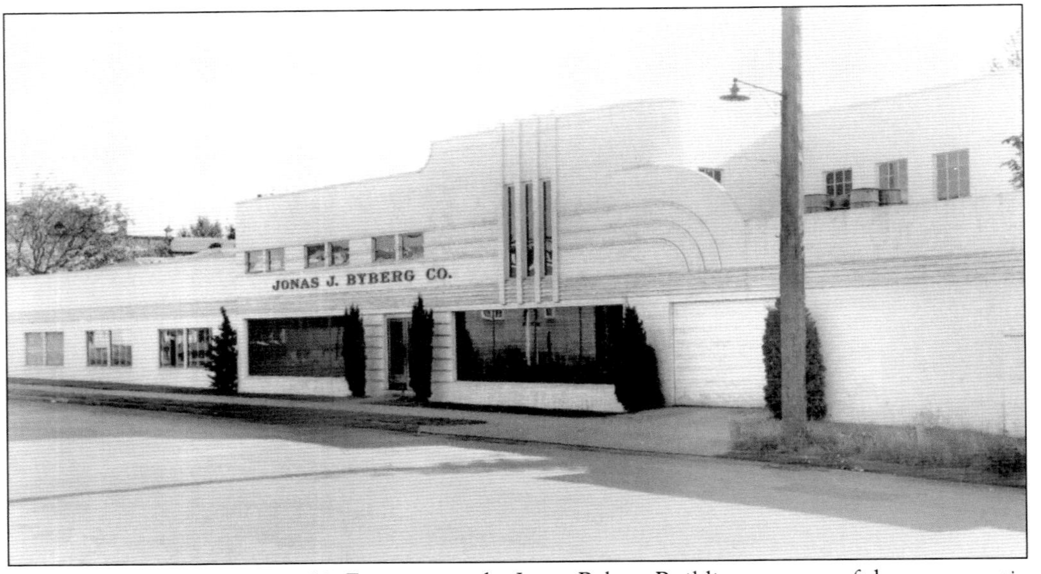

JONAS BYBERG BUILDING, 1950. For its time, the Jonas Byberg Building was one of the more exotic structures ever built in town. Its sweeping style and curving lines seemed to imply that the whole place was about to speed off down the road. It was torn down in the 1980s to make room for the new post office. (Bill Hanson photograph; courtesy of Curt Almquist.)

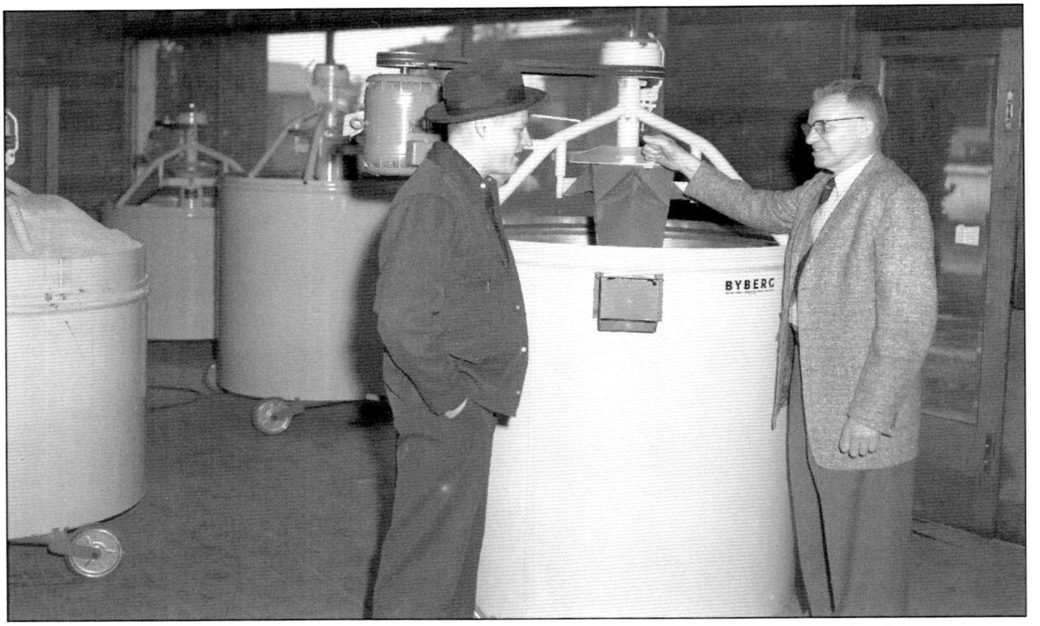

JONAS J. BYBERG, 1950. Jonas J. Byberg (right) was an unassuming genius. He built a career on the invention and the construction of agricultural machinery. The J.J. Byberg Company created such exotic devices as filbert nut harvesters and bean pickers. He held numerous patents and prefabricated his modest ranch-style home in his shop on North Water Street before it was assembled on his lot at the corner of Cherry and Welch Streets. (Bill Hanson photograph; courtesy of Curt Almquist.)

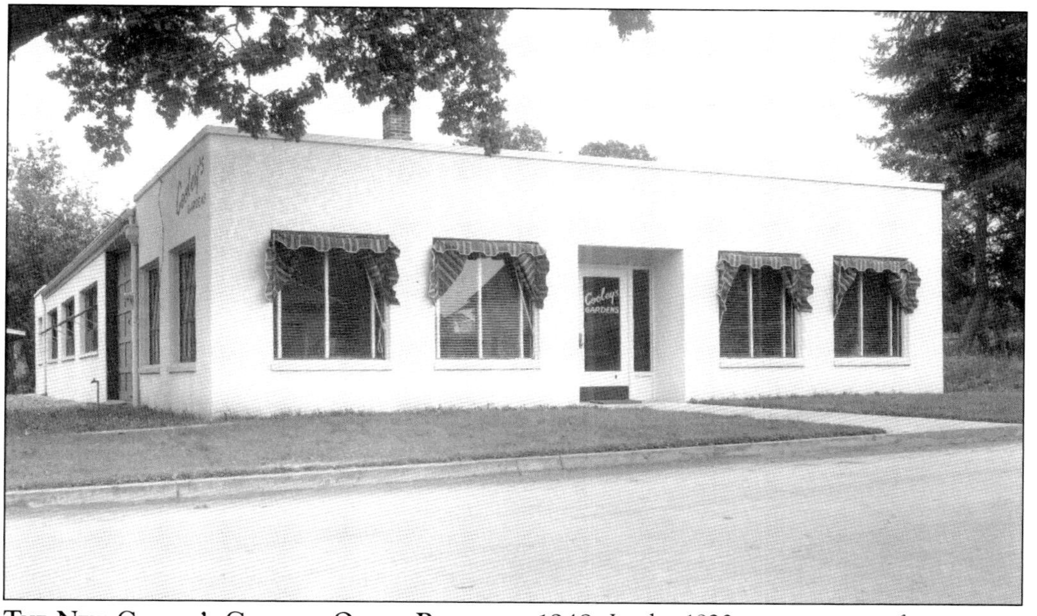

The New Cooley's Gardens Office Building, 1948. In the 1920s, a new type of crop came to Silverton. Financed by a loan from his father, Rholin Cooley turned his hobby of hybridized bearded iris into a lucrative, multigenerational family business. The building constructed in 1948 now houses Almquist Photography Studios. Cooley's Gardens relocated out of town on an expanded complex that includes a bearded iris display garden. (Courtesy of Cooley's Gardens.)

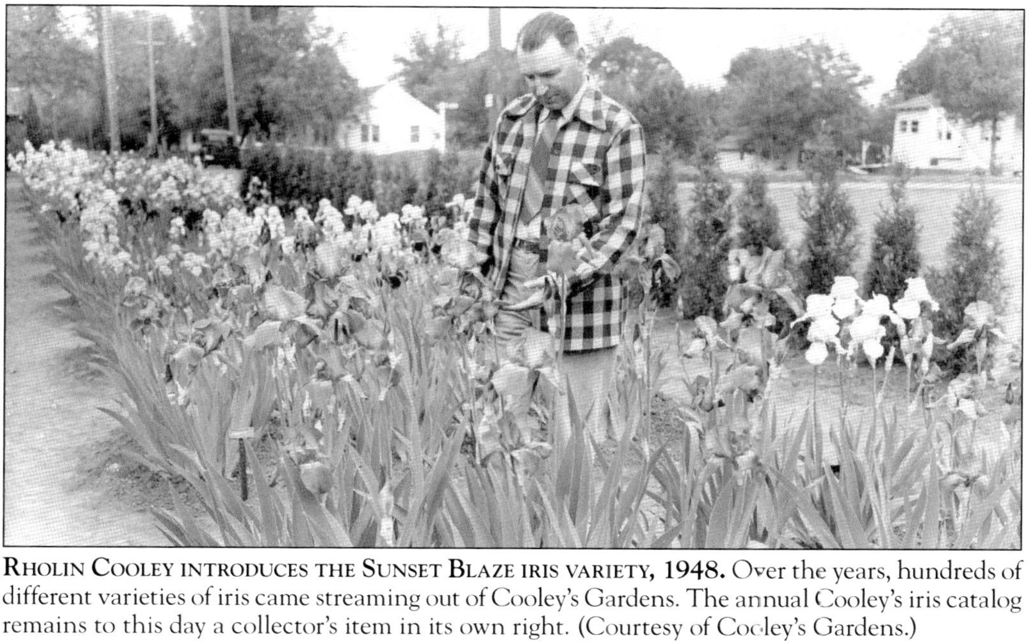

Rholin Cooley introduces the Sunset Blaze iris variety, 1948. Over the years, hundreds of different varieties of iris came streaming out of Cooley's Gardens. The annual Cooley's iris catalog remains to this day a collector's item in its own right. (Courtesy of Cooley's Gardens.)

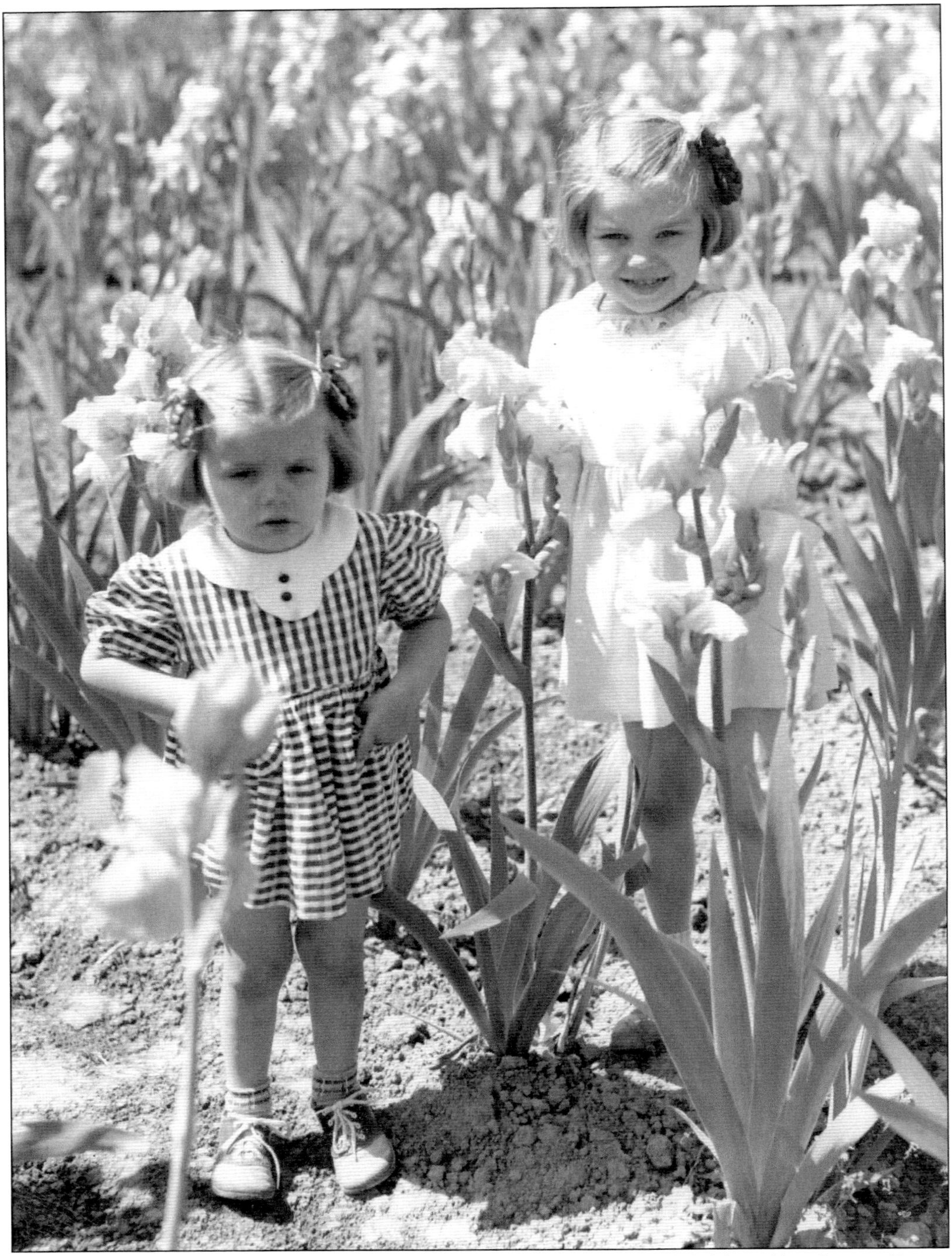

GEORGIE AND JUDY ERNST IN THE FIELD, 1949. Two of Rholin's grandchildren (daughters of Larry Ernst and Rholin's daughter Miriam) mug it up among the flowers. With their brother Rick, the Cooley iris tradition continued into a new millennium. Although now retired, Georgie and Judy both worked at Cooley's Gardens for many years and remain active in the community. (Courtesy of Cooley's Gardens.)

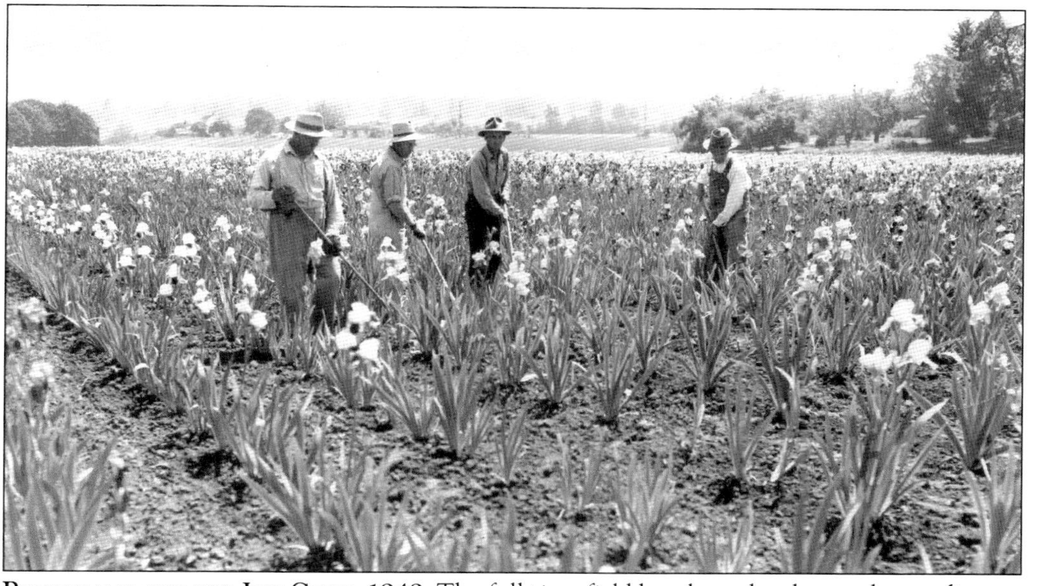

Beauchamp and the Iris Crew, 1949. The full-time field hands are hard at work rounding up stray iris. Their names are lost to time, except for that of the foreman, Mr. Beauchamp, on the left. Like most agricultural operations, the roundup time would depend upon various factors, including field size, weather, and labor. (Courtesy of Cooley's Gardens.)

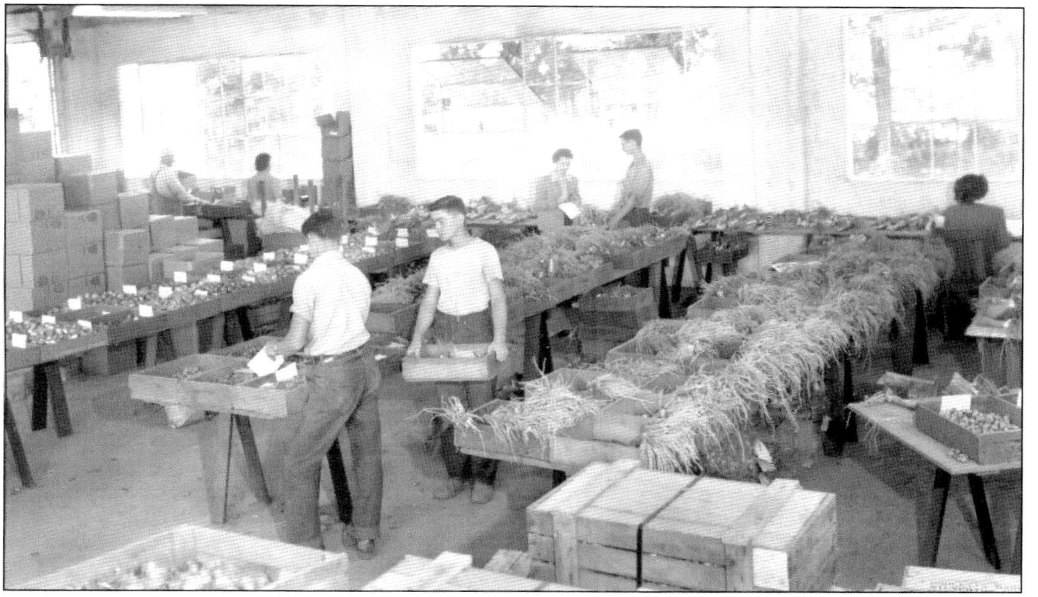

Shipping Spring Iris and Daffodils, 1950. Much of the seasonal labor on the farms of the 1940s consisted of local youth. It was a tried and true method to earning some spending money. Here is a view of the back warehouse where bulbs and rhizomes are prepped for shipment around the world. (Courtesy of Cooley's Gardens.)

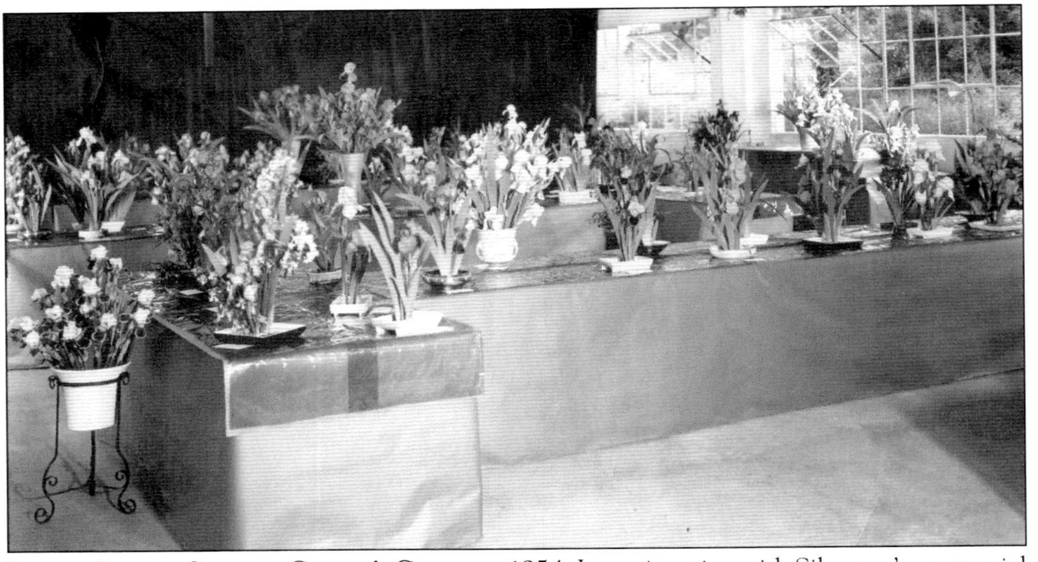

INDOOR FLOWER SHOW AT COOLEY'S GARDENS, 1954. In conjunction with Silverton's centennial celebration, Cooley's Gardens hosted an indoor flower show featuring a wide variety of exotic bearded iris blooms. (Courtesy of Cooley's Gardens.)

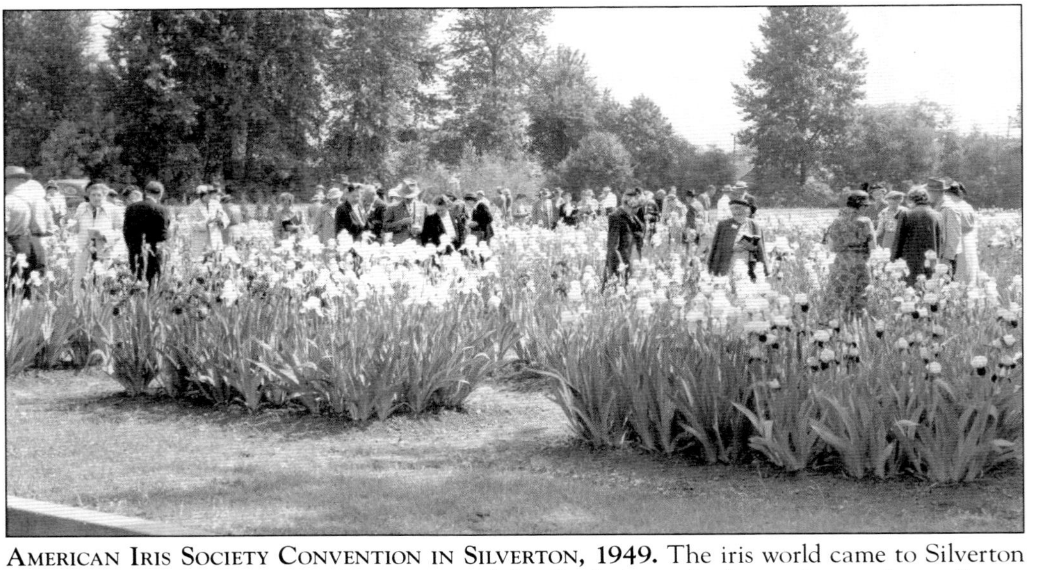

AMERICAN IRIS SOCIETY CONVENTION IN SILVERTON, 1949. The iris world came to Silverton in this image. The nation's iris fanciers toured the Cooley's iris display gardens on James Street. (Courtesy of Cooley's Gardens.)

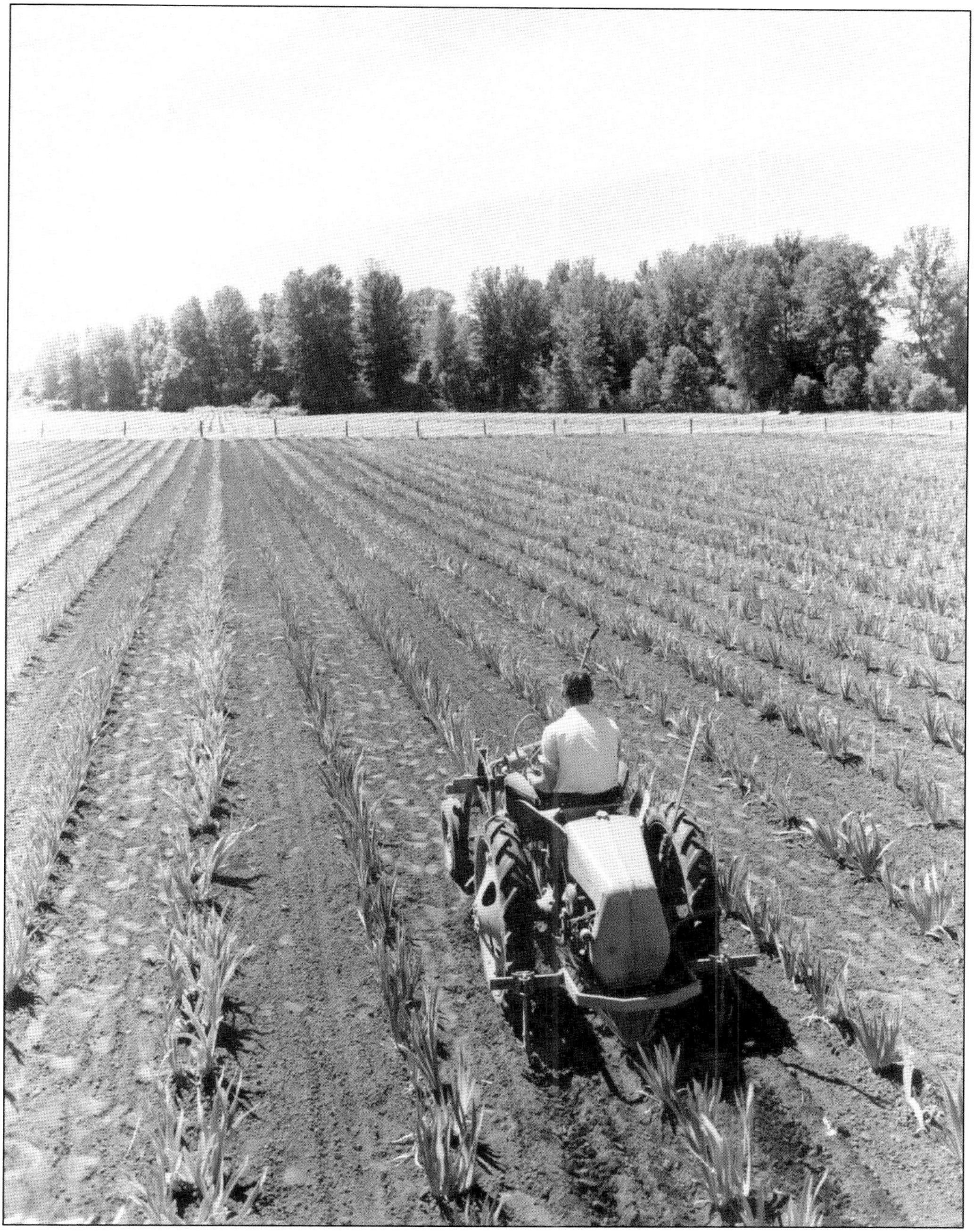

LARRY ERNST ON THE MODEL G, 1949. The Allis-Chalmers Manufacturing Company came to Cooley's Gardens to promote their new Model G tractor. Rholin Cooley's son-in-law Larry Ernst takes it for a spin in this image. For years, Larry took all of the beautiful iris shots for the catalog. His son, the late Rick Ernst, carried on the tradition in the digital realm. (Courtesy of Cooley's Gardens.)

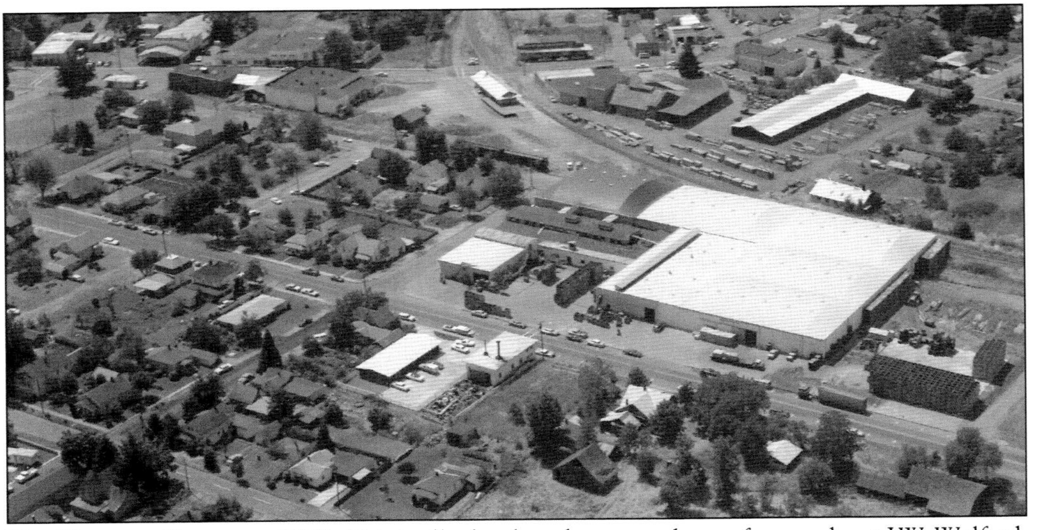

The Kolstad Cannery, 1963. Originally developed as a warehouse for merchant J.W. Wolfard, this property grew over the years and eventually served as a cannery. This low oblique aerial view was taken prior to the building of Roth's Grocery Store Complex, which would be in the lower right of this image. (Bill Hanson photograph; courtesy of Curt Almquist.)

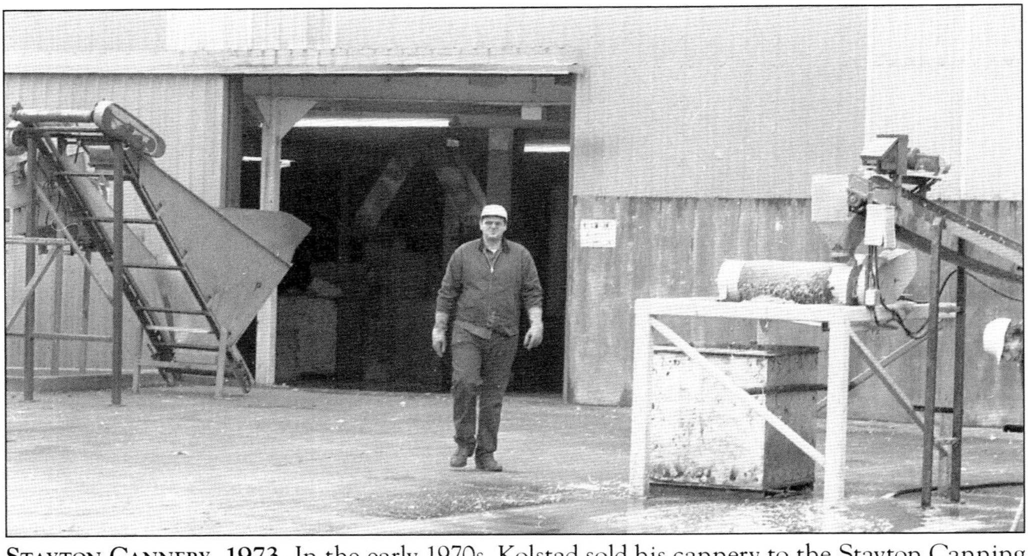

Stayton Cannery, 1973. In the early 1970s, Kolstad sold his cannery to the Stayton Canning Company headquartered in the community of Stayton, a dozen miles south of Silverton. Here is sanitation foreman Harold Adams walking out after his shift. (Gus Frederick photograph.)

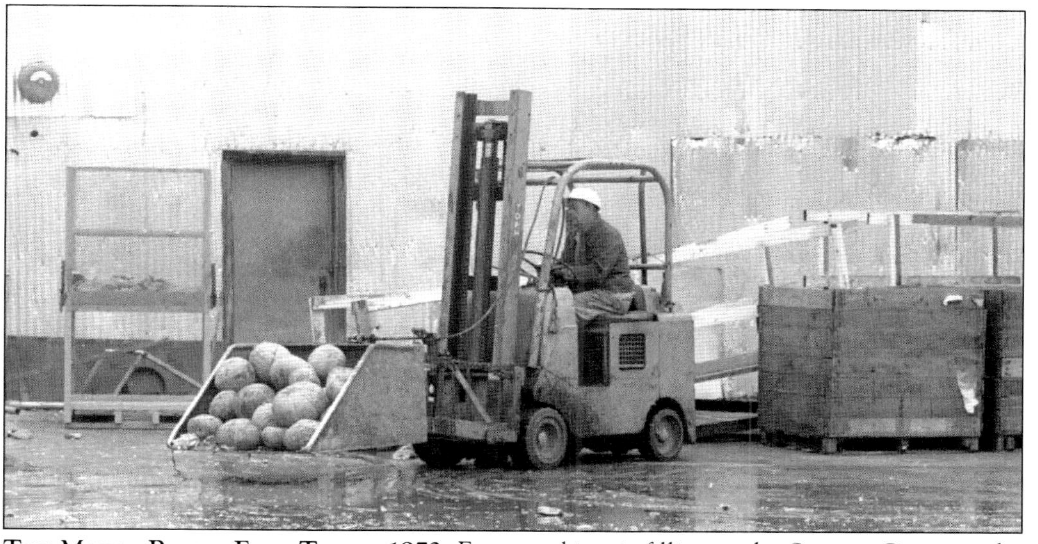

TOW MOTOR BRAND FORK TRUCK, 1973. For pumpkin pie filling at the Stayton Cannery, the meatier squash pumpkin is used. Huge piles of squash pumpkin would be stacked in three-sided bins. Then they would be scooped up with this modified forklift, which dumped them into the washer. (Gus Frederick photograph.)

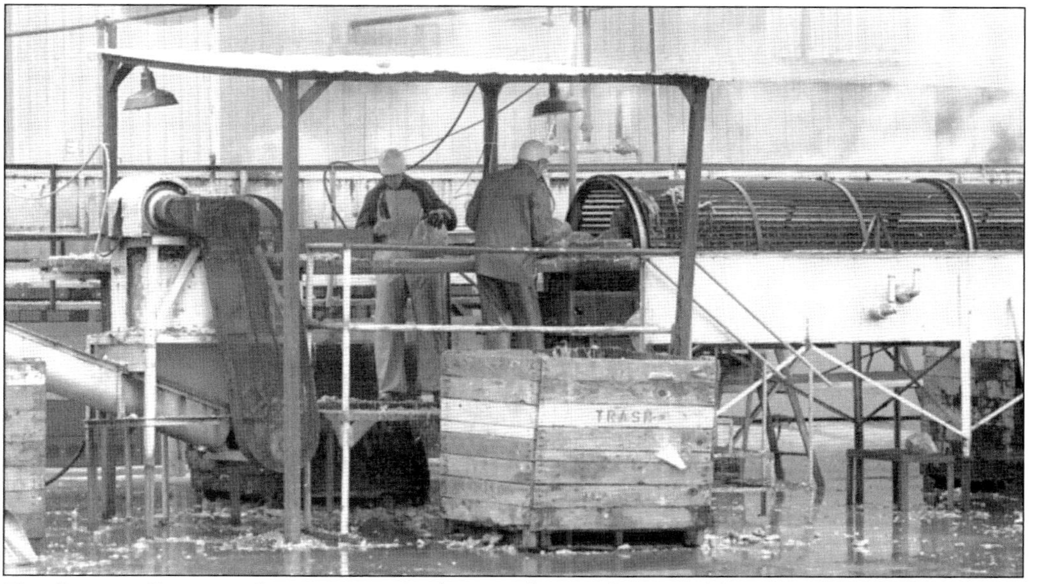

THE SQUASH CARVING CREW, 1973. As the squash pumpkins tumble out of the rotating washer, they are grabbed by one of the two squash carvers, but there is no time for these squash pumpkins to be transformed into jack-o'-lanterns. These pumpkins receive a couple of quick whacks to remove the stalks and bottoms and are then placed in the grinder. (Gus Frederick photograph.)

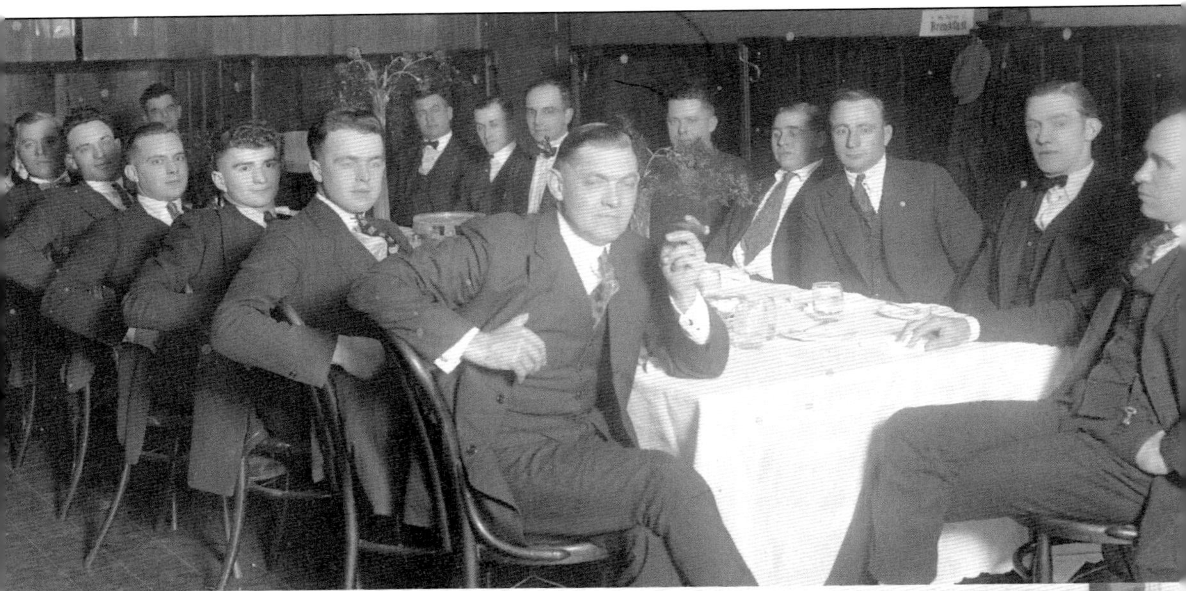

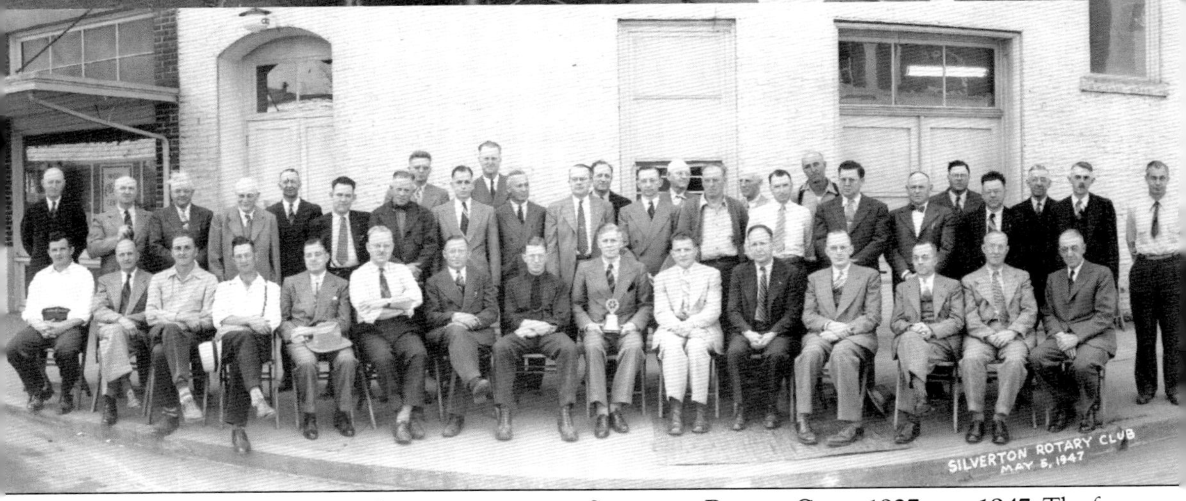

SILVERTON CHAMBER OF COMMERCE AND THE SILVERTON ROTARY CLUB, 1927 AND 1947. The face of Silverton's business community has changed repeatedly over the years. The bend of the curb in the lower image is an artifact of the specialized panoramic camera used. Actually, the chairs are arranged in a semicircle along First Street, next to the Odd Fellows Building. The major change today is the fact that women make up a significant portion, if not the majority, of Silverton's business community. (Top, courtesy of SCHS; bottom, courtesy of Stu Rasmussen.)

Four

Schools and Education

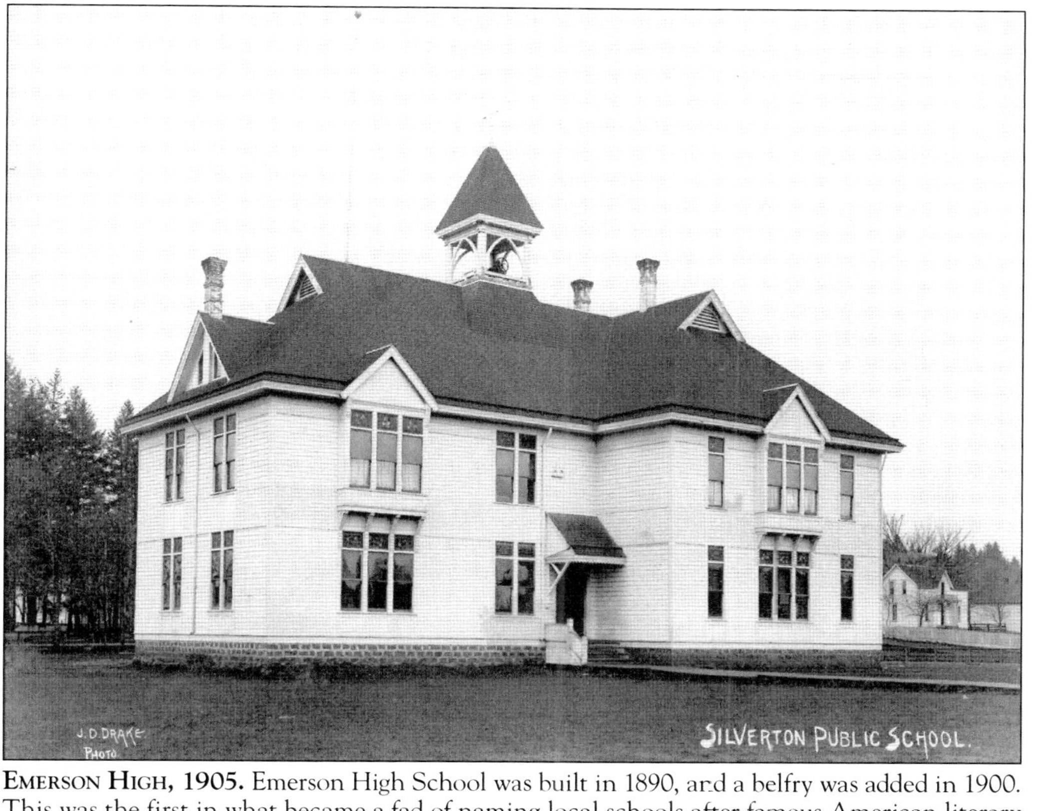

Emerson High, 1905. Emerson High School was built in 1890, and a belfry was added in 1900. This was the first in what became a fad of naming local schools after famous American literary greats. The Emerson Building burned down in 1929. Eugene Field School, Robert Frost Elementary, and Mark Twain Junior High are still going strong. (Courtesy of SCHS.)

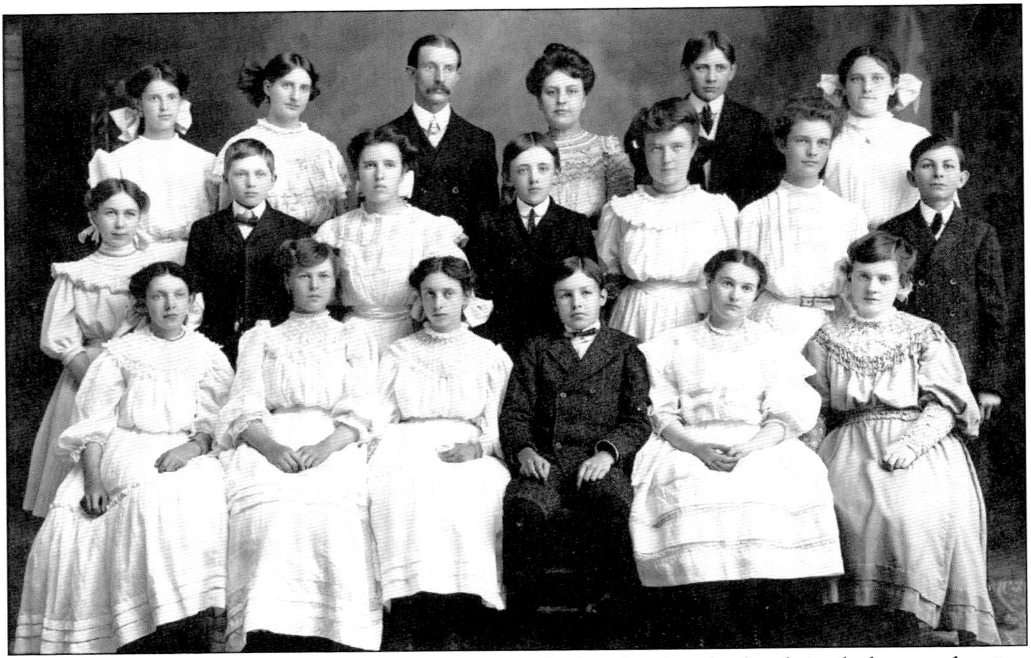

Silverton Eighth-Grade Graduation, 1905. To this day, local schools include a graduation ceremony for students completing the eighth grade. This started in an era when most students did not even get that far. (Courtesy of SCHS.)

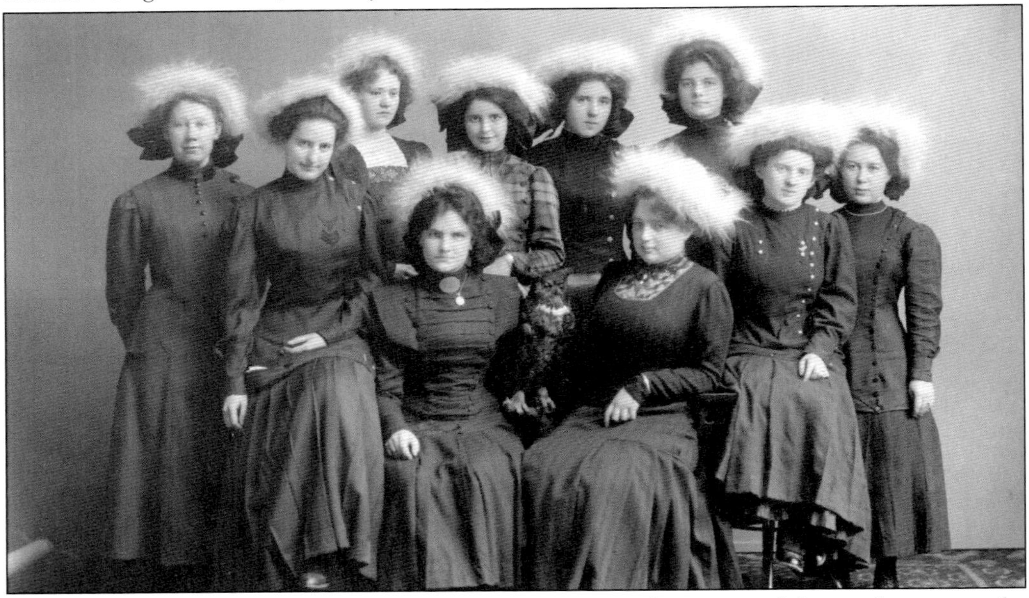

Silverton High School Honor Society, 1910. Here is the cream of the academic crop for 1910. Those pictured are, from left to right, (first row) Ethel Larrabee, Minnie Mascher, Bess Cowdar, Luanna Evans, Letha Cavender, and Krettle Hicks; (second row) Melvina Gjertsen, Virie Mascher, Anna Hammond, and Edna Steen. Minnie Mascher went into the field of education, teaching for many years at Evergreen School about a mile south of town on the Cascade Highway. (Courtesy of SCHS.)

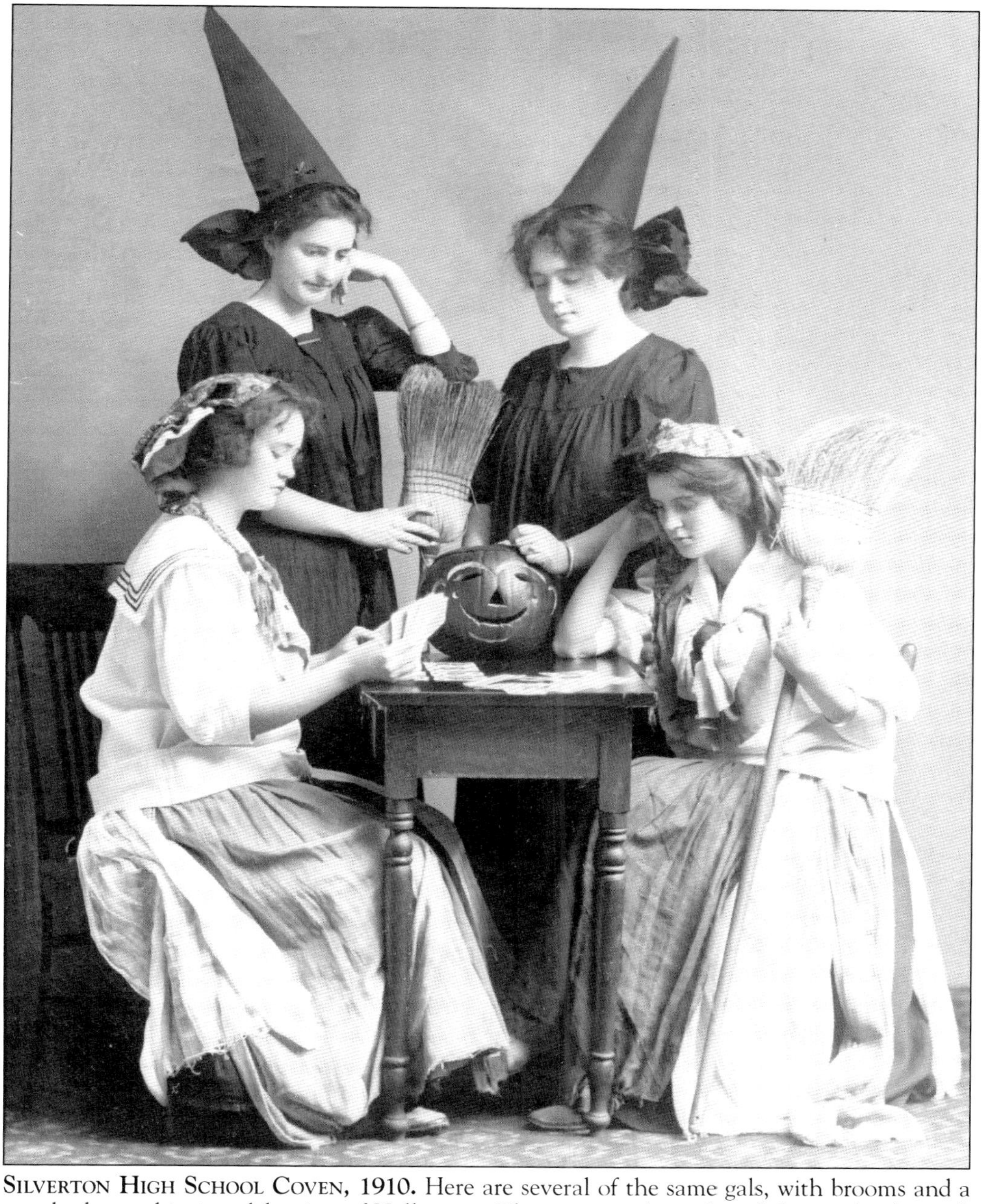

SILVERTON HIGH SCHOOL COVEN, 1910. Here are several of the same gals, with brooms and a standard pumpkin in celebration of Halloween. Those pictured are, from left to right, (seated) Virgie Mascher and Melvina Gjertsen; (standing) Minnie Mascher and Luanna Evans. (Courtesy of SCHS.)

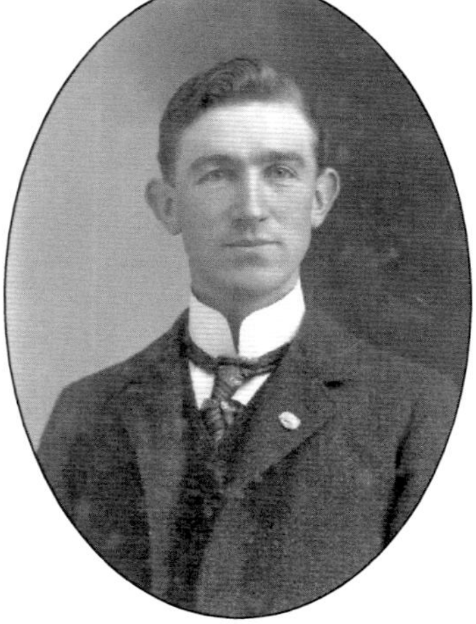

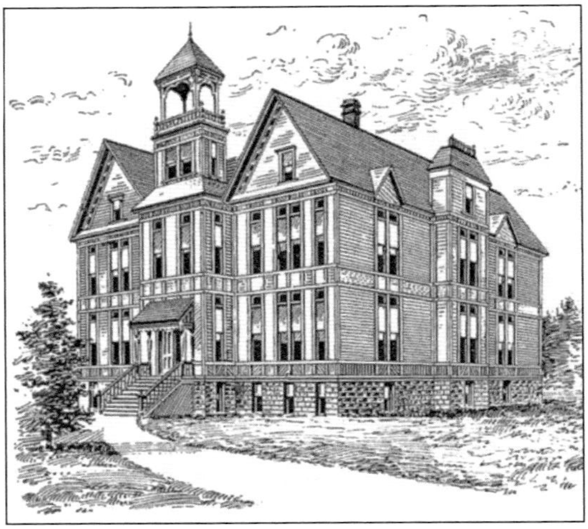

LIBERAL UNIVERSITY OF OREGON. Homer Davenport's cousin Pearl W. Geer stayed true to his family's secular roots and became interested in education. Geer was able to assemble a team of like-minded people to establish the first institute in the state not affiliated with a religious organization. The Liberal University of Oregon (LUO) Building, depicted in this illustration by Samuel Ames, was a beautiful Victorian structure. (Left, courtesy of the Geer family archives; right, from *Free Thought Magazine*, 1897.)

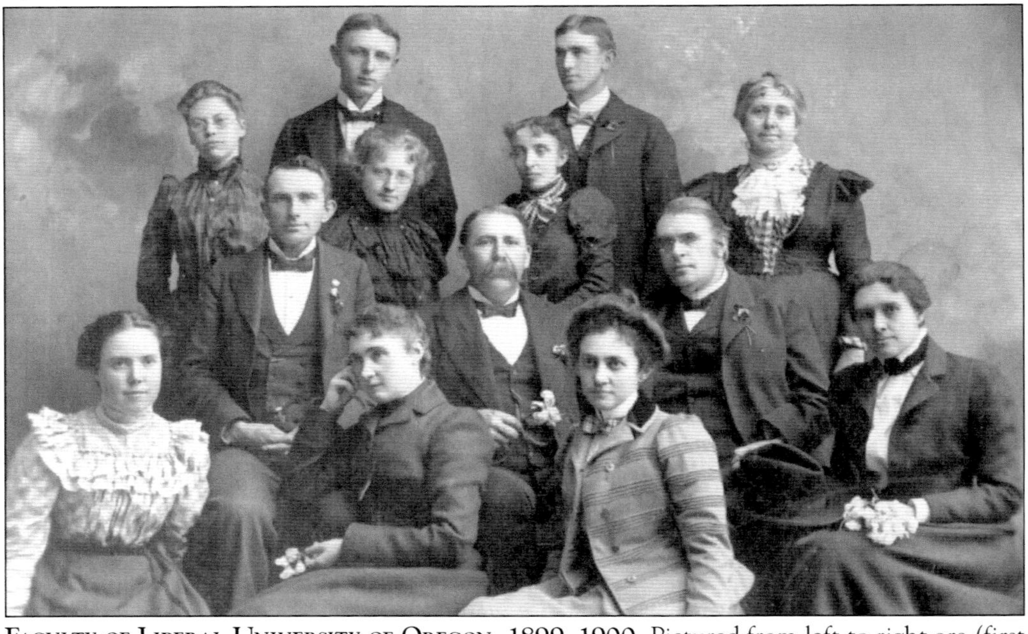

FACULTY OF LIBERAL UNIVERSITY OF OREGON, 1899–1900. Pictured from left to right are (first row) Lora Ames (physiology and hygiene), Minnie P. Hosmer (history, English, botany, and music), Sophie Wolf (piano, elocution, and English literature), and Clara Wakeman (art); (second row) Pres. John E. Hosmer, A.A. Leonard (anatomy, physiology, hygiene, and electricity), and Thaddeus B. Wakeman (history, society, law, ethics); (third row) Katie Mattesan (librarian), Alice Davenport (shorthand and typing), Minnie Preston (primary and kindergarten), and Emily L. Wakeman (girl's matron); (fourth row) Louis Raush (bookkeeping) and Pearl W. Geer (secretary and lecturer). (Courtesy of SCHS.)

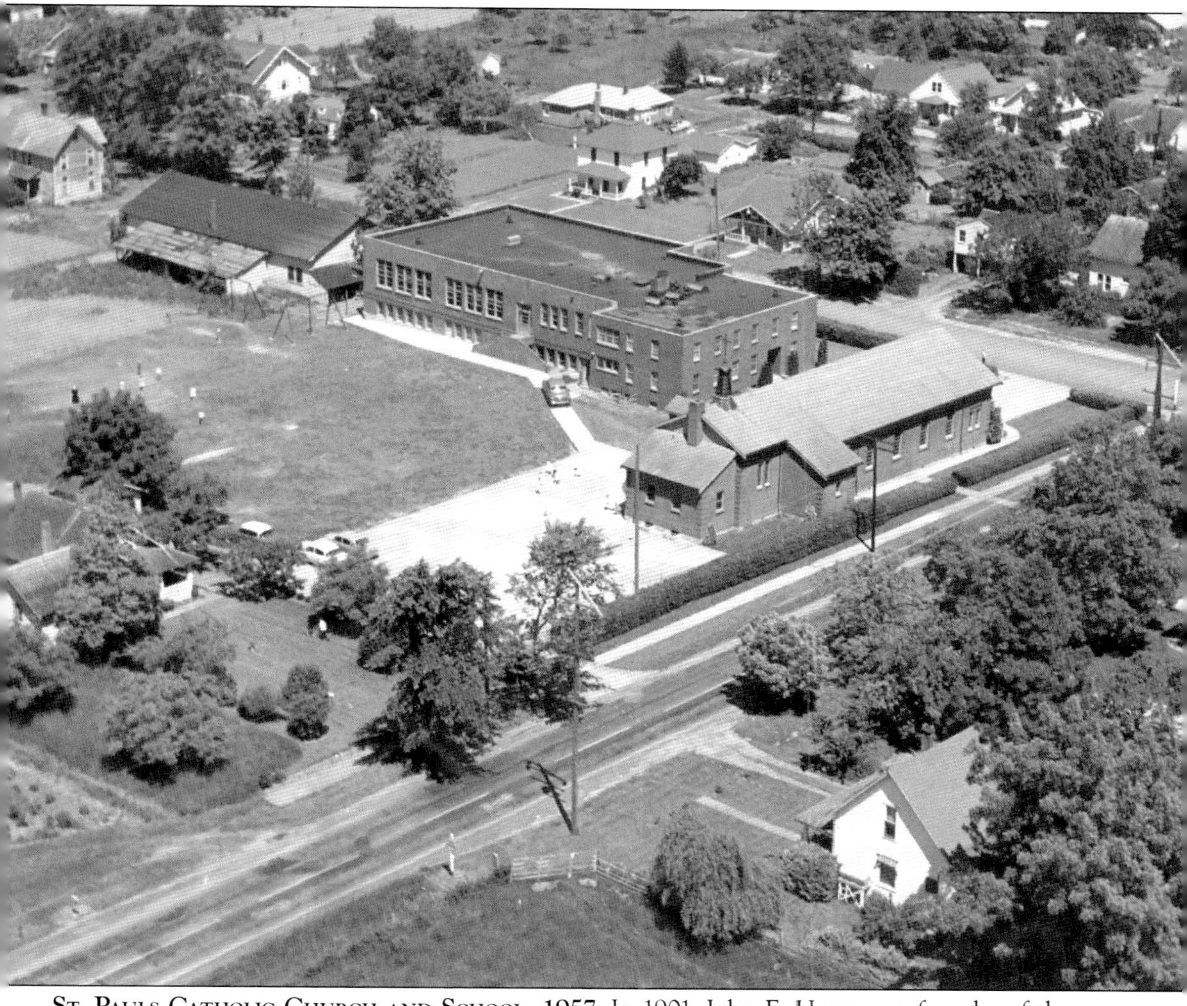

St. Pauls Catholic Church and School, 1957. In 1901, John E. Hosmer, cofounder of the Liberal University of Oregon, demanded to be bought out so that he and his wife, Minnie, could move to California to start over. Pearl Geer mortgaged his farm to buy him out. However, Hosmer instead remained in town and purchased the *Silverton Appeal* newspaper. He sold the *Silverton Appeal* several years later and then started the *Silverton Journal*. That publication ended with a lawsuit for libel from the Catholic Church in response to Hosmer's 1914 pamphlet, *The Escaped Nun from Mount Angel Convent*. In spite of the hard work of his defense attorney, Robert H. Down, Hosmer lost and served 100 days in jail. After 1902, the LUO school building sat vacant until the archdiocese of Oregon City purchased it in 1920. In a bit of ironic history, it became a private Catholic school. It was eventually torn down and replaced by the structure shown in this low oblique aerial view. (Madelyn Studios photograph; courtesy of SCHS.)

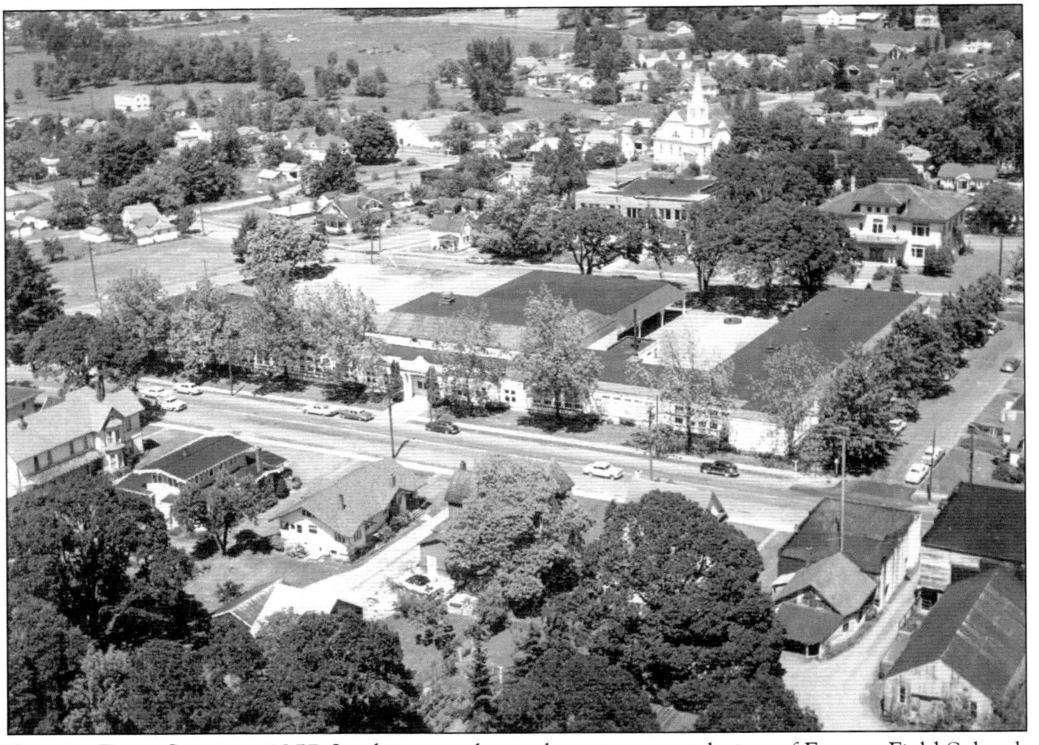

EUGENE FIELD SCHOOL, 1957. Looking northeast, here is an aerial view of Eugene Field School. Designed in 1921 by Portland architect C.N. Freeman, Eugene Field School was a modern marvel of educational design. Its unique single-story design eliminated the need for stairs. (Madelyn Studios photograph; courtesy of SCHS.)

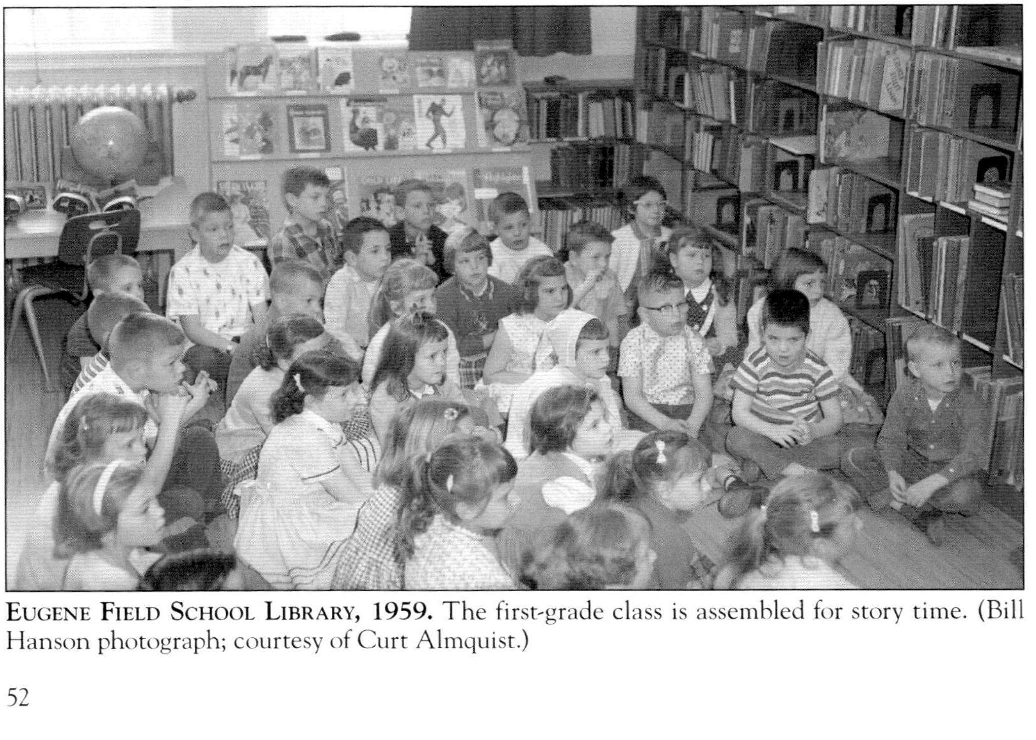

EUGENE FIELD SCHOOL LIBRARY, 1959. The first-grade class is assembled for story time. (Bill Hanson photograph; courtesy of Curt Almquist.)

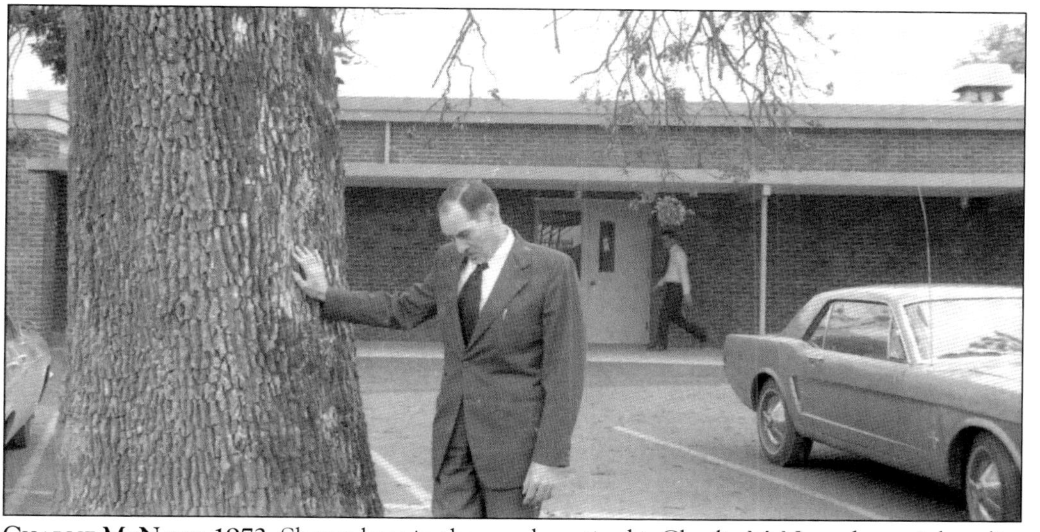

Charlie McNatt, 1973. Shown here in the year he retired is Charlie McNatt, the social studies teacher at Silverton Union High School (SUHS). Originally from Oklahoma and of Native American descent, he was an inspiration to countless students. Both Charlie and the oak he is leaning on are now gone. (Gus Frederick photograph.)

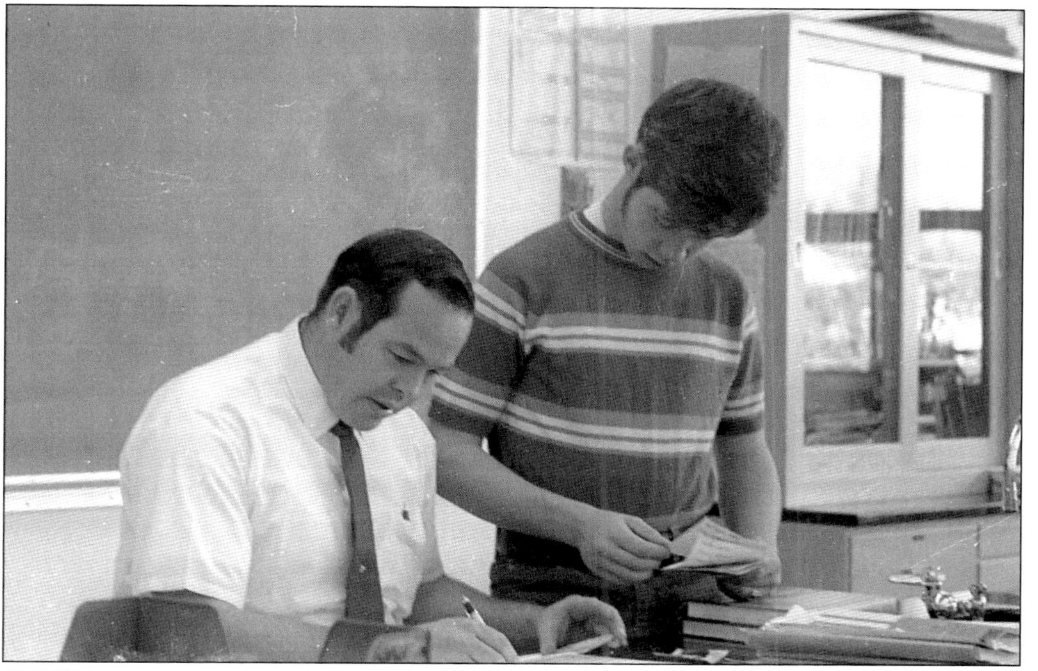

SUHS Science Class, 1973. Shown at the old Schlador Street campus, science teacher Lowell Swanson and student Arlan Gilmore discuss an assignment. (Gus Frederick photograph.)

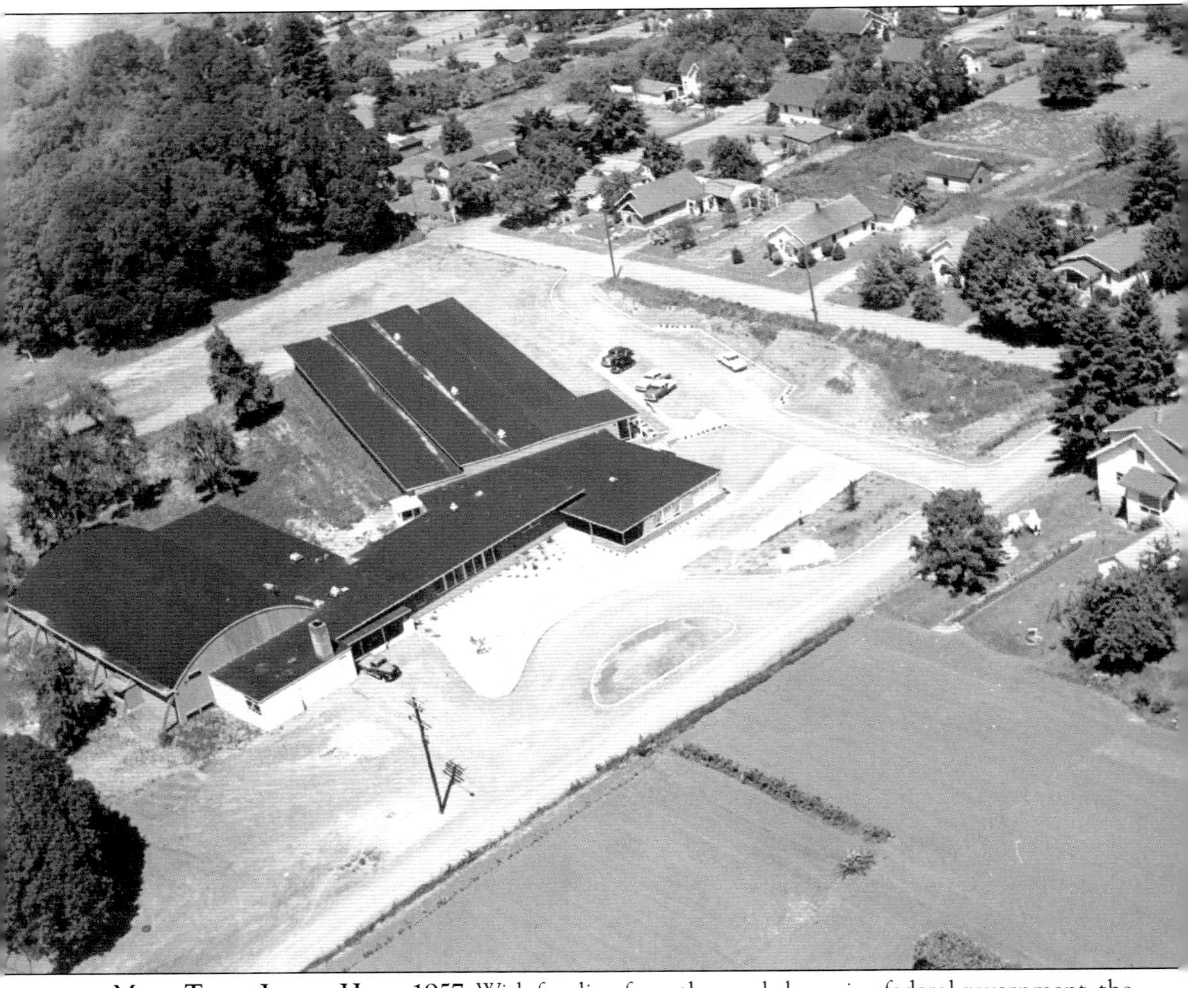

Mark Twain Junior High, 1957. With funding from the newly booming federal government, the Silverton School District decided to add another school to the system. Construction started in the fall of 1956 and was pretty far along by the spring of 1957 when this shot was taken. Located on property that used to be part of DeGuire's dairy pasture on West Hill, it overlooked the vanishing ruins of the Silver Falls Timber Company mill located just to the north. Mark Twain Junior High is one of 10 in the Silver Falls School District. It serves 272 students in grades seven and eight. (Madelyn Studios photograph; courtesy of SCHS.)

Five

The Business Community

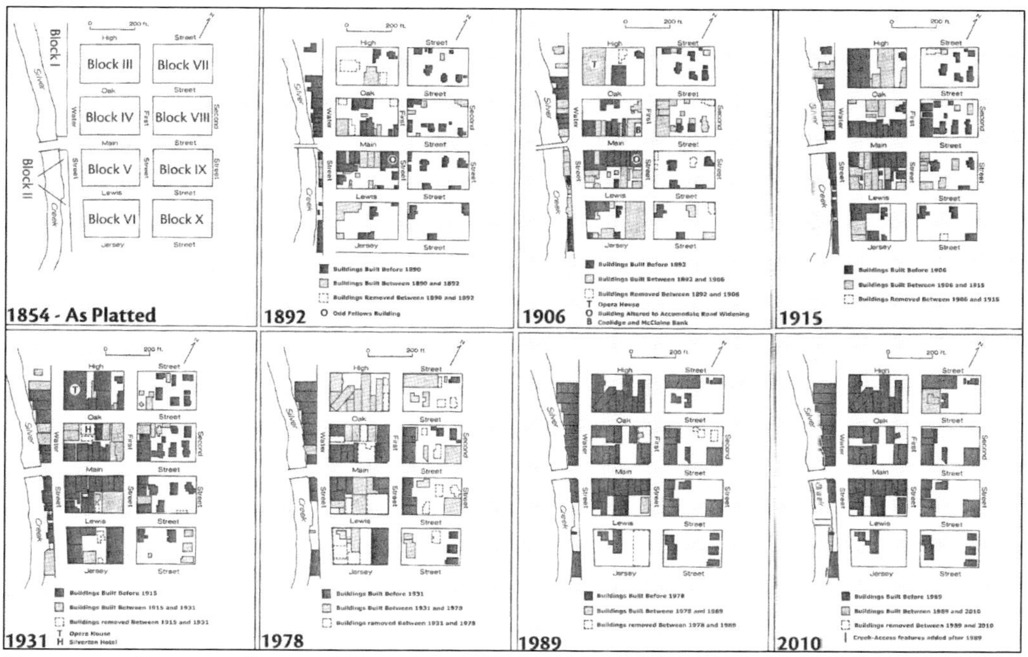

Downtown Business Core, 1854 to 2010. These diagrams show the ebb and flow of Silverton's downtown business district. Note the addition of multiple creek access features, which were added between 1989 and 2010. (Courtesy of P. McEachern; modified by Gus Frederick.)

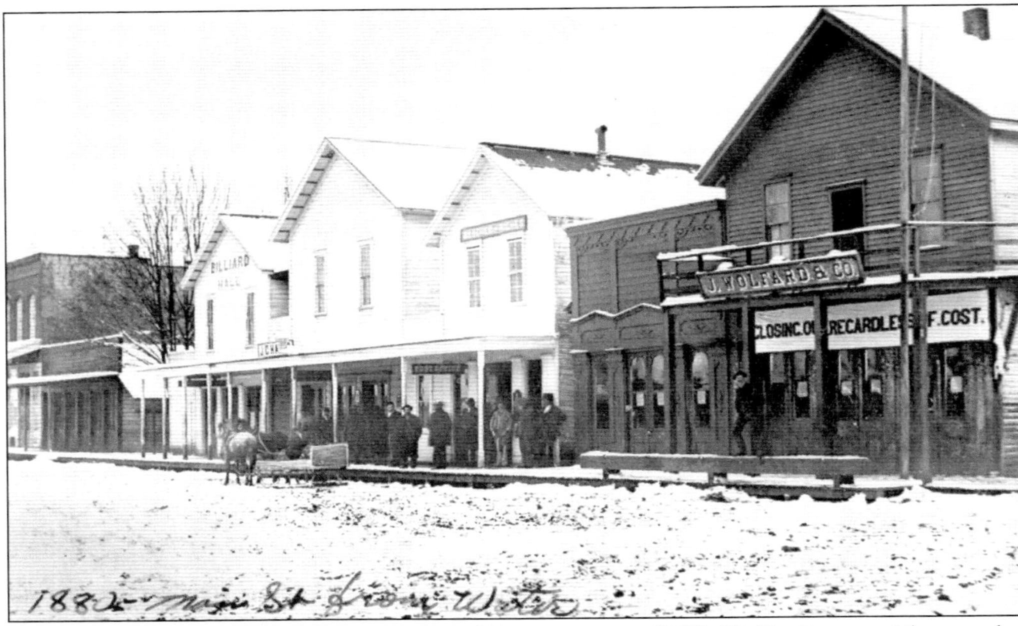

Main Street from Water Street, 1880. Here is a view of J.W. Wolfard's store. The wooden structure was replaced several years later with the brick structure that is still in use today. (Courtesy of SCHS.)

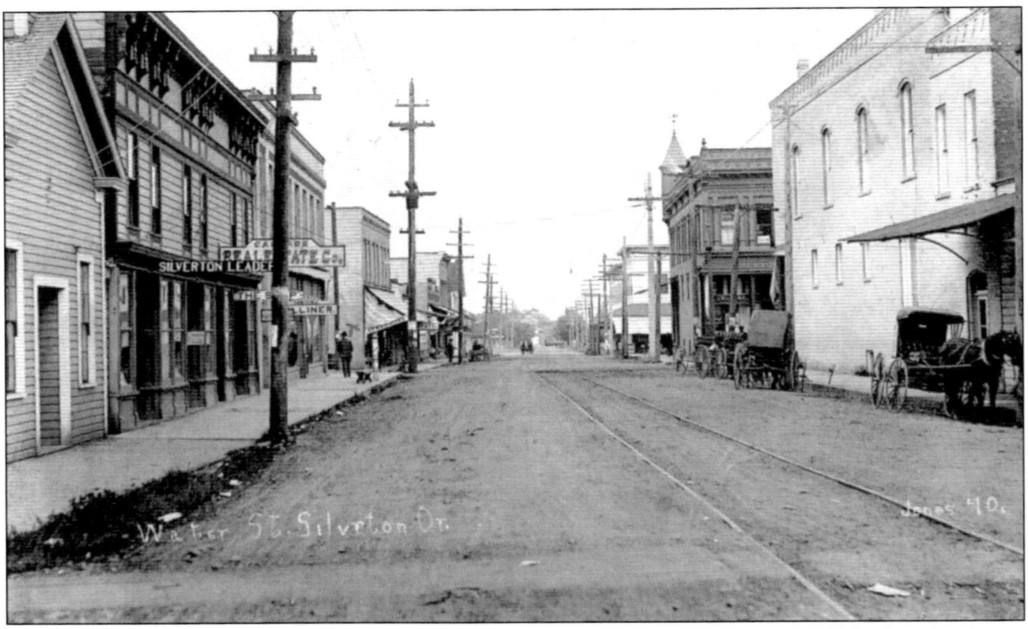

Water Street, Looking North, 1890. Here is a north view of the second block. The Ames Building on the left housed Dr. A.E. Wrightman's office on the top floor for close to 20 years. (Courtesy of SCHS.)

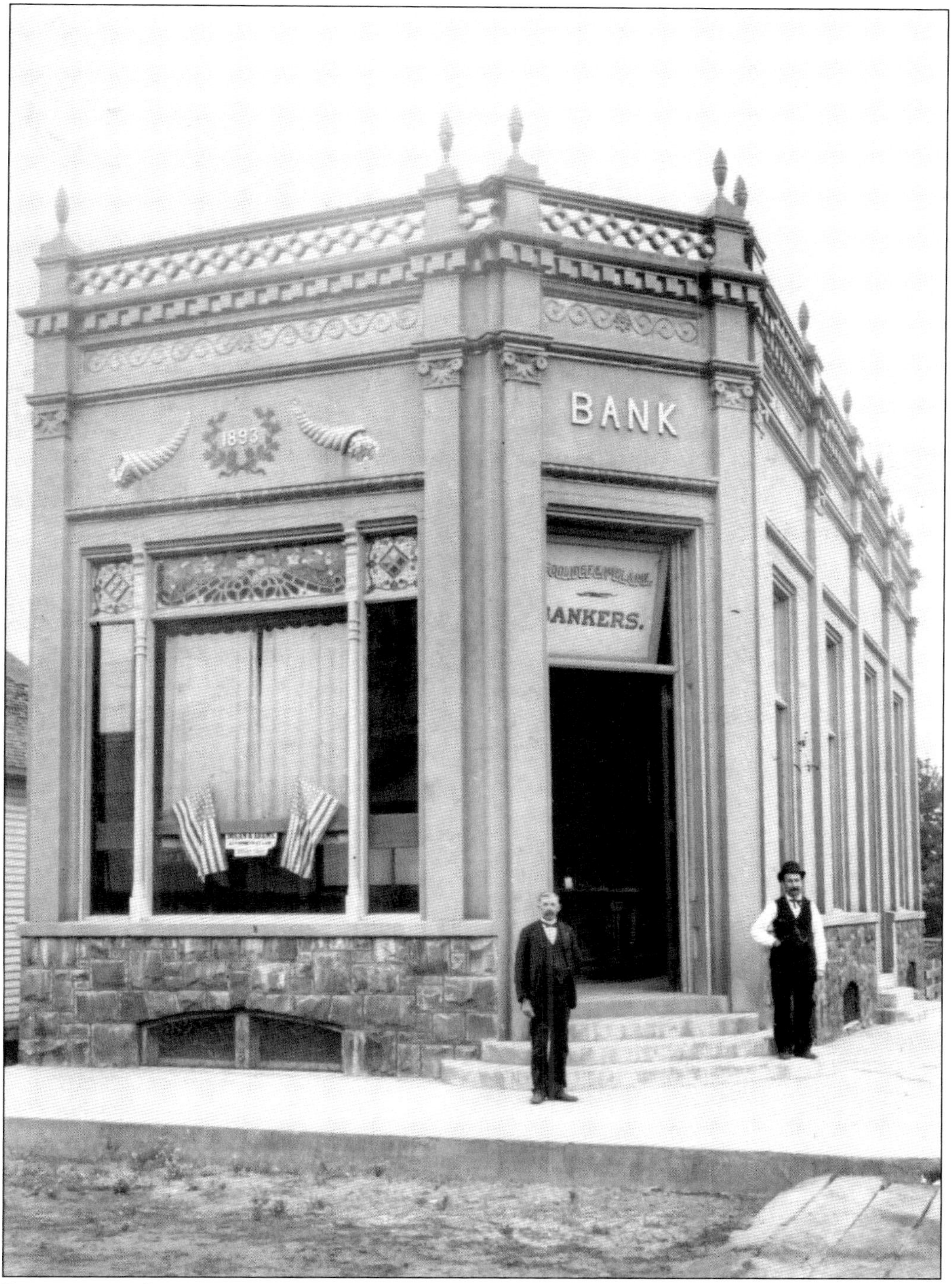

Exterior of Coolidge-McClaine Bank, 1893. On the northwest corner of First and Main Streets, Silverton's original financial institution, built in 1893, is shown. Coolidge-McClaine Bank survived and prospered for many years until falling victim to the Great Depression. The current Citizens Bank Building replaced this one in 1922. (Courtesy of SCHS.)

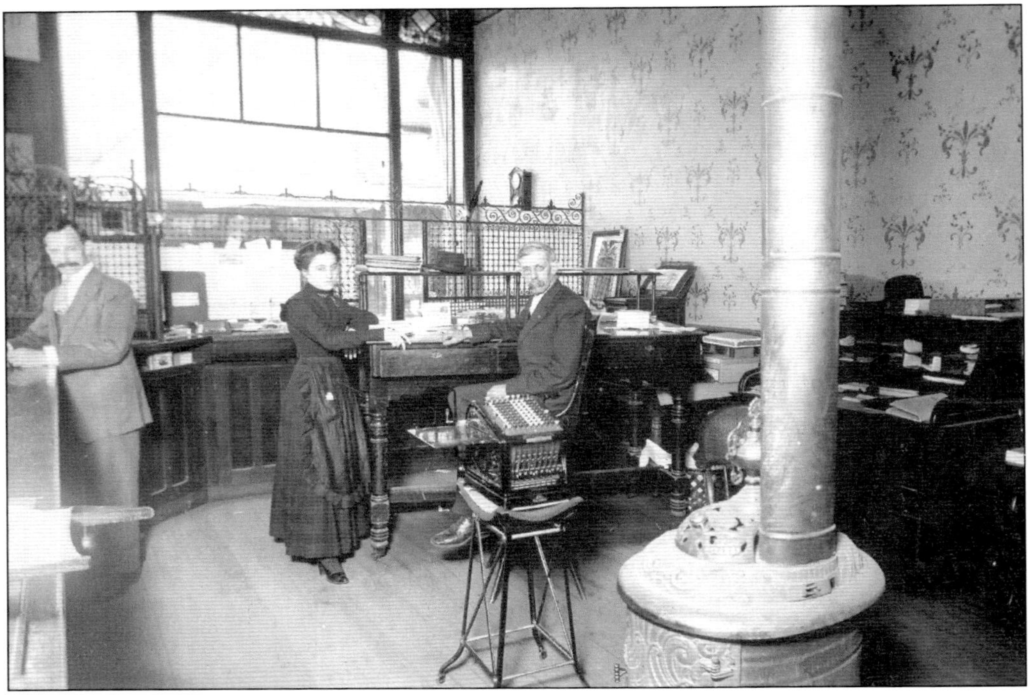

INTERIOR OF COOLIDGE-MCCLAINE BANK, 1890S. All the latest conveniences are visible in this magnesium-flash scene. Powdered magnesium metal would be lit, creating a brilliant flash, flooding the room with enough light to expose the plate. Those pictured are, from left to right, Ed Adams, Alpha Smith, and Martin Adams. (Courtesy of SCHS.)

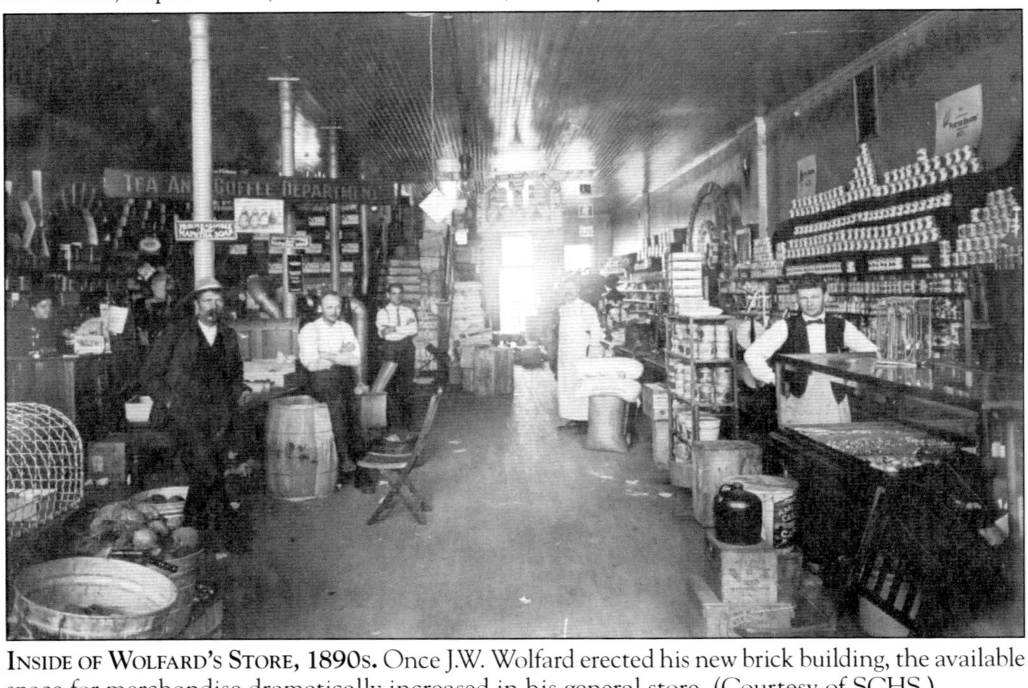

INSIDE OF WOLFARD'S STORE, 1890S. Once J.W. Wolfard erected his new brick building, the available space for merchandise dramatically increased in his general store. (Courtesy of SCHS.)

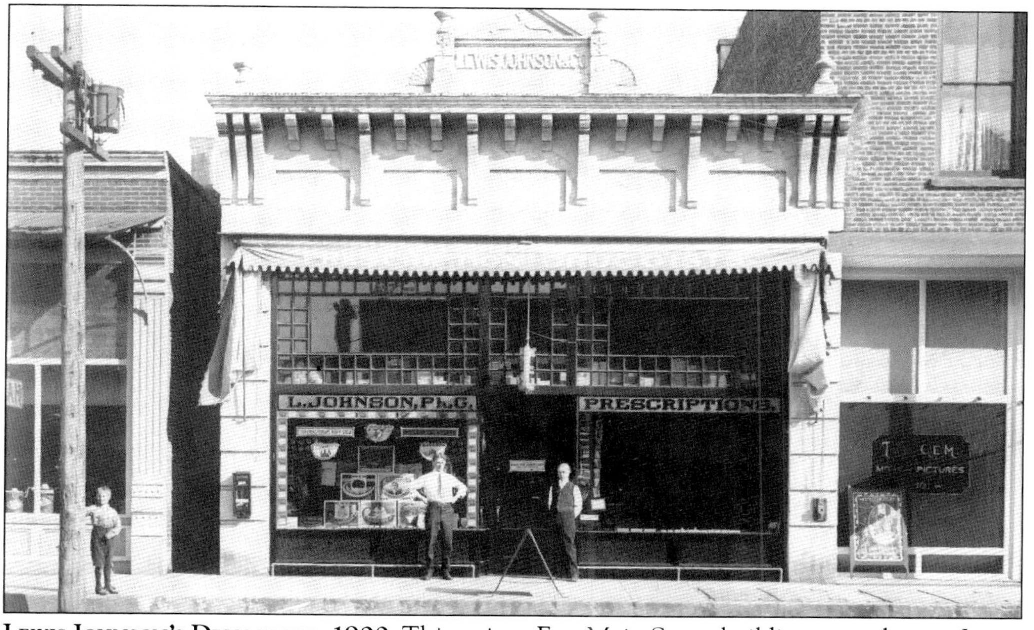

LEWIS JOHNSON'S DRUGSTORE, 1900. This unique East Main Street building started out as Lewis Johnson's Drugstore. Since then, it has been a jewelry store and currently hosts one of Silverton's finer gourmet bistros, the Silver Grill. (Courtesy of SCHS.)

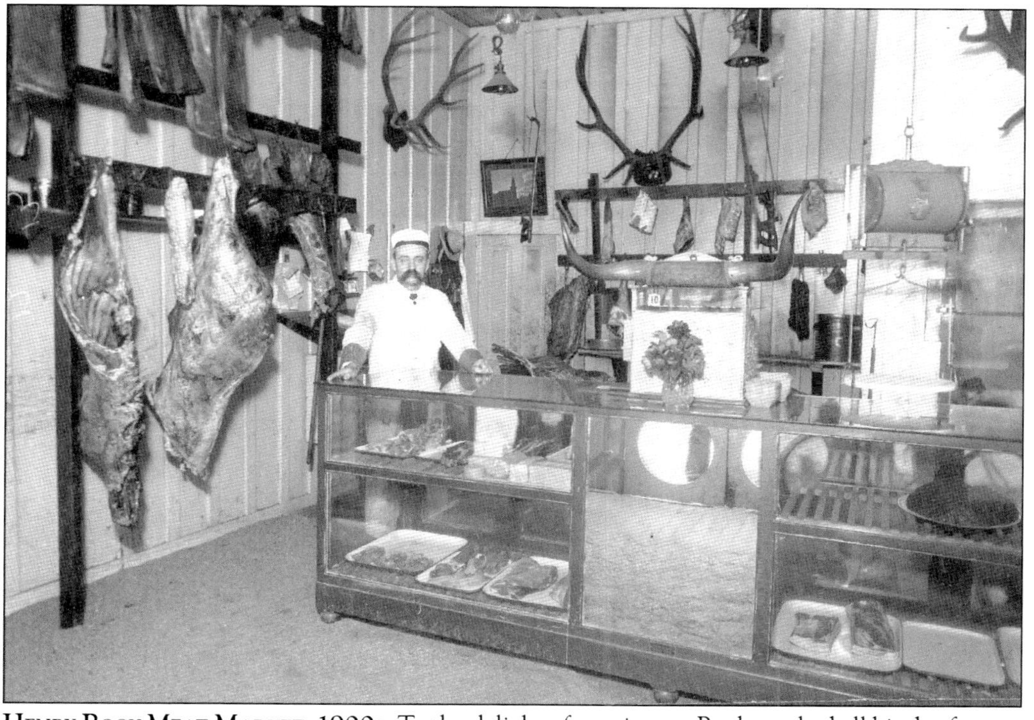

HENRY BOCK MEAT MARKET, 1900s. To the delight of carnivores, Bock stocked all kinds of meats and even did custom butchering and packing orders for local hunters and cattlemen. (Courtesy of SCHS.)

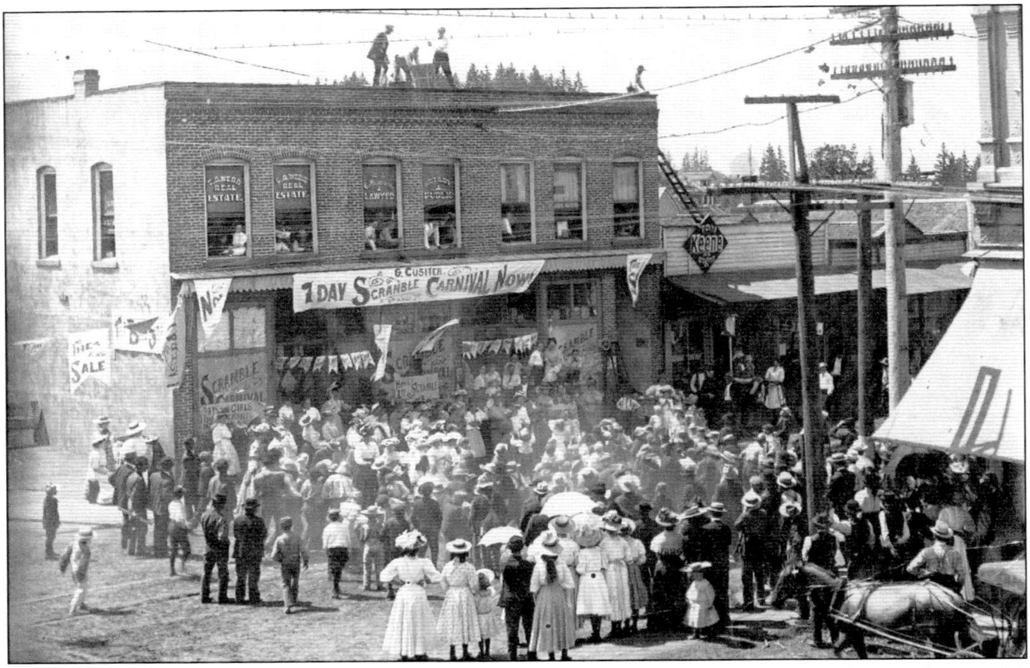

Seven-Day Scramble Carnival, 1900s. George Cusiter's store seems to be employing the c. 1973 National Lampoon Radio Dinner "catch it and you keep it" approach to marketing. Apparently, special coupons were thrown from the roof of the Water Street store, and those lucky enough to catch the coupon received a good deal. (Courtesy of SCHS.)

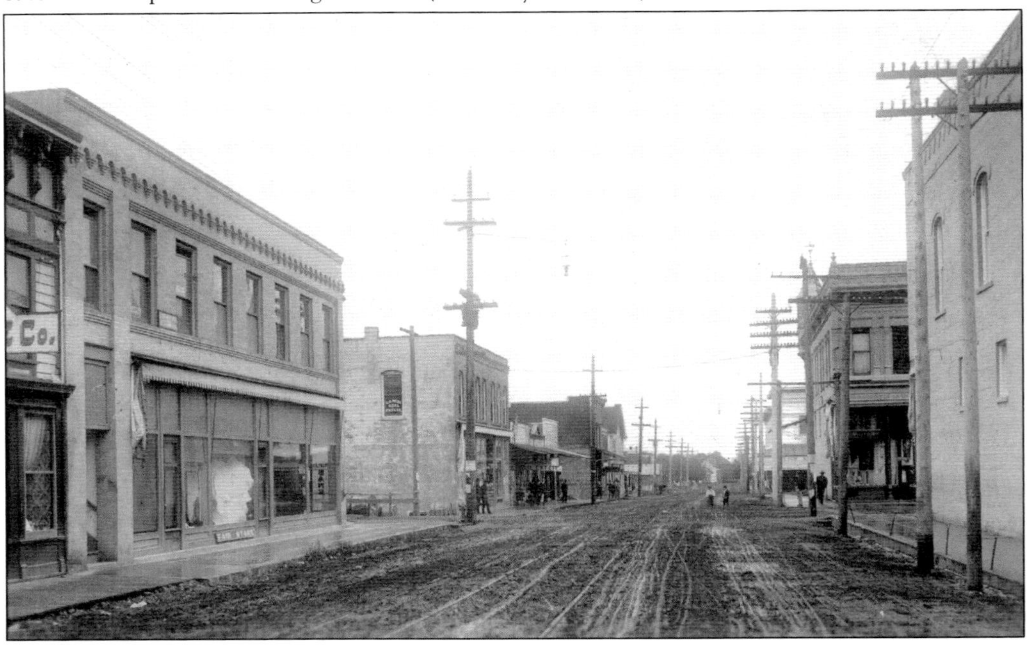

Water and Main Streets, Looking North, 1900s. This photograph shows Cusiter's store (from the previous image) on the left. Note the train tracks for the Fischer Flouring Mill spur running down the center of the street. (Courtesy of SCHS.)

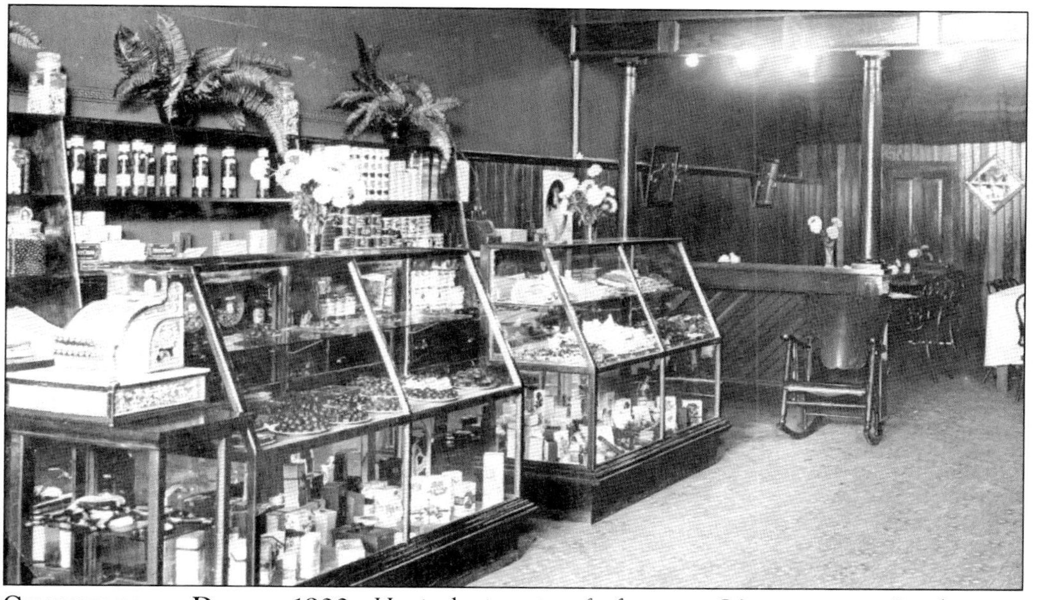

Confections on Display, 1900s. Her is the interior of a forgotten Silverton store. Candy stores were popular, as the town hosted several confectioneries. (Courtesy of SCHS.)

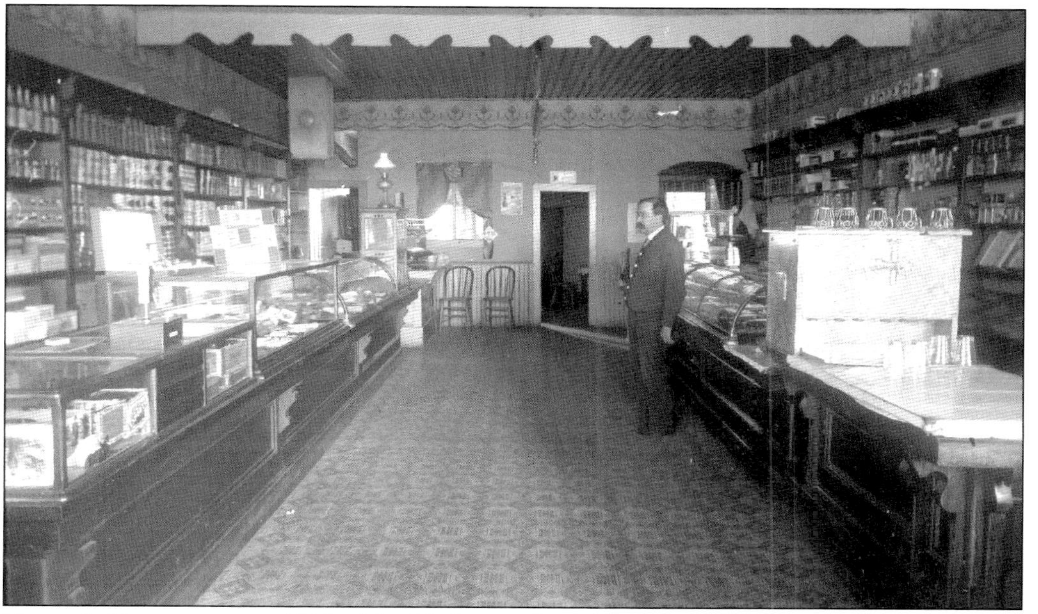

Morley's Confectionery, 1900s. John Morley stands ready to serve his customers. His confectionery was located on North Water Street, next to Cusiter's Market. John was a descendant of Silverton pioneer Moses Morley. (Courtesy of SCHS.)

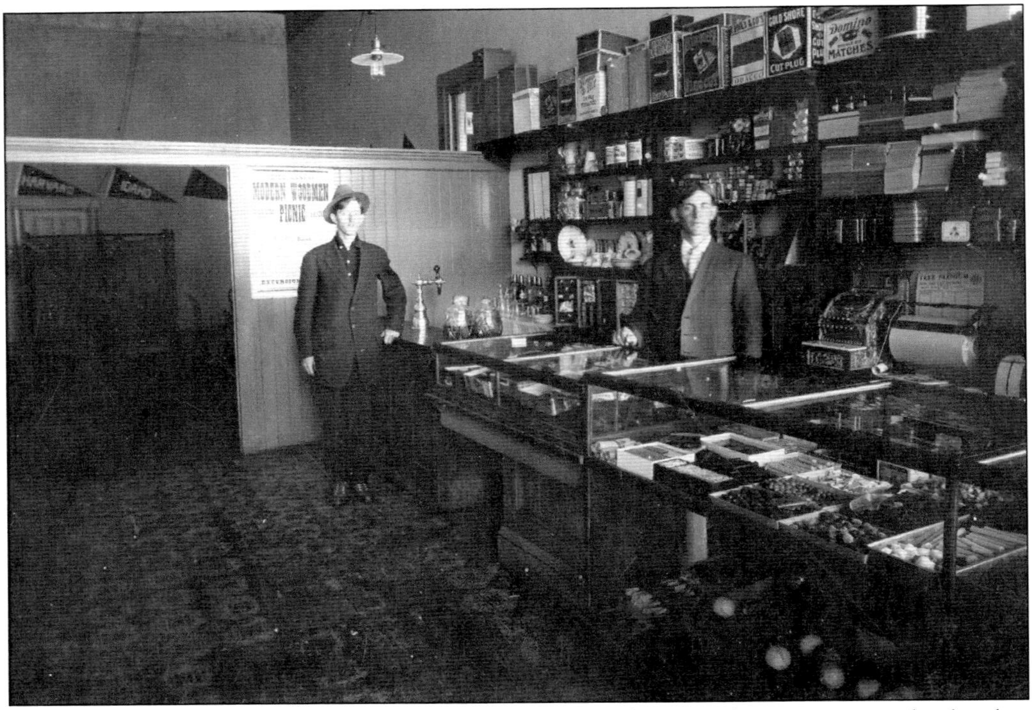

First Street Ice Cream and Candy Store, 1902. Mack Opsund is seen visiting his brother Robert (behind the counter). Even before Prohibition, Silverton was a dry community. Many of the merchants employed a "candy is dandy" approach to sales. (Courtesy of SCHS.)

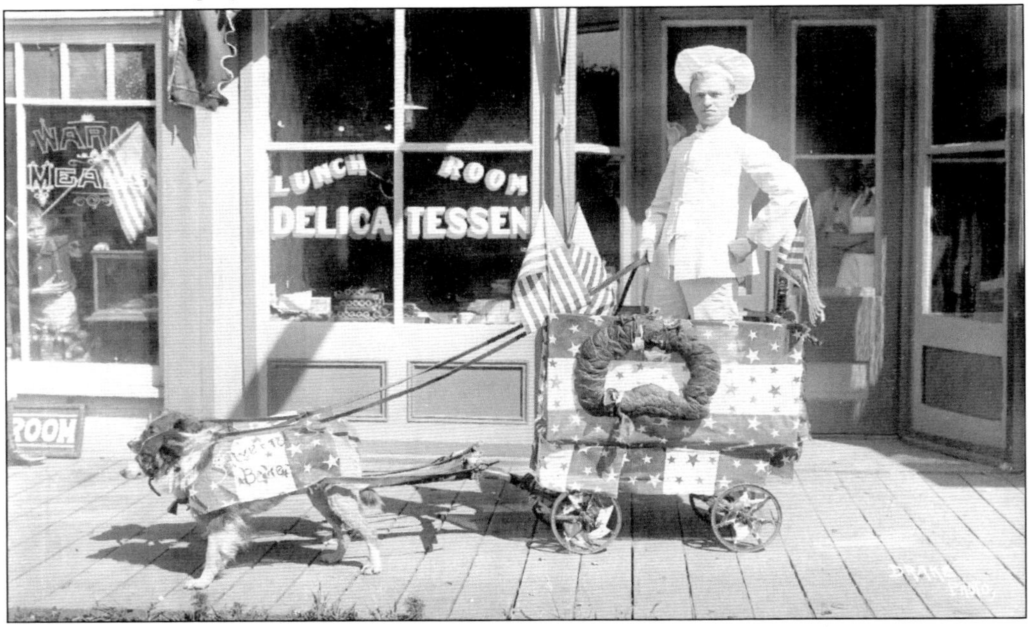

Hot Dogs for Lunch, 1904. The unidentified chef of the Lunchroom Delicatessen on Main Street is prepared for the annual Fourth of July Parade with his dog-powered wagon. (Courtesy of SCHS.)

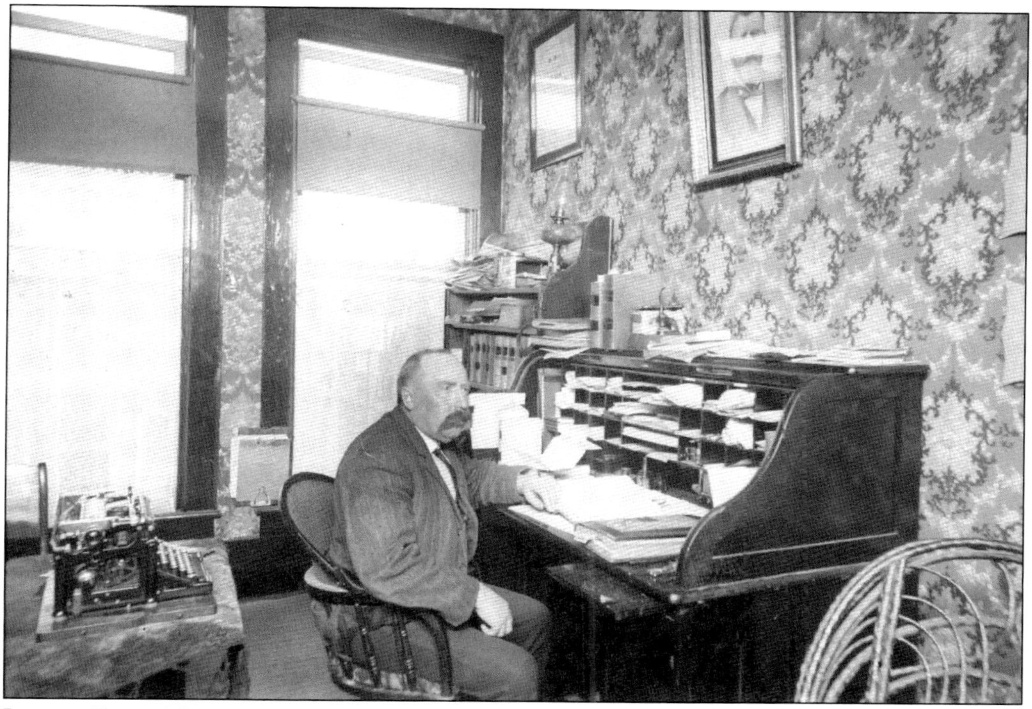

Justice Earle Hammond, 1906. His honor poses at a rolltop desk in his office. The roll-down cover, when locked tight, served the same function as a computer password today. (Courtesy of SCHS.)

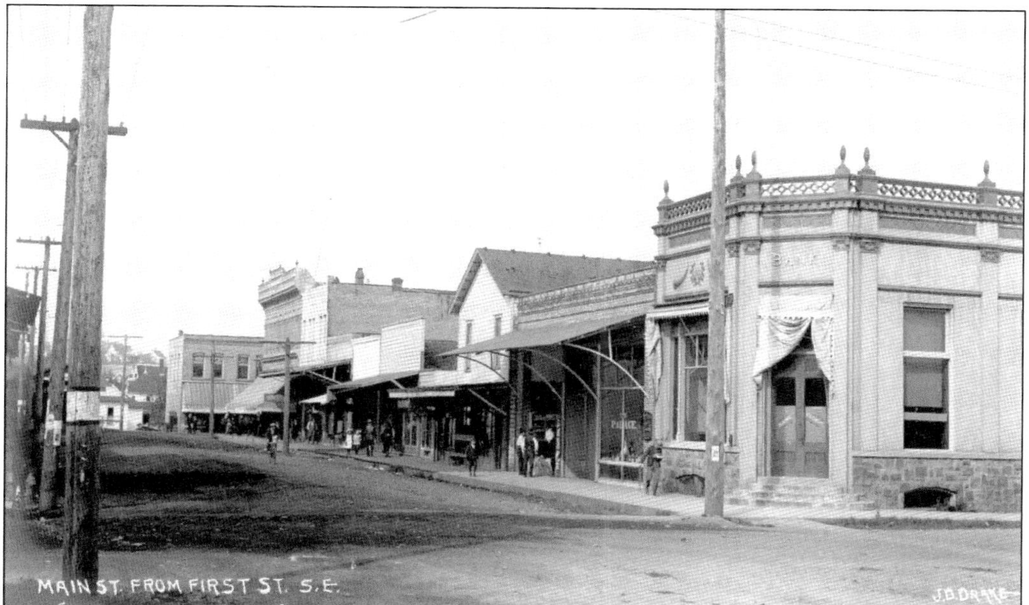

Main Street from First Street, 1907. On the right is the Coolidge-McClaine Bank. At far left is Cusiter's store, and West Hill is beyond. (Drake Brothers photograph; courtesy of SCHS.)

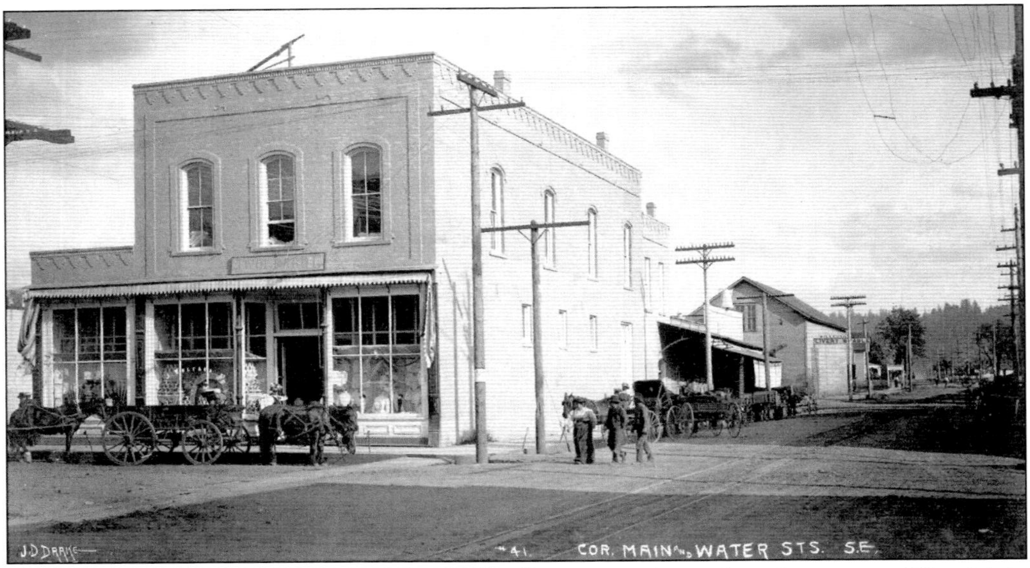

MAIN AND WATER STREETS, 1907. John Wolfard's store was located on the corner of East Main and Water Streets. This was just before the addition that expanded the building to the left of this view. Today, the lower portion houses El Toro, one of Silverton's finest family restaurants. It has a dance studio upstairs. (Drake Brothers photograph; courtesy of SCHS.)

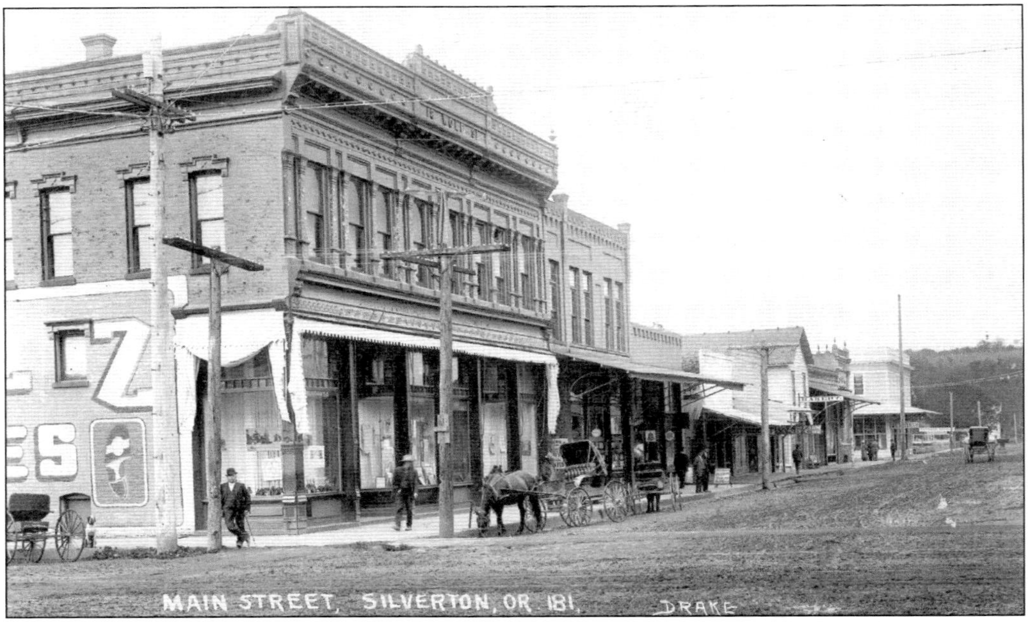

ADOLF WOLF BUILDING, 1911. Across the street from Wolfard's sits one of Silverton's most unique historic buildings, the 1890 Adolf Wolf Building. It started as, and remained, a hardware store for much of its history. Wolf Hardware became Wolf and Sons, then Ames Hardware, and finally Hande Hardware. Today, with its exterior largely unchanged, the Adolf Wolf Building serves as an anchor business in the downtown core and encloses a unique Victorian mall of small shops within. The top floors sport modern apartments and office space. (Drake Brothers photograph; courtesy of SCHS.)

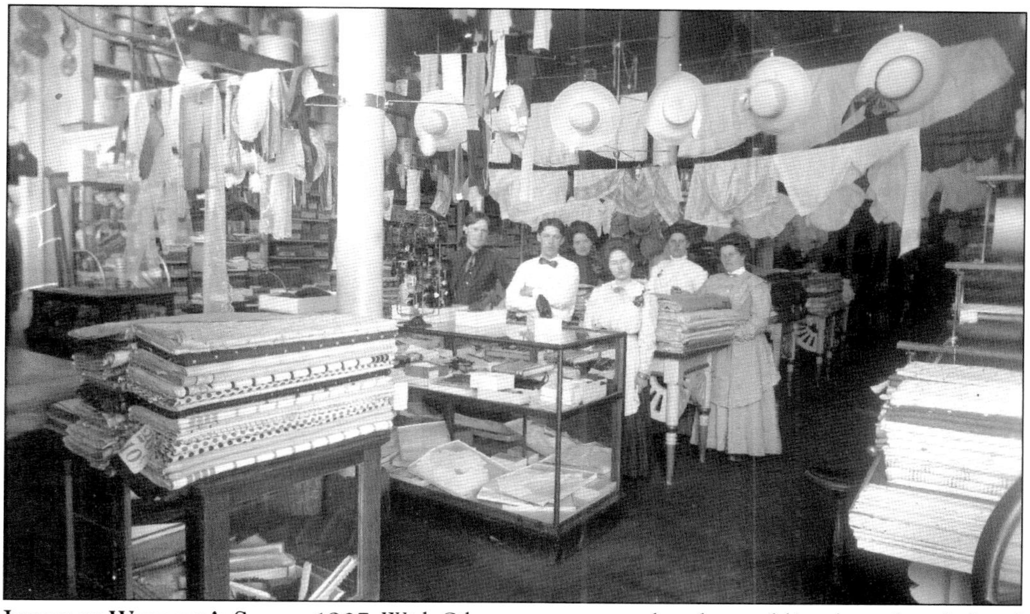

INSIDE OF WOLFARD'S STORE, 1907. With Silverton connected to the world by the railroads, local merchants were able to provide many goods that had been unheard of luxuries just several years earlier. John Wolfard was on top of his game and built a large warehouse, blocking Front Street on the north side of town near the train depot. Wolfard's warehouse eventually became the cannery, now housing Bruce Pack Meat Product Designers. (Courtesy of SCHS.)

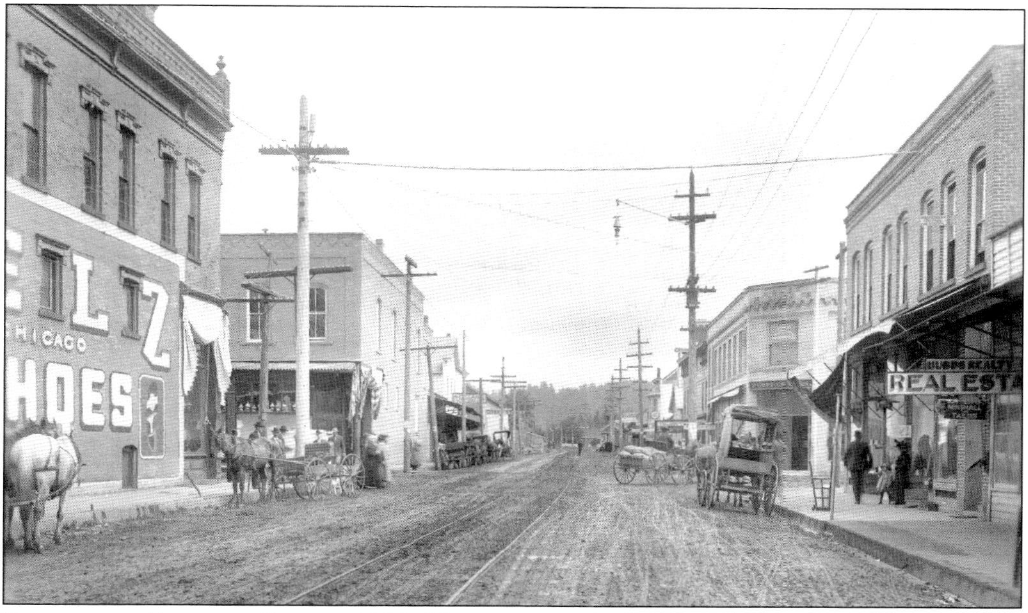

DOWNTOWN, LOOKING SOUTH, 1909. Here is a view looking south down Water Street. The Adolf Wolf Building is on the left, with Wolfard's store across the street. The Fischer Flouring Mill railroad spur is visible going down the center of the street. The rails were paved over and eventually removed in the 1980s during a major sewer upgrade. A portion of the original rails can be seen outside the Silverton Country Historical Society Museum. (Courtesy of SCHS.)

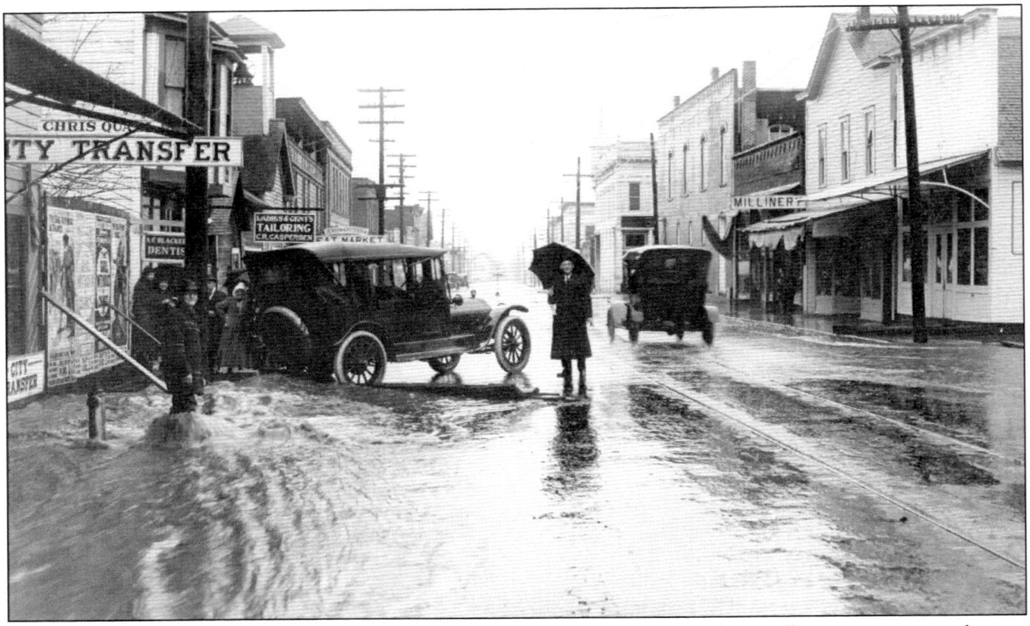

WATER ON WATER STREET, 1920s. Silver Creek tops its banks and overflows into town during a winter flood. The view is looking north, with the Wolf and Wolfard Buildings in the center. The *Bobbie the Wonder Dog* mural by Silverton artist Lori Webb is currently on the left side of this view. (Courtesy of SCHS.)

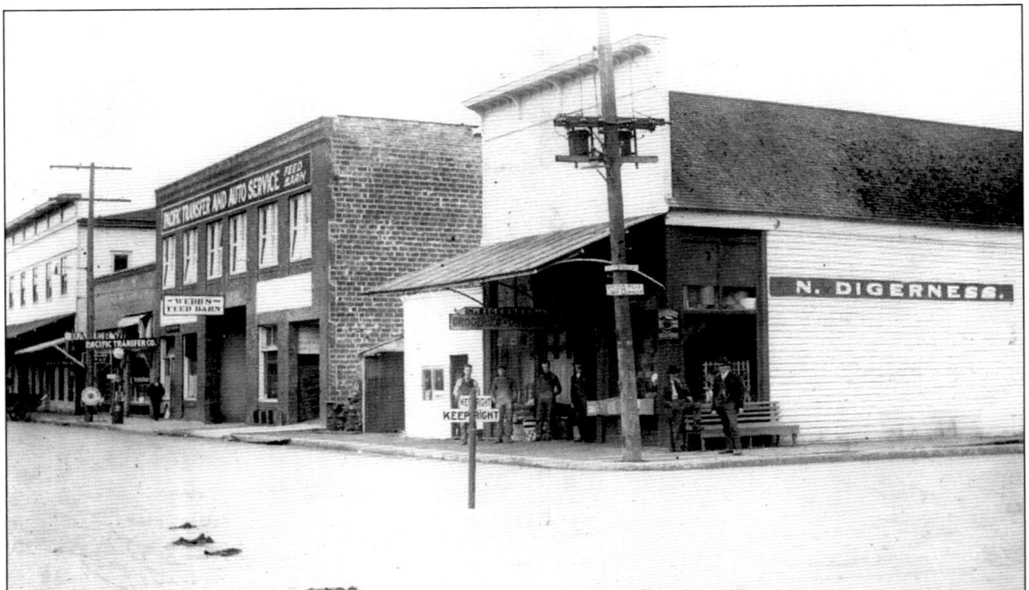

OAK STREET, 1914. On the corner of Oak and First Streets, the Digerness Store is next door to the Pacific Transfer and Auto Service and Webb's Feed Barn. This is an interesting visual indicator of society's change from a horse-drawn to an auto-centric world. The building was gutted by the opera house fire of 1935. (Courtesy of SCHS.)

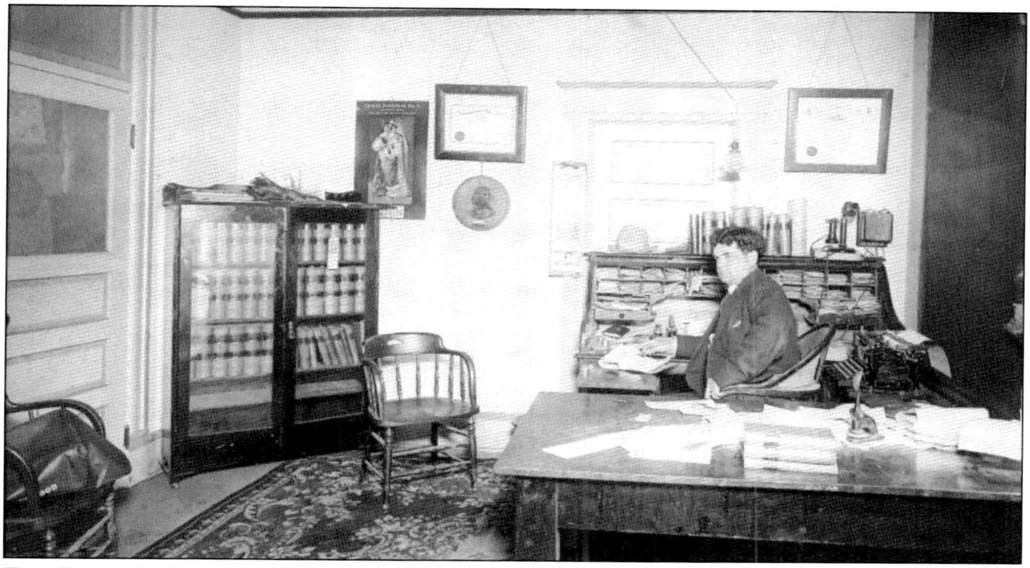

The People's Council, 1912. Silverton attorney Van Valkenberg sits in his office for this unique electric-arc flash image. Unlike the soft, even lighting from magnesium powder, the arc flash created a smaller, brighter source of light, making more pronounced shadows and luminous highlights. It only required the push of a button, instead of igniting a narrow tray of explosive powdered metal. (Courtesy of SCHS.)

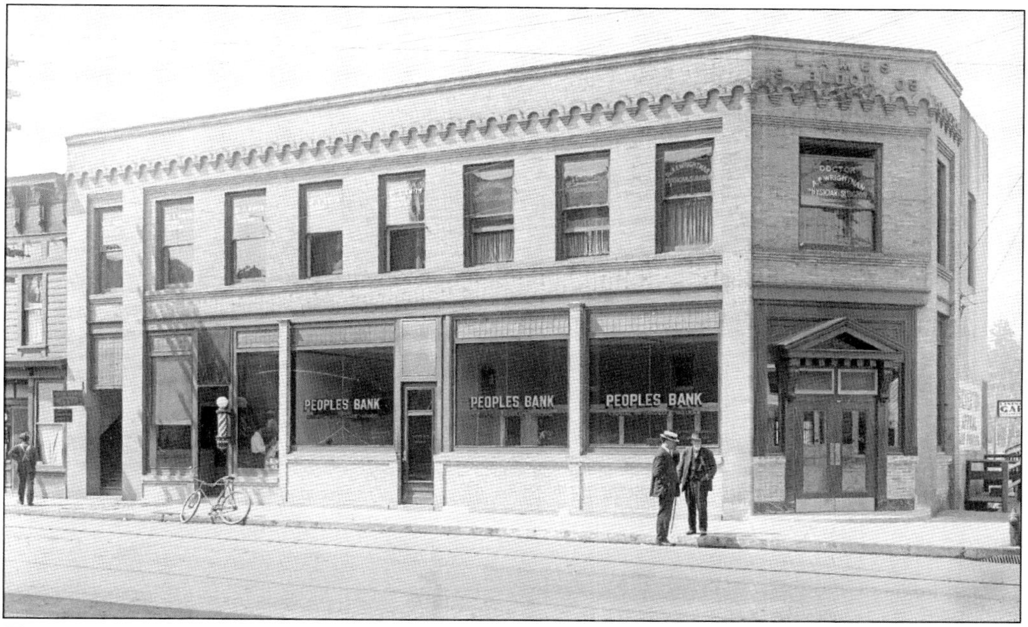

The L. Ames Building, 1914. Here is the Peoples Bank, on the corner of Water and Main Streets. Dr. A.E. Wrightman, a physician and surgeon, had an office on the second floor. First National Bank took over several years after this photograph was captured. Currently, the building houses the Larson and Flynn Insurance Agency. In the 2001 comedy *Bandits*, it was used as a bank. Filmed in and around the Silverton area, *Bandits* was directed by Barry Levinson and starred Bruce Willis, Billy Bob Thornton, and Cate Blanchett. (Courtesy of SCHS.)

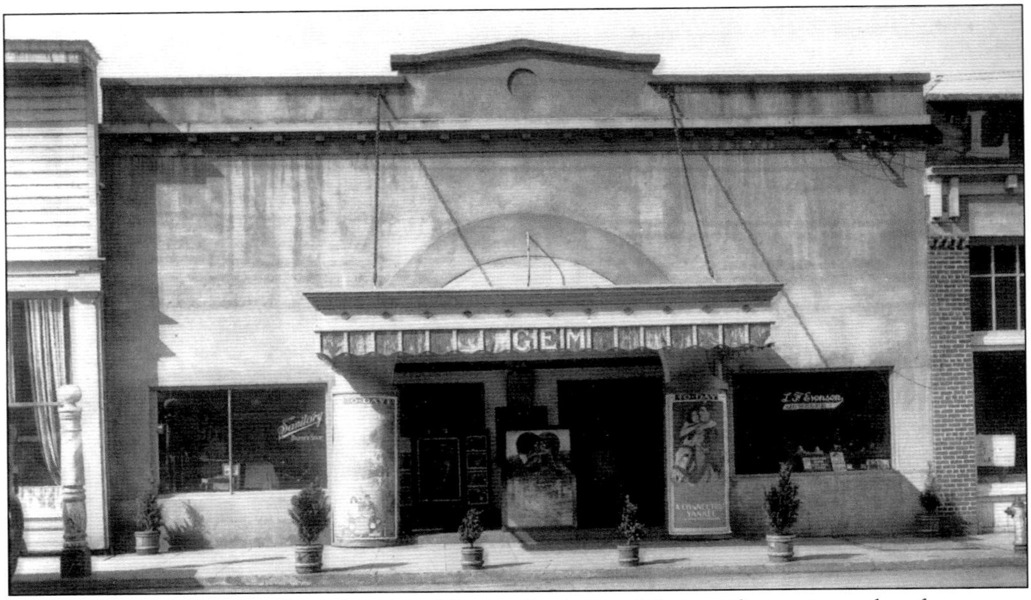

THE GEM THEATER, 1914. Over the years, Silverton had several theaters for movies and performances. The Gem Theater on North Water Street was situated across the street from the much larger Palace Theater, which was called the opera house. The Gem remained in operation after the fire of 1935, as did the rebuilt Palace Theater. When M.G. Cooley, the owner of the Gem, decided to retire, Al Adams, the owner of the Palace, bought it and closed it down. It is currently the Red Bench antique store. (Courtesy of SCHS.)

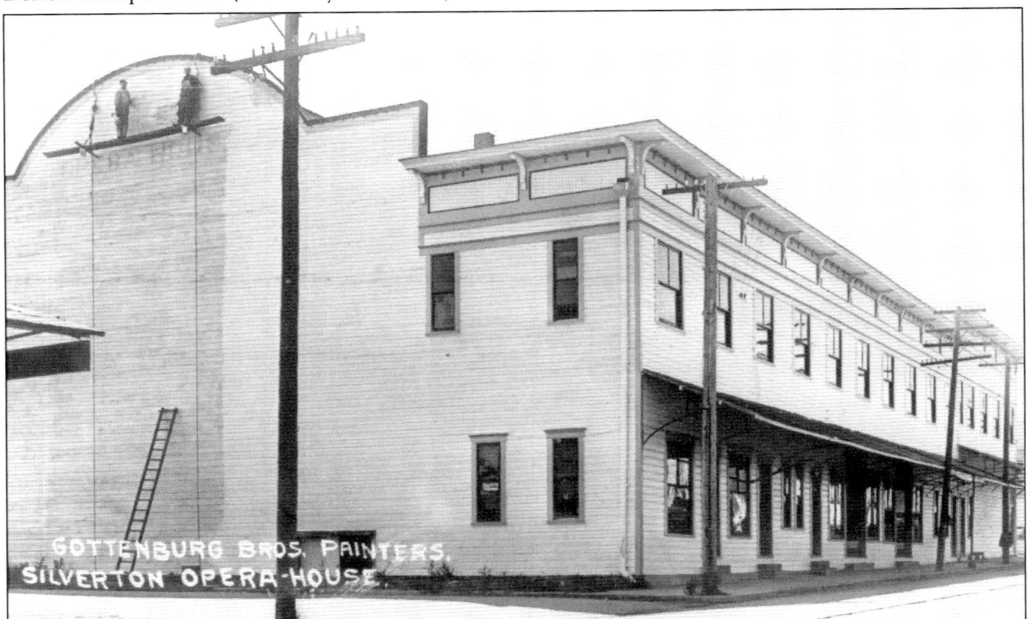

THE OPERA HOUSE, 1914. A massive structure taking up half the block, the original Palace Theater offered a unique challenge to the Gottenburg brothers (seen here painting the building). The theater was used for live shows and also motion pictures. (Courtesy of SCHS.)

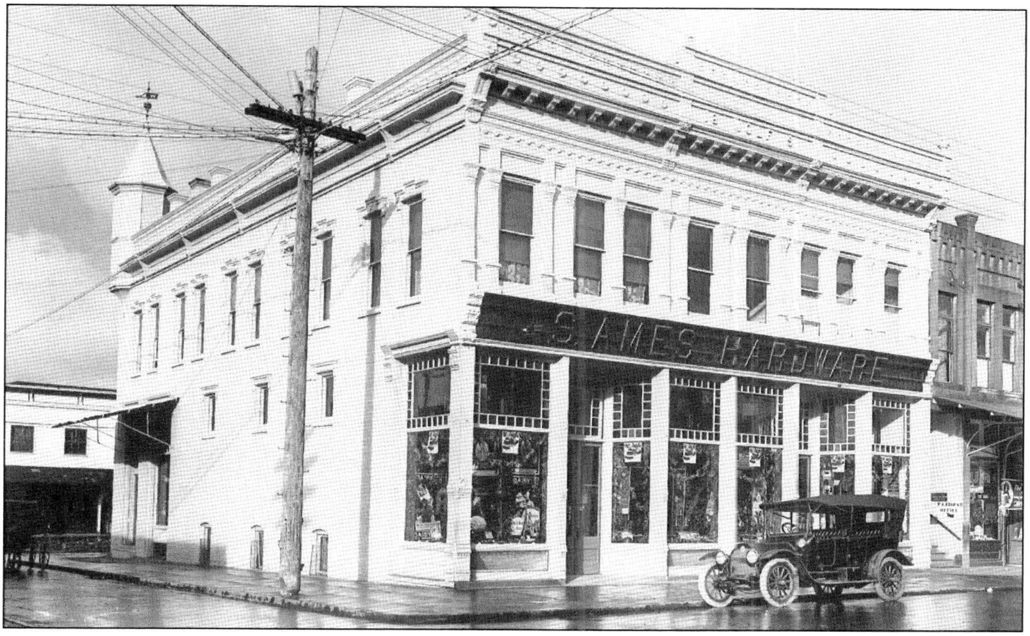

AMES HARDWARE, 1919. The Adolf Wolf Building is now home to Samuel Ames's hardware. Samuel was the artist who sketched the illustration on page 50 of the Liberal University. Ames's son Norris took over the business. Norris retired to the Ames River Ranch along the banks of the Abiqua Creek. Carl Hande expanded his already thriving hardware business and moved into the building. Carl operated it until his retirement in the 1980s. (Courtesy of Almquist Studios.)

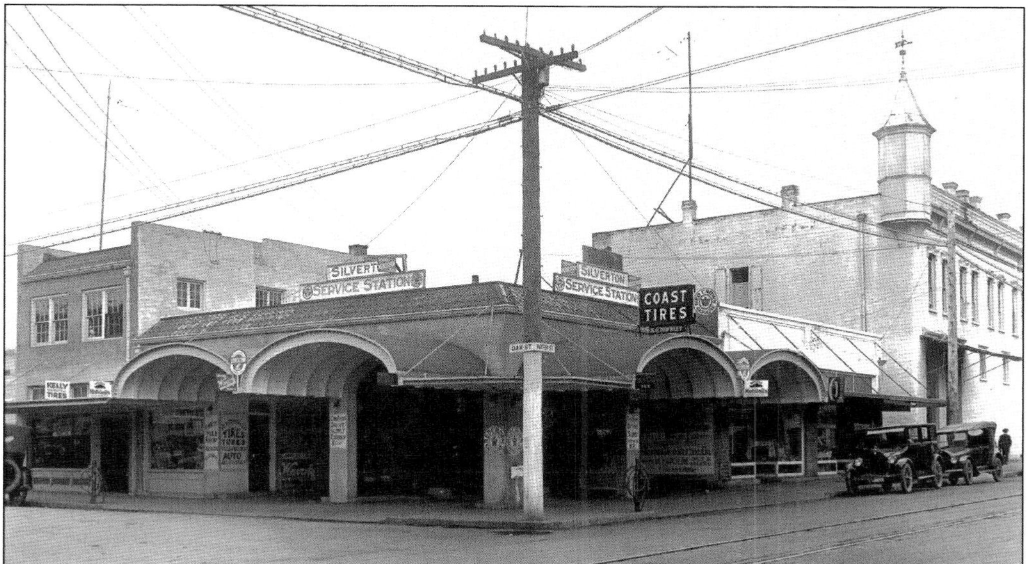

SILVERTON SERVICE STATION, 1924. Joe Uphoff opened the first dedicated automotive service station in town. Located on the corner of Oak and North Water Streets, it sits just behind the Adolf Wolf Building, which is visible on the right side of this image. A cluster of small shops now occupies this corner, including a barber, hair stylist, and collectible fossil and lapidary supply store. (Courtesy of SCHS.)

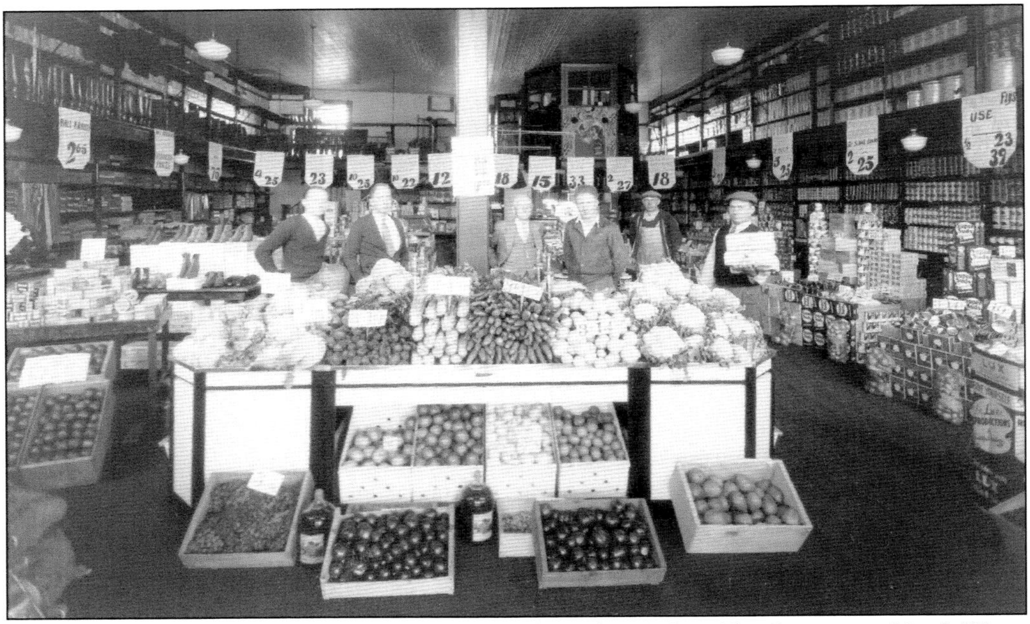

Julius Alm Grocery, 1920s. In the heyday of fresh produce, Julius Alm Grocery on North Water Street offered a wide variety of locally grown organic produce. Those pictured are, from left to right, Elmer Peterson, Otto Alm, Julius Alm Sr., Ben Tolstad, and two unidentified customers. (Courtesy of SCHS.)

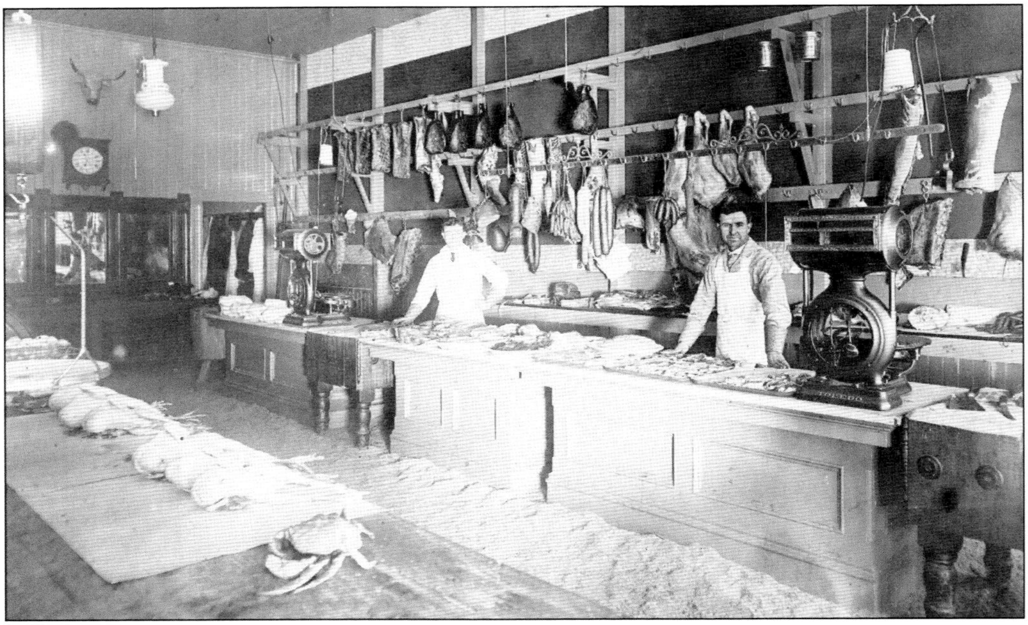

Garver and Glenn Tucker, Butchers, 1919. The product of an electric-arc flash, this photograph shows the inside view of the Tucker Brothers Butcher Shop. The store sold not only meat from land animals but also fresh seafood, such as salmon and Dungeness crab. (Courtesy of SCHS.)

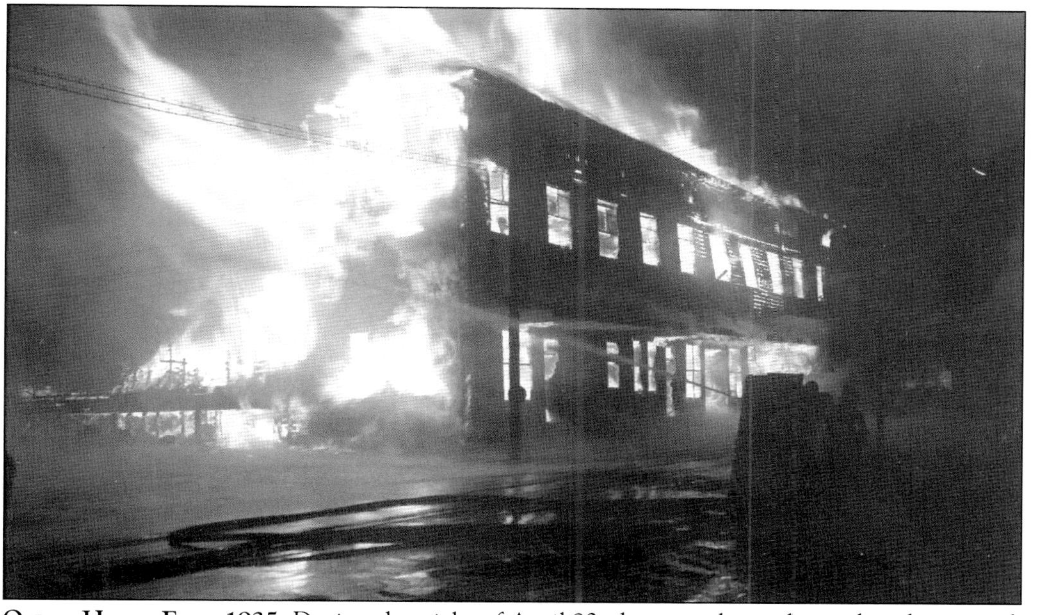

Opera House Fire, 1935. During the night of April 23, the opera house burned to the ground, gutting many of the structures on the block between North Water and First Streets. Notice the large shields protecting firemen on the right side of the image. Al Adams built the current Palace Theater on the same spot the following year. First-run movies are still shown seven days a week. (Courtesy of SCHS.)

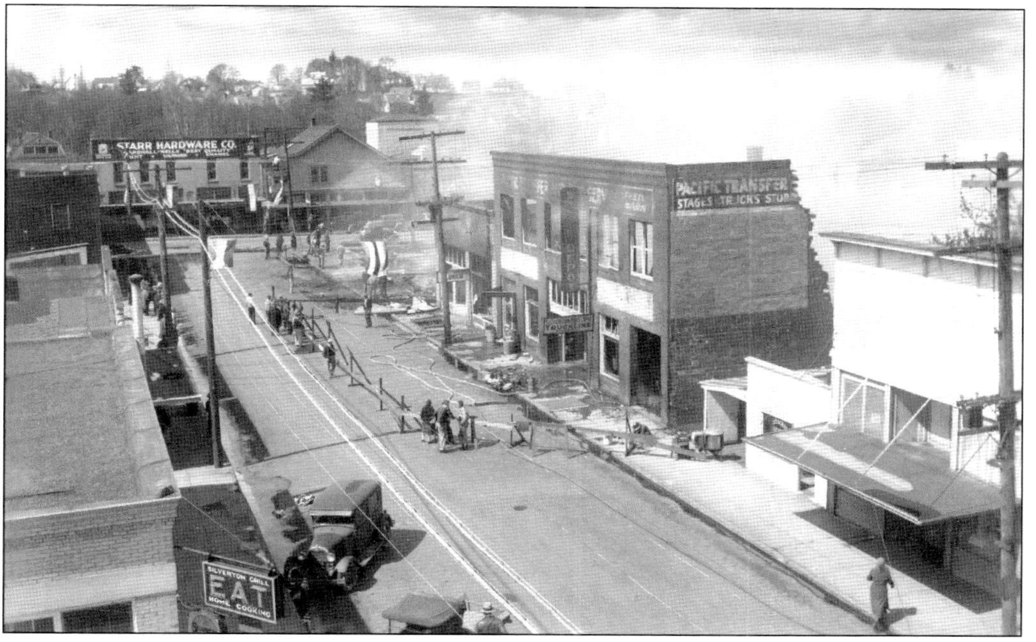

Opera House Fire, the Day After, 1935. The sun rose on a changed city. The historic wooden theater, the Pacific Transfer Building, and most of the buildings on the block were gone. The heat from the burning building was so intense that several structures across the street were damaged beyond repair and had to be removed. (Courtesy of SCHS.)

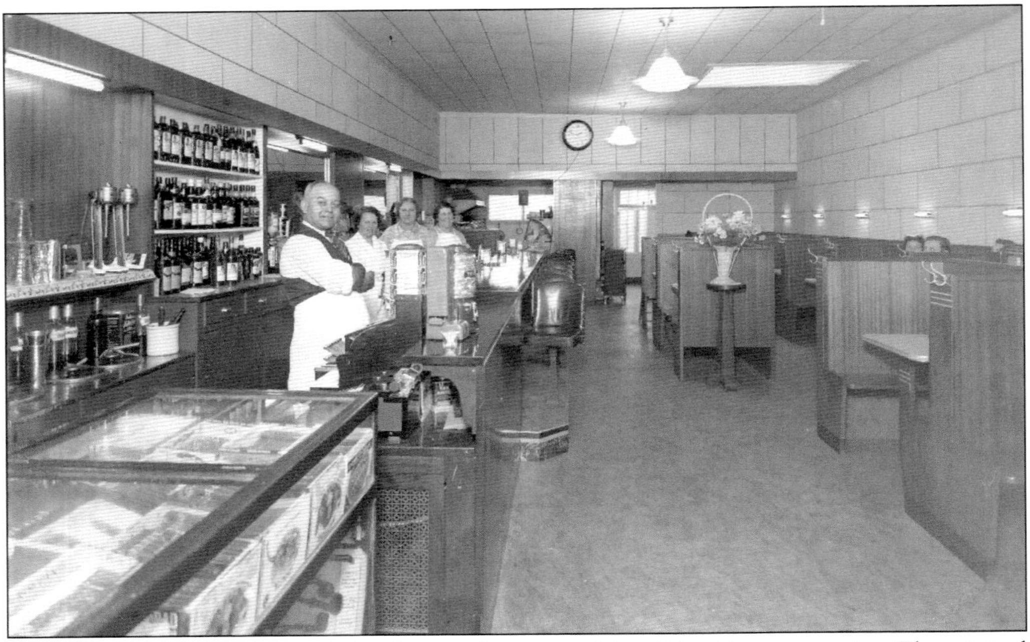

George's Café, 1946. George Manolis proudly presents his café in this postwar view. The original building has since been replaced, and O'Brien's Family Restaurant now occupies this location. (Courtesy of SCHS.)

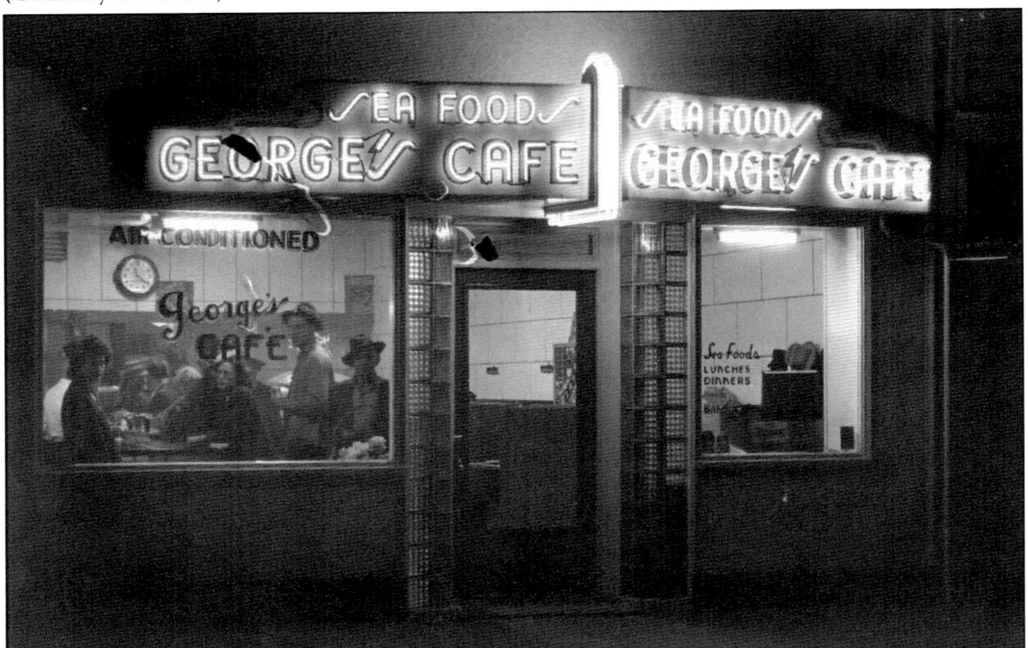

George's Café at Night, 1946. Here is a night view of the café on Water Street. Neon lights and glass blocks were popular to include in the facades of buildings during this time. After the building burned down, the new structure housed a sporting goods store, which was eventually replaced by a series of restaurants. (Courtesy of SCHS.)

Six

Transportation Changes

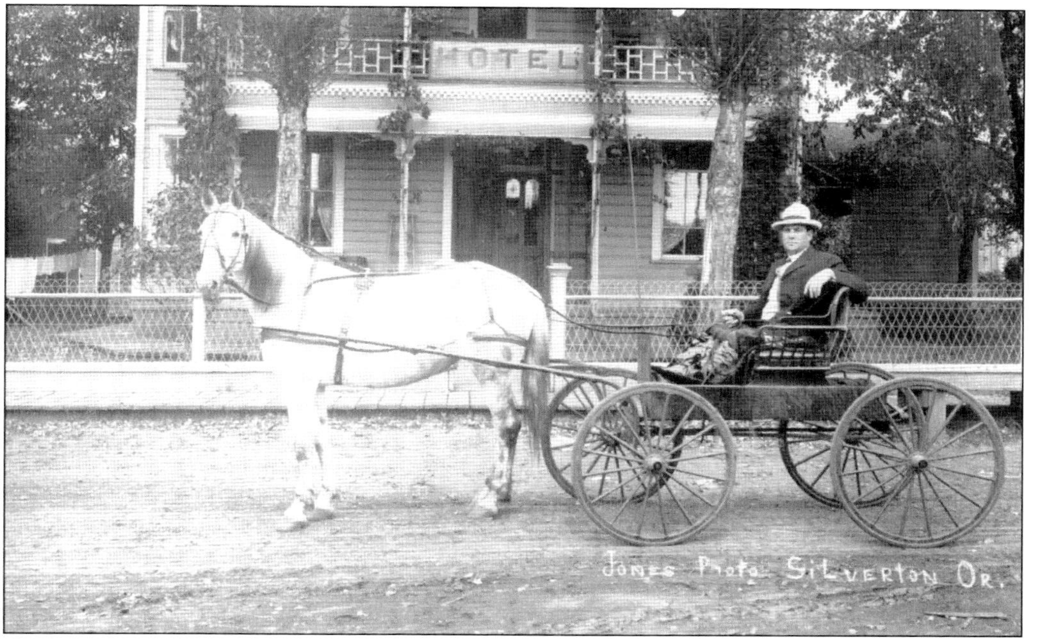

Horse and Buggy, 1903. Silverton started out as a pedestrian community: people either walked or were transported by animal-drawn vehicles. Like elsewhere, transportation technology slowly changed the town from a citywide pedestrian mall to one that catered to transportation hardware. (W. Jones photograph; courtesy of SCHS.)

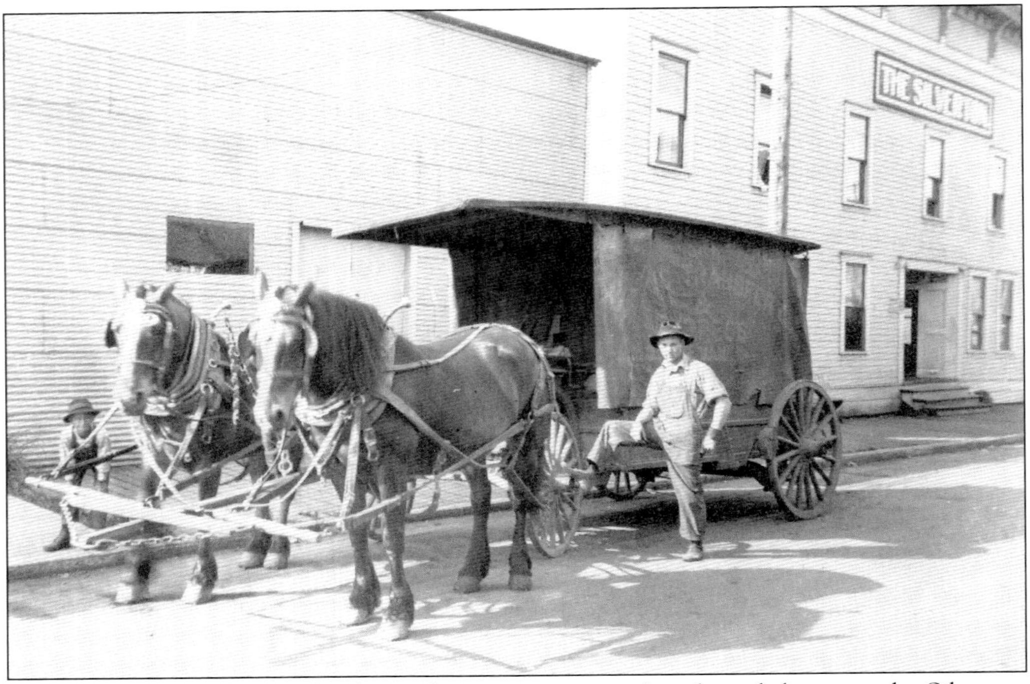

TRANSFER WAGON, 1919. This horse-drawn service transferred goods between the Silverton Railroad Depot and the community. As materials needed to be shipped out of town or delivered to a business, farm, or home, the wagon would appear to pick up or drop off the material. (Courtesy of SCHS.)

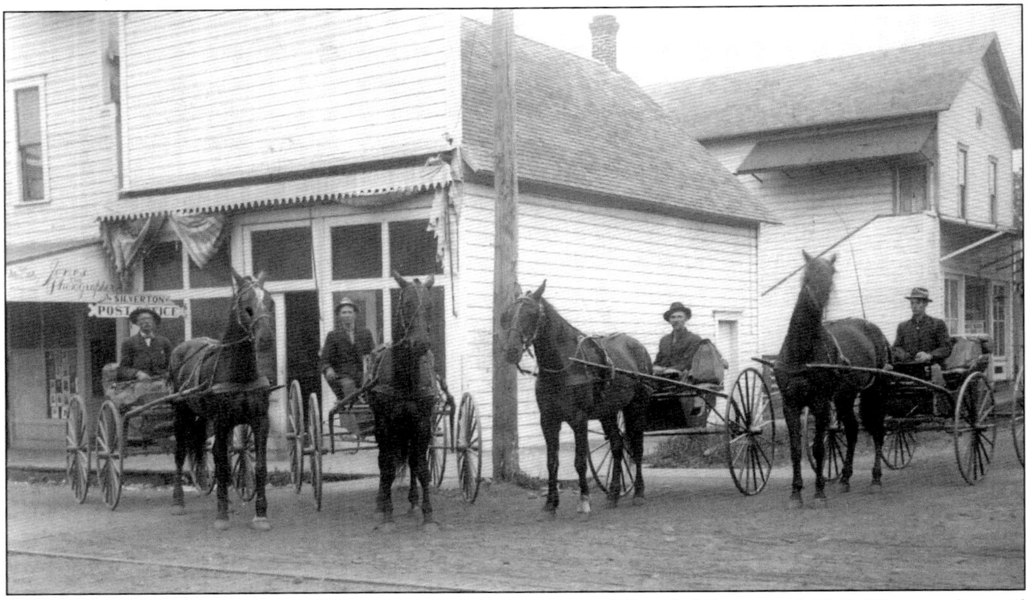

THE BUGGY BRIGADE, 1901. This scene of the corner of North Water and Oak Streets showed the quickest means of local transport at the time. The vehicle's power source was self-fueling and required minimal mechanical maintenance. The "exhaust" could be repurposed to grow more fuel, and the top speed was adequate for local use. (W. Jones photograph; courtesy of SCHS.)

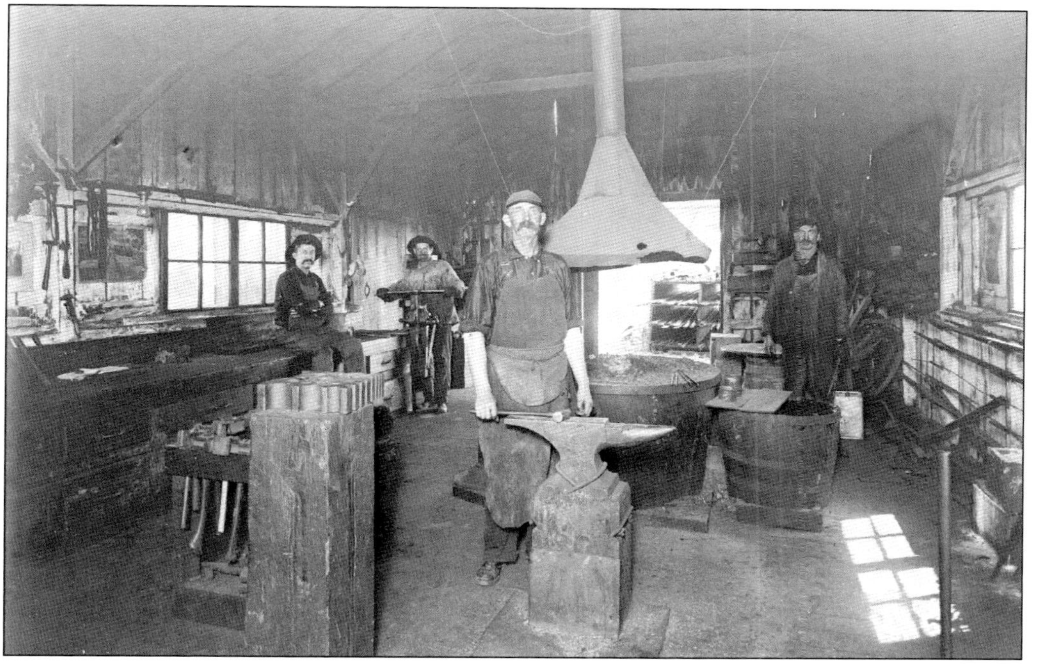

TILL HUTTON (CENTER) AND FELLOW BLACKSMITHS, 1900S. Every transportation system requires its own unique support infrastructure. Livery stables and blacksmiths kept things moving before cars. (Courtesy of SCHS.)

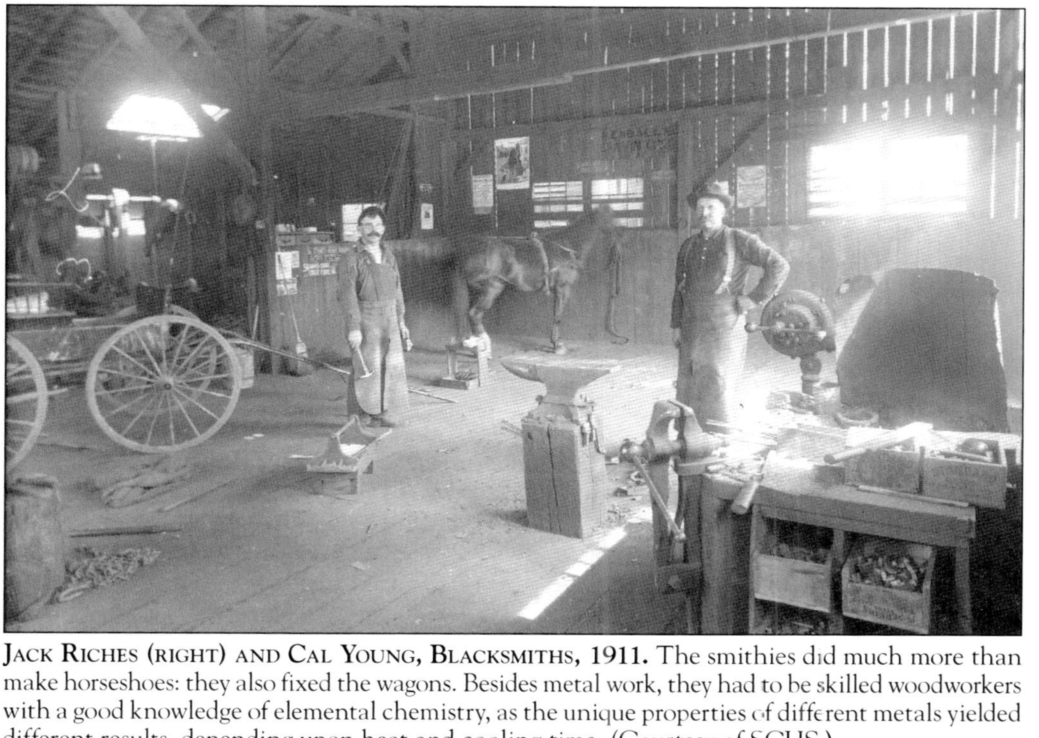

JACK RICHES (RIGHT) AND CAL YOUNG, BLACKSMITHS, 1911. The smithies did much more than make horseshoes: they also fixed the wagons. Besides metal work, they had to be skilled woodworkers with a good knowledge of elemental chemistry, as the unique properties of different metals yielded different results, depending upon heat and cooling time. (Courtesy of SCHS.)

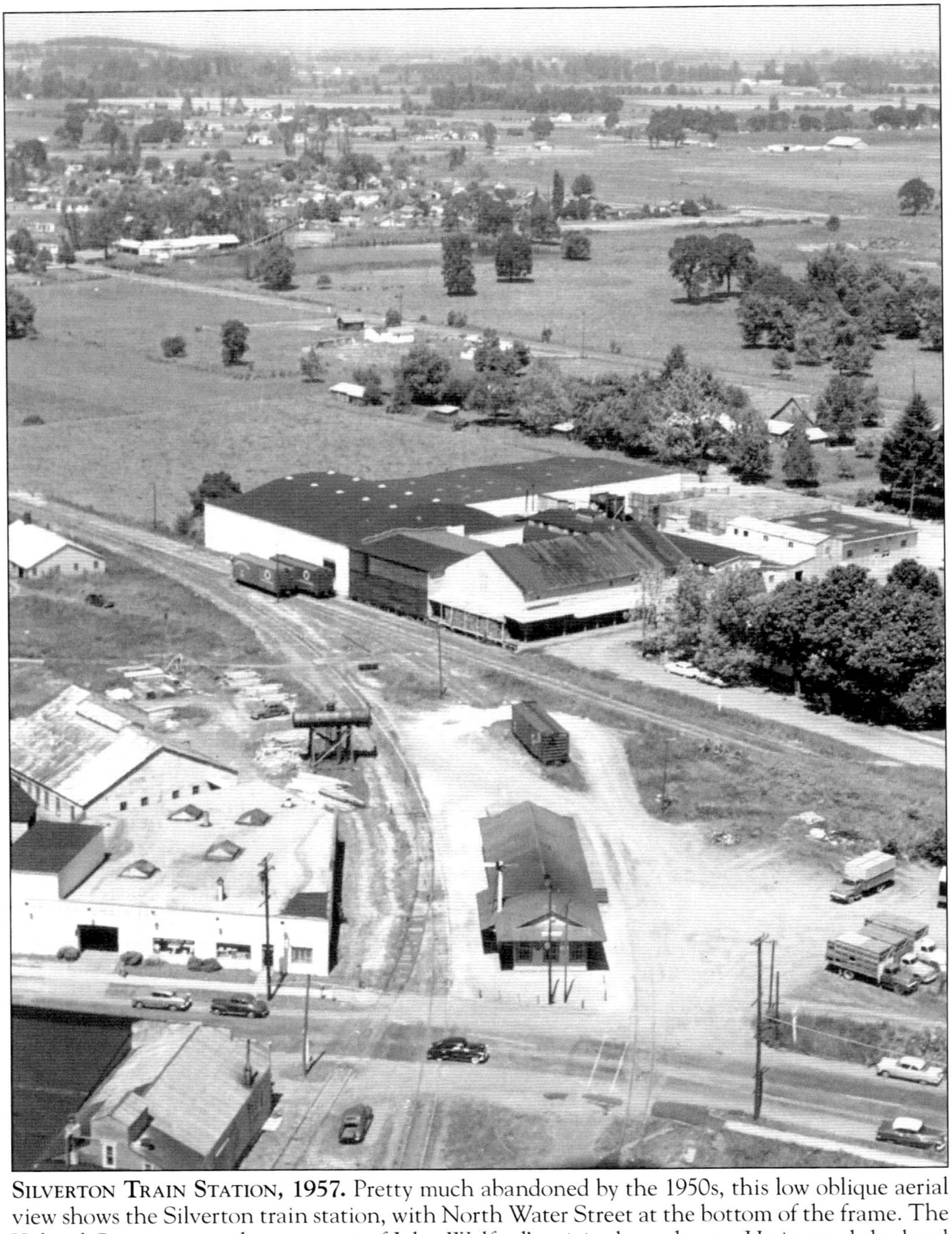

SILVERTON TRAIN STATION, 1957. Pretty much abandoned by the 1950s, this low oblique aerial view shows the Silverton train station, with North Water Street at the bottom of the frame. The Kolstad Cannery complex grew out of John Wolfard's original warehouse. He ignored the local Front Street right-of-way and built over the area to get closer to the train tracks. As a result, Front Street effectively ends at the cannery. In the original plat of the area, Front Street was the natural choice for a north entrance to town, with subsequent commercial development along the length of the street, but because of Wolfard's warehouse, this honor was shifted one block over to First Street. (Madelyn Studios photograph; courtesy of SCHS.)

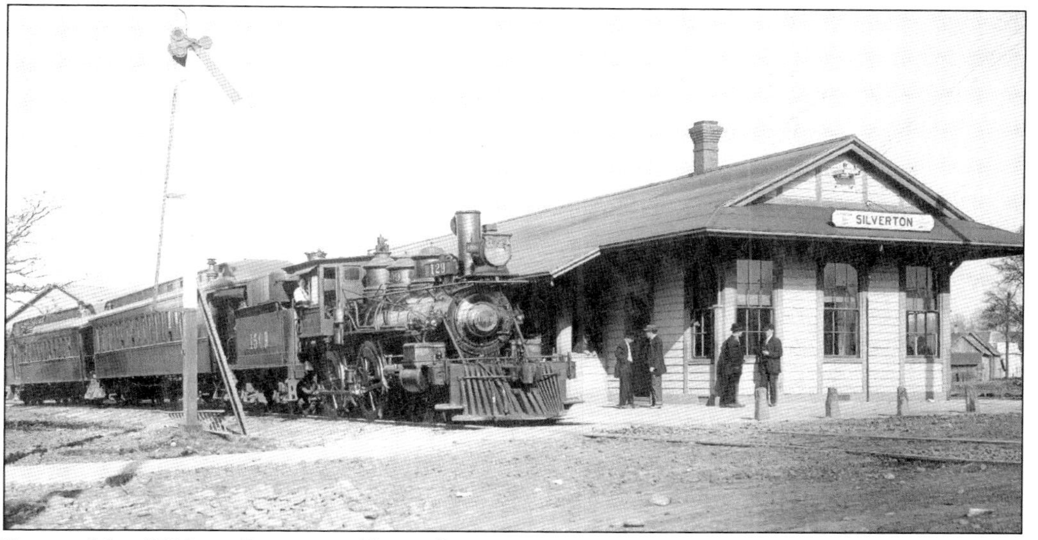

ENGINE NO. 1509 AT SILVERTON TRAIN STATION, 1913. Here is a quintessential Western scene. This particular view is looking toward the depot from the southwest. The depot was moved across the street in the late 1960s and later moved across town to its present location next to the Silverton Country Museum. The Silverton Chamber of Commerce is housed there now. (Courtesy of SCHS.)

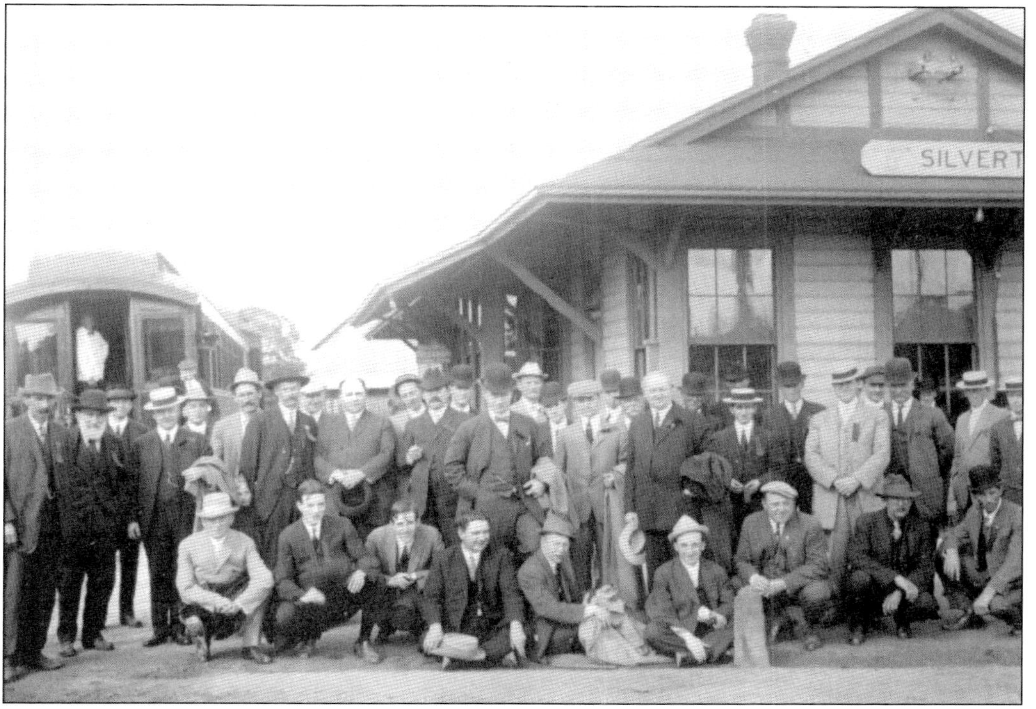

WHEN DAVENPORT COMES TO TOWN, 1908. Even though he was now a successful cartoonist with his own Arabian horse ranch in Morris Plains, New Jersey, Homer Davenport often found time to return to the town he loved. Here is the end of one such visit, as many of the town's movers and shakers have shown up to see him off. (Courtesy of SCHS.)

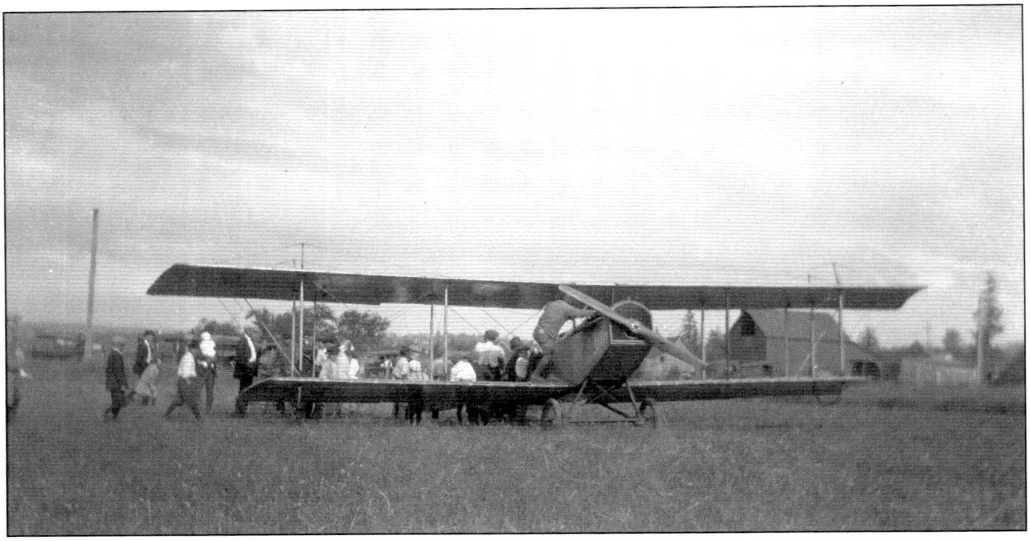

"Jenny" at the Airport, 1920s. As the 20th century progressed, so did Silverton's place in it. Several enterprising citizens started flying airplanes in and out of a flat field west of town near Bethany. This particular craft is a vintage, World War I Curtis JN, also known as a "Jenny." (T.P. Trix Heidenstrom photograph; courtesy of Almquist Studios.)

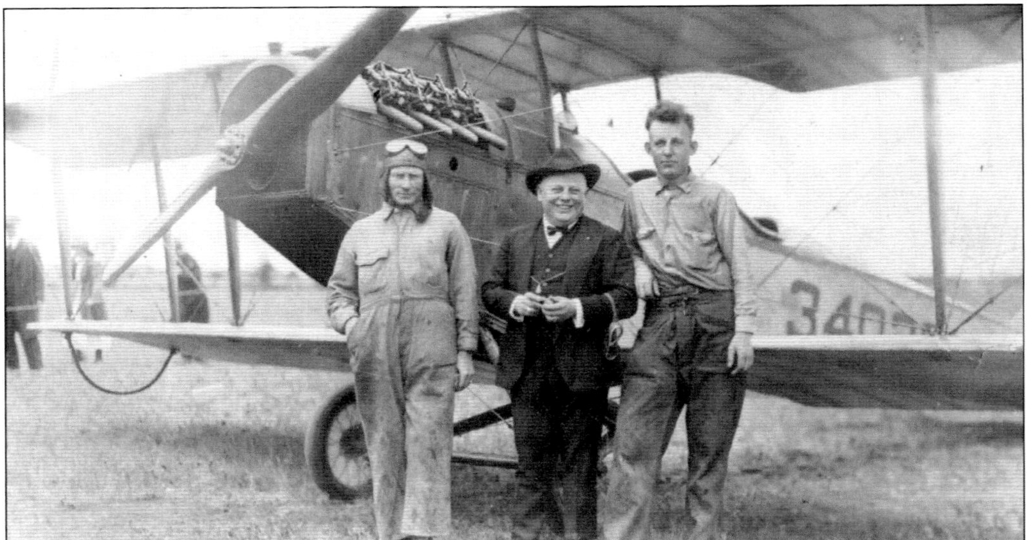

Reynolds at the Airport, 1920s. Pilot Charley Reynolds (left), a former Silverton High School basketball star, is seen with the same Jenny from the previous picture. The others shown are unidentified. Reynolds often sold rides in his planes. The passengers would ride in the front cockpit while Reynolds controlled the craft from the rear. (Courtesy of SCHS.)

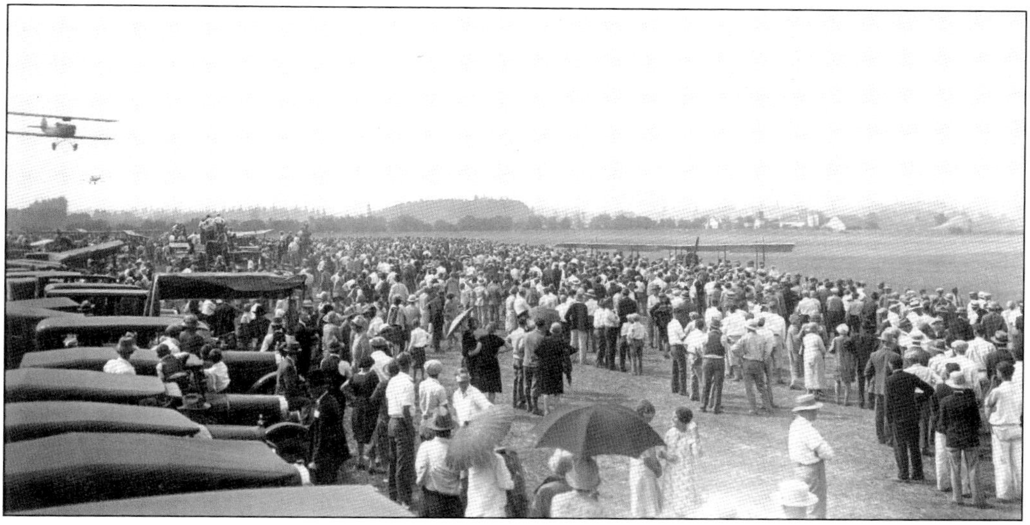

Air Show at Silverton Airport, 1928. As more and more planes flew in and out of Silverton Airport (SLV), the interest in aviation grew. The 1928 *Silvertonia*, the Silverton High School yearbook, was dedicated to aviation. That same year, the first of several air shows was held at the aerodrome. As seen in these images, the crowds were quite big. There is no doubt that local merchants welcomed air shows. (Both, courtesy of SCHS.)

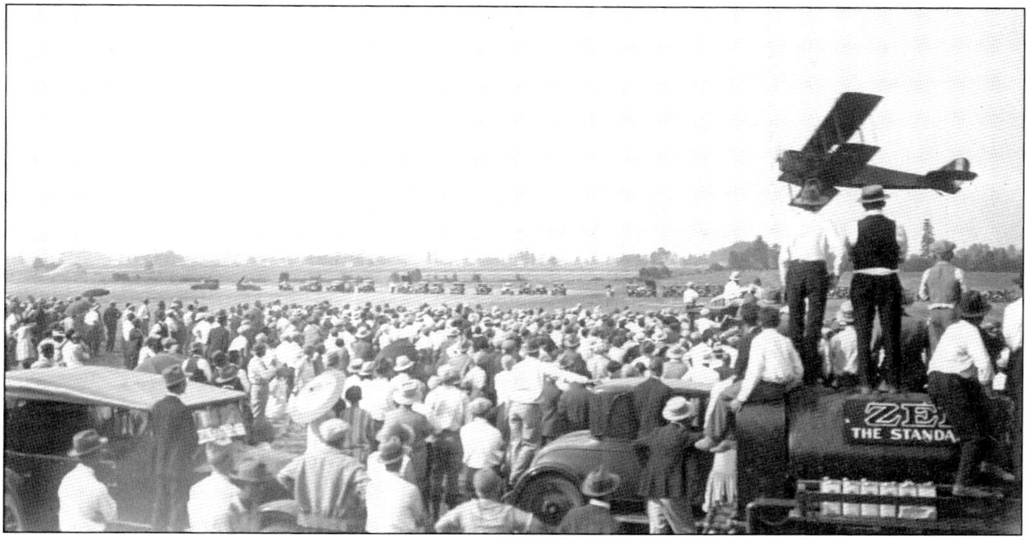

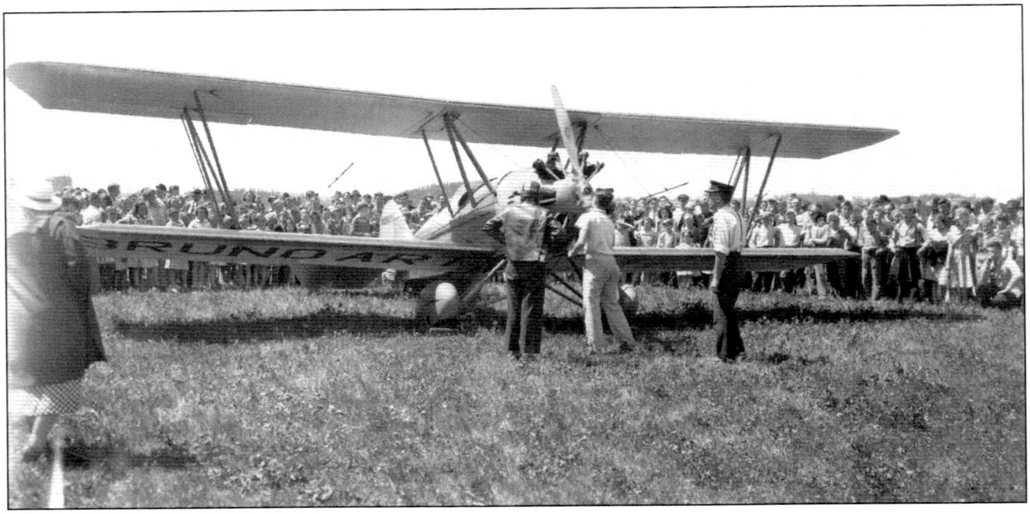

USPS Airmail Plane The *Eagle Rock* at Silverton Airport, 1938. On May 19, 1938, during National Airmail Week, 1,700 special one-day-only flights were made to pick up airmail letters from cities across the country. Forty-seven of these flights were flown by women pilots. Silverton was one of these locations, and Bessie Halladay, a well-known Oregon woman pilot, flew the *Eagle Rock* to Silverton. The flight started in Marshfield (Coos Bay area) en route to Portland, with stops in Eugene, Albany, Salem, Silverton, and Troutdale. Silverton was one of about 10,000 cities that prepared a special cachet for their airmail letters. The Silverton cachet was designed by Dr. Keene and featured a picture of Silver Falls with an airplane. The cachet was stamped on the airmail envelopes used for that day's mail. The Silverton Chamber of Commerce paid for the pickup of the airmail. (Both, courtesy of SCHS.)

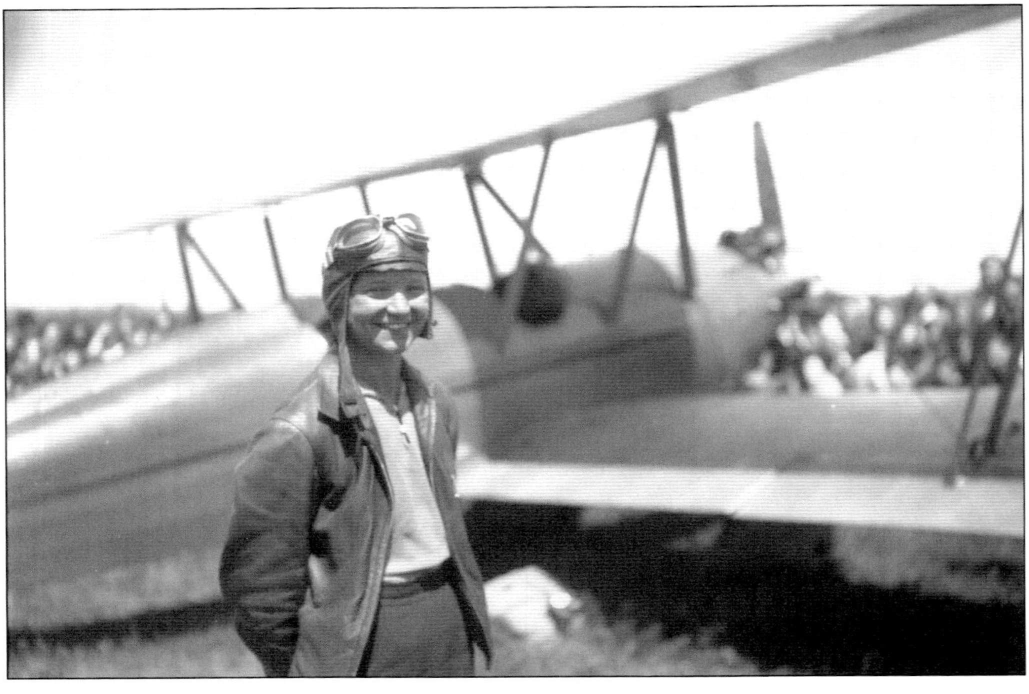

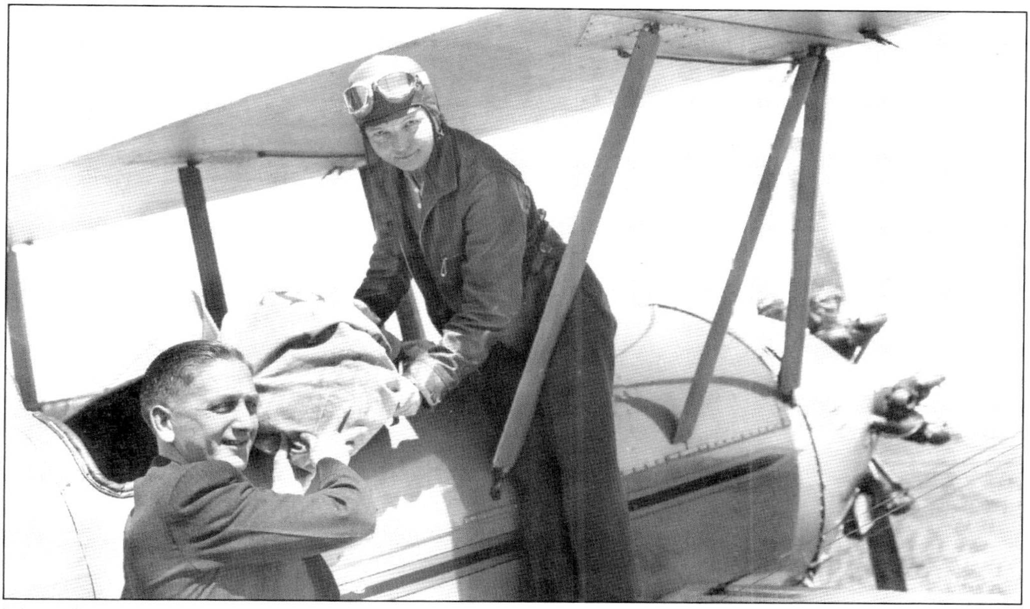

MAIL CALL AT SLV, 1938. Silverton postmaster Henry Alm presents Halladay with the first 750 pieces of airmail at the Silverton Airport. It remains the only airmail to fly out of Silverton. The *Eagle Rock* was made by the Alexander Aircraft Company of Denver, Colorado, and was powered by a Wright radial engine. (Courtesy of SCHS.)

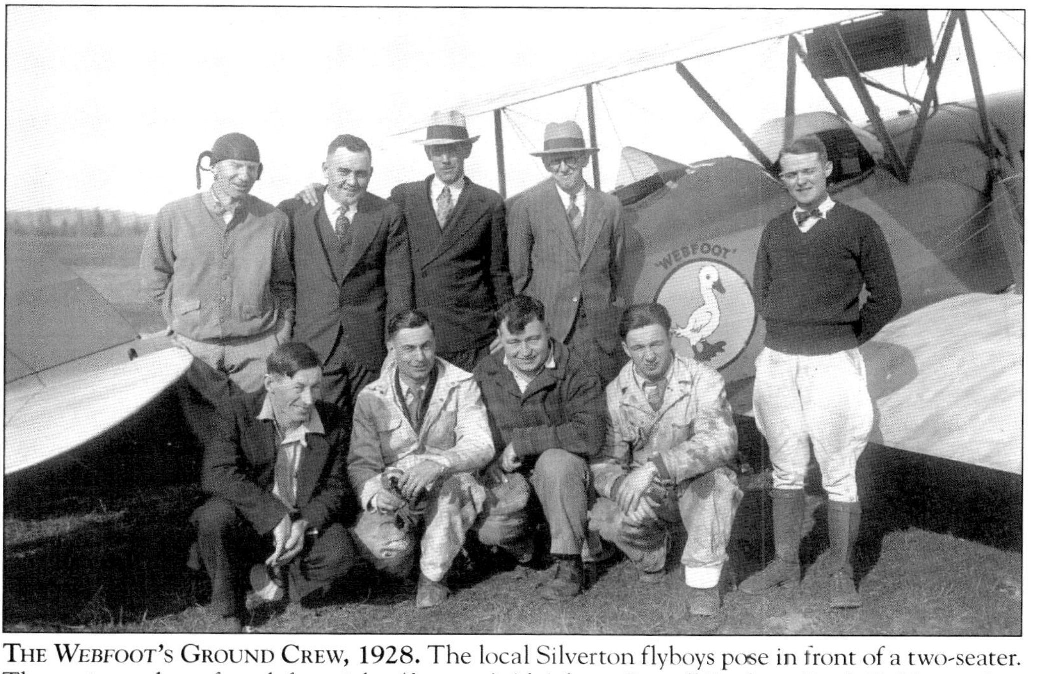

THE *WEBFOOT*'S GROUND CREW, 1928. The local Silverton flyboys pose in front of a two-seater. Those pictured are, from left to right, (first row) Al Adams, Russell Boelster, Brick Hoblet, and an unidentified mechanic; (second row) Charley Reynolds, Earl Hartman, John Small, Bill McClary, and Jim Hollingsworth. The aircraft seems to be a New Standard D-25 with a water-cooled, five-cylinder radial engine. (Courtesy of SCHS.)

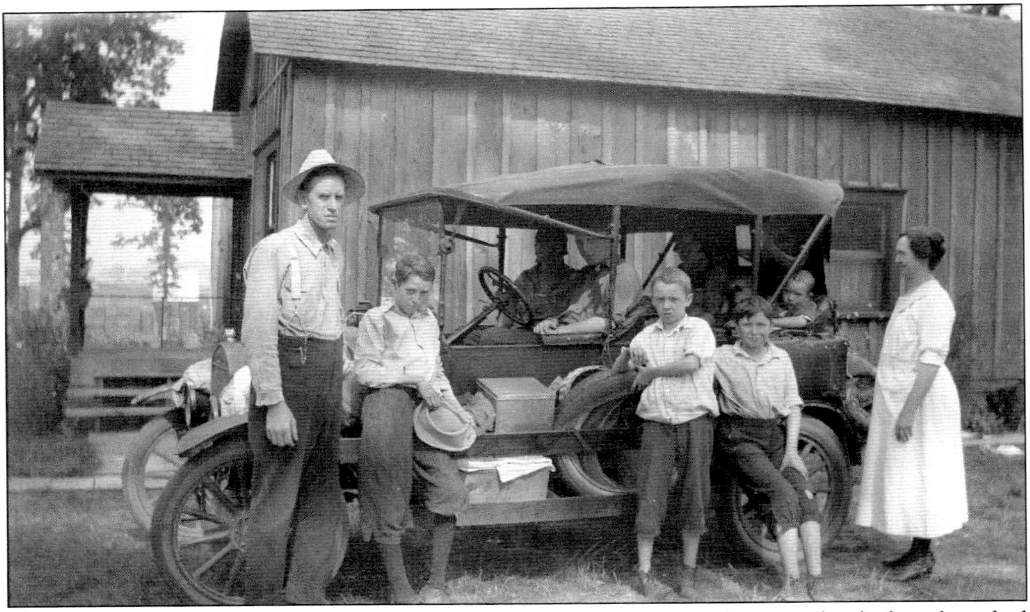

Visitors in a Car, around 1918. The Almquist family says farewell to a carload of unidentified friends. Those pictured (standing in front of the car) are, from left to right, George, Clifford, Elvin, Paul, and Henrietta Almquist. Like the rest of the country, Silvertonians soon found the conveniences of automobiles irresistible. With mass production, Henry Ford, and cheap gasoline, even the skies seemed limitless. (Courtesy of Curt Almquist.)

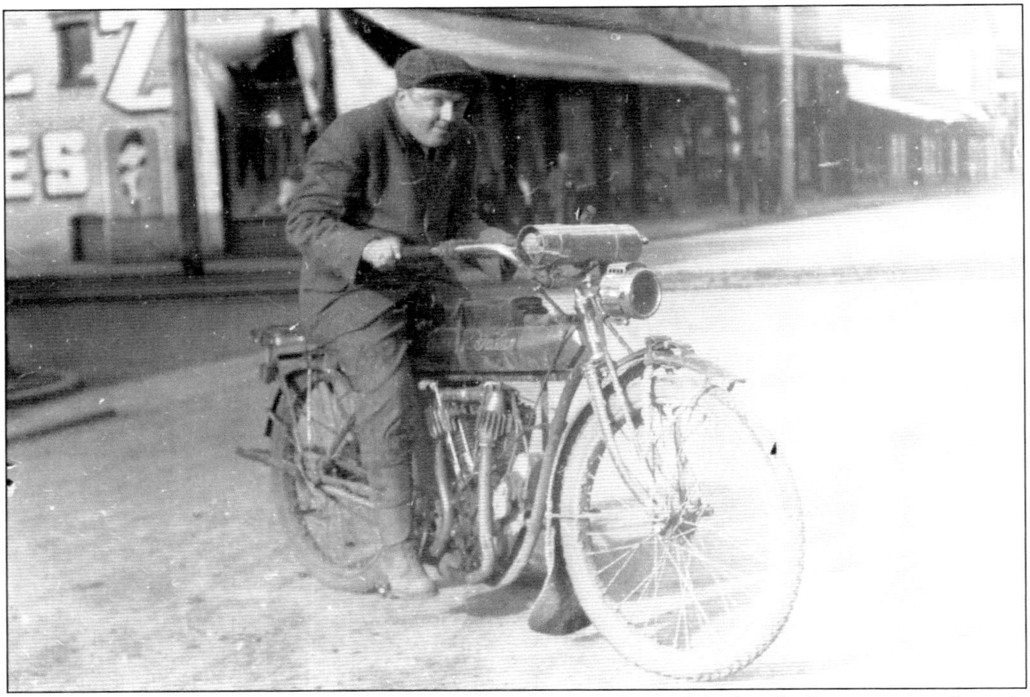

An Indian Biker on Main Street, 1913. Here is an early model of an Indian motorcycle with an unidentified rider. The Wolf Building is behind him. (Courtesy of SCHS.)

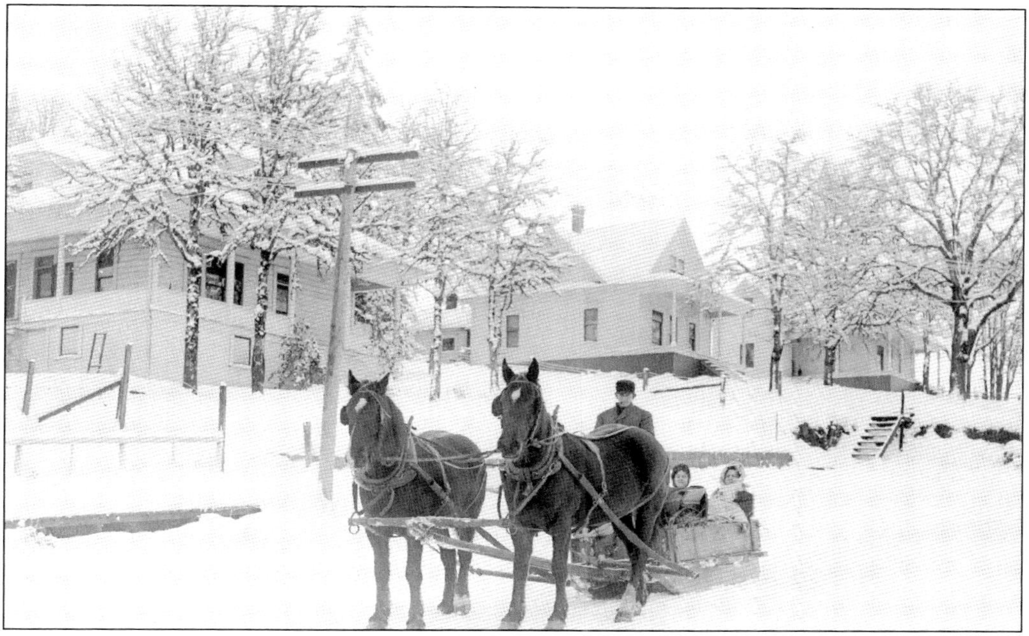

HORSE-DRAWN SLEIGHS, 1909. In spite of new paved roads and gas-powered automobiles, the horse, when it came to snow, could not be beat. During the blizzard of 1909, people were able to get around town by hitching sleds to horses, as seen in these two images. The sled shown above seems to be homemade, while Dr. Chase's sled seen below was a commercial model. Dr. Chase was the large-animal veterinarian in Silverton. (Both, courtesy of SCHS.)

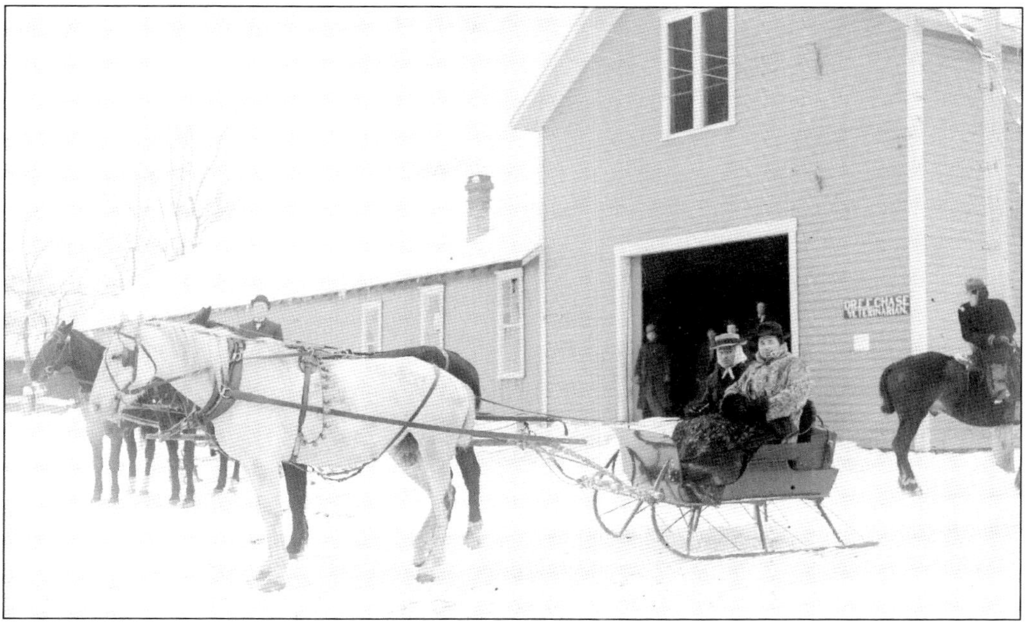

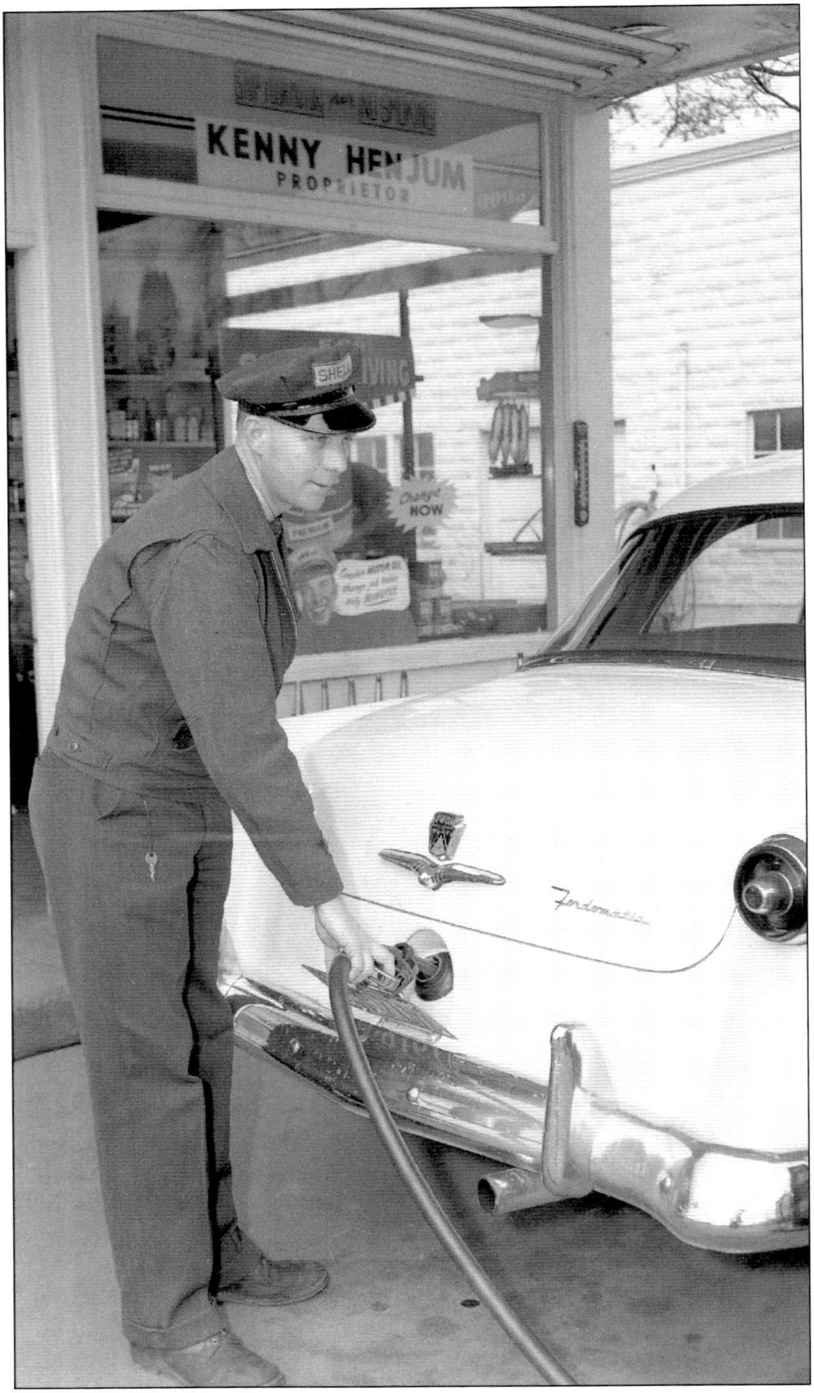

KEN HENJUM SHELL STATION, 1958. The new transportation support system takes over. By the 1950s, one would be hard-pressed to find any commercial activity dealing with horse-drawn transport. Kenny Henjum fills up another customer's tank at his Shell station. (Bill Hanson photograph; courtesy of Curt Almquist.)

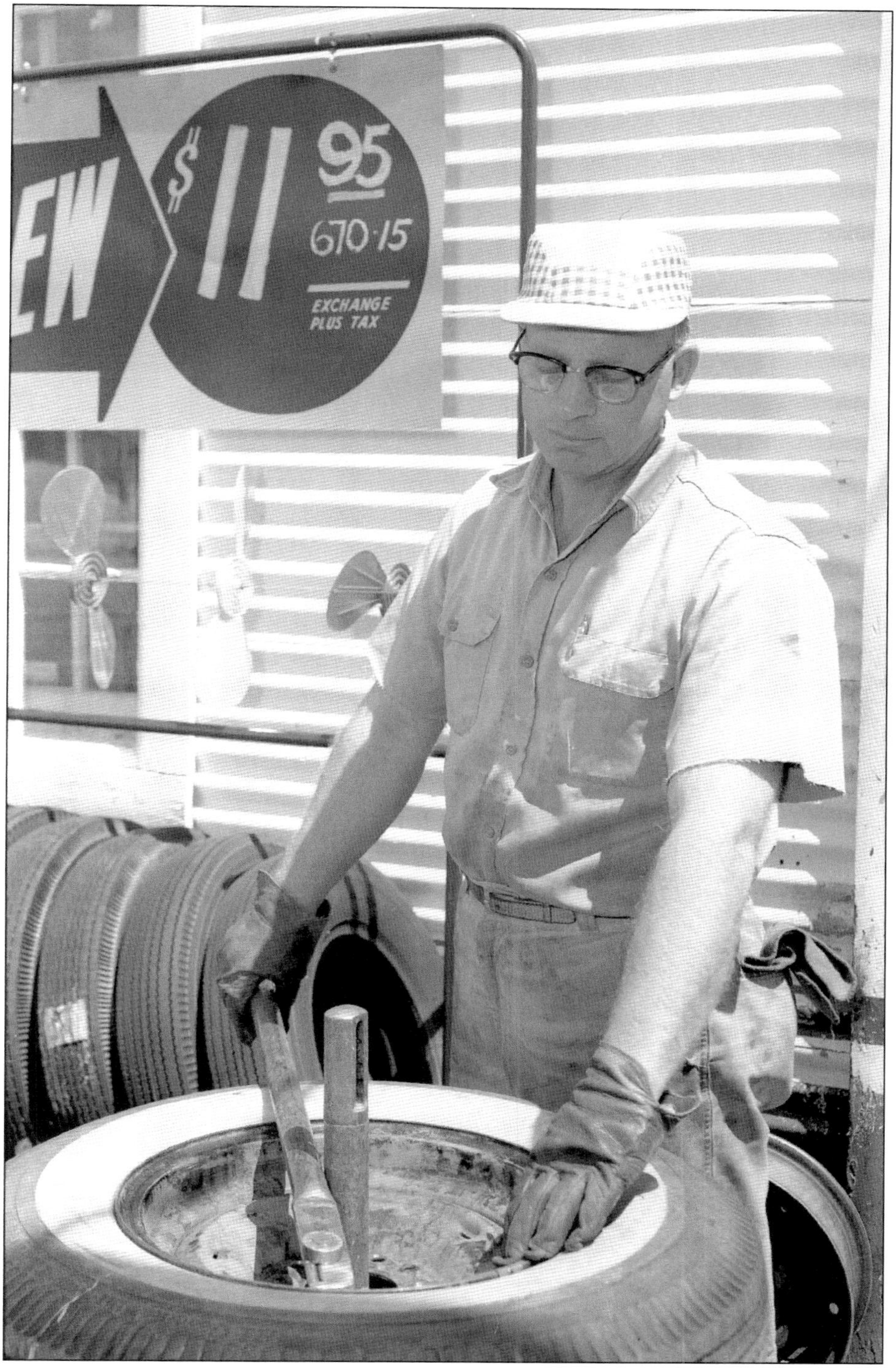

OK Rubber, 1958. Even though blacksmithing became a niche service, the "horse" still needed "shoes." The OK Rubber Tire Shop was the place to go for new treads, including whitewalls. (Bill Hanson photograph; courtesy of Curt Almquist.)

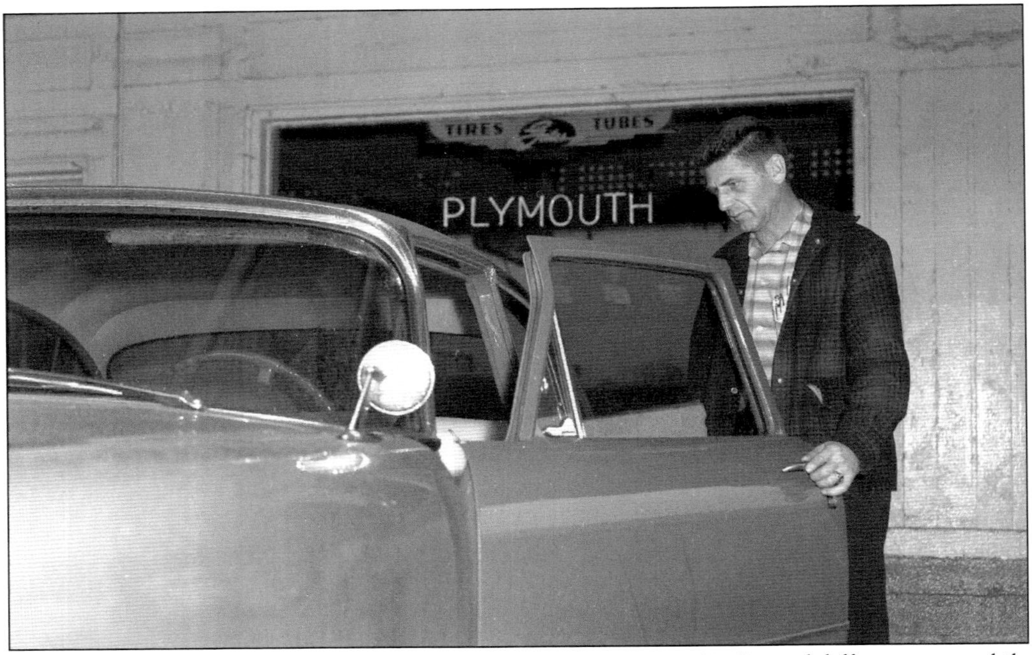

Seifer-Moll Motors, Chrysler and Plymouth Dealership, 1958. Several different automobile dealerships flourished in Silverton. Hank Moll is shown inspecting a new Plymouth. His business partner, Al Seifer, went on to found Cascade Farm Machinery. His son Roger Seifer is the current owner. (Bill Hanson photograph; courtesy of Curt Almquist.)

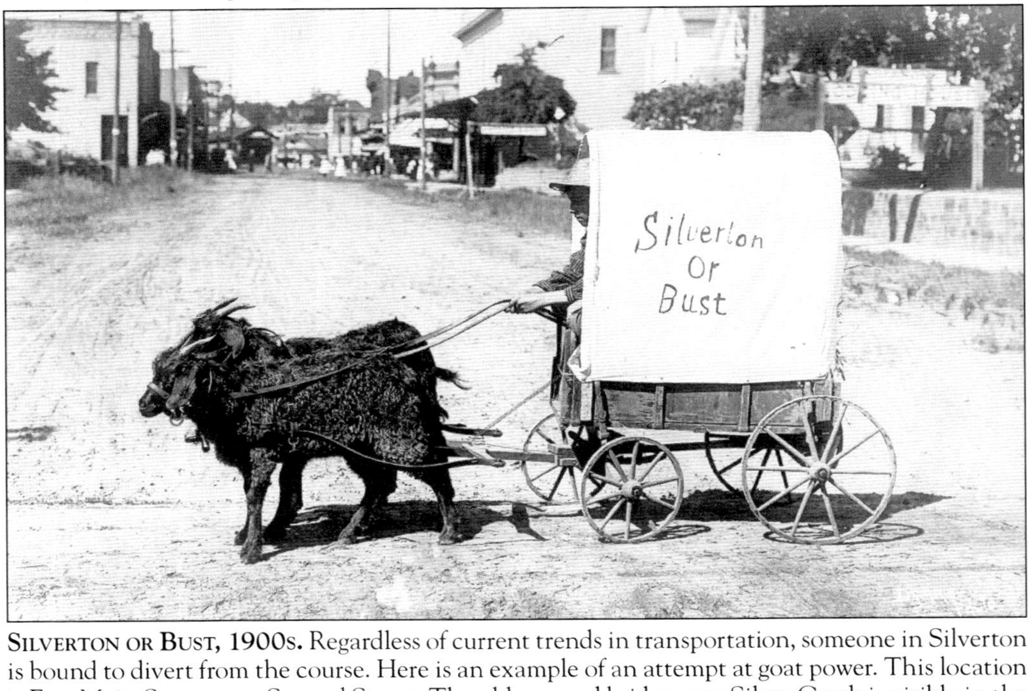

Silverton or Bust, 1900s. Regardless of current trends in transportation, someone in Silverton is bound to divert from the course. Here is an example of an attempt at goat power. This location is East Main Street near Second Street. The old covered bridge over Silver Creek is visible in the distance. (Courtesy of SCHS.)

Seven

Music, Sports, and Theater

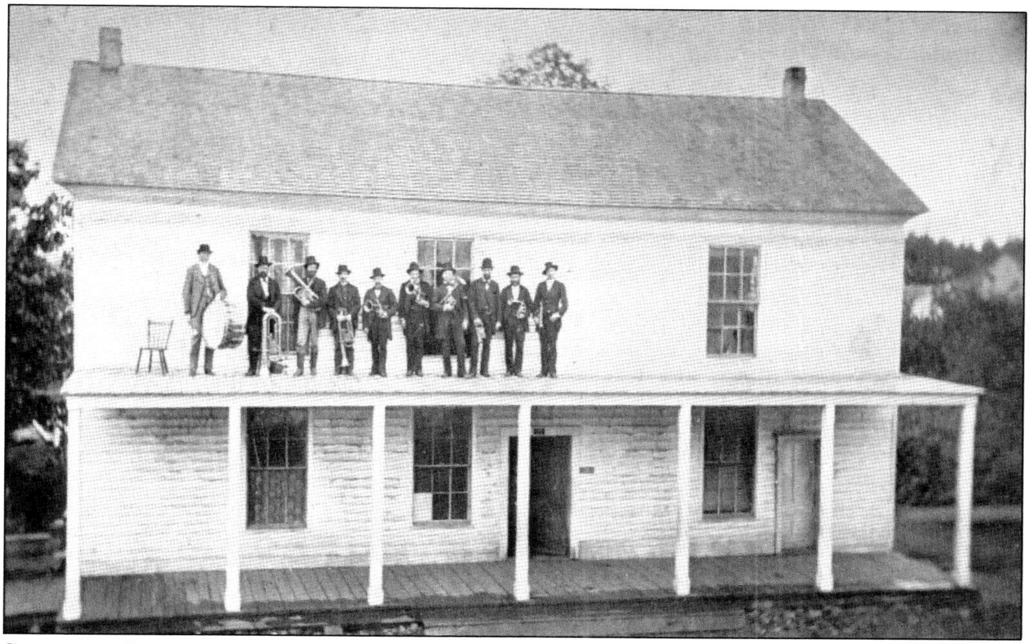

Silverton Band, 1879. A loose-net unit of 10 pieces, this band is assembled on the awning of the old Silverton School. Constructed in 1866, it was moved several times and currently resides on Third Street. This is the oldest building in Silverton. (Courtesy of SCHS.)

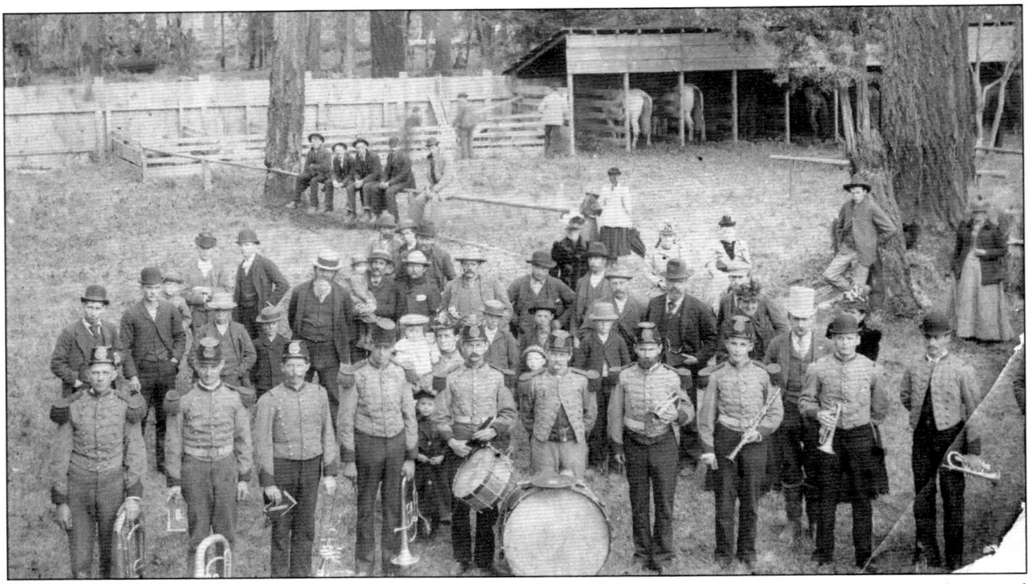

Silverton Trombone Band in the Park with Jake McClaine, Late 1880s. Banker and community benefactor Uncle Jake McClaine is shown here with members of the Silverton Trombone Band, which he helped finance. Uncle Jake is the gentleman with the white beard and straw hat located behind the third band member, Ernest Hodges (valve trombone), from the left. With horse stalls and compost bins in the background, the location looks like it is adjacent to a livery stable. (Courtesy of SCHS.)

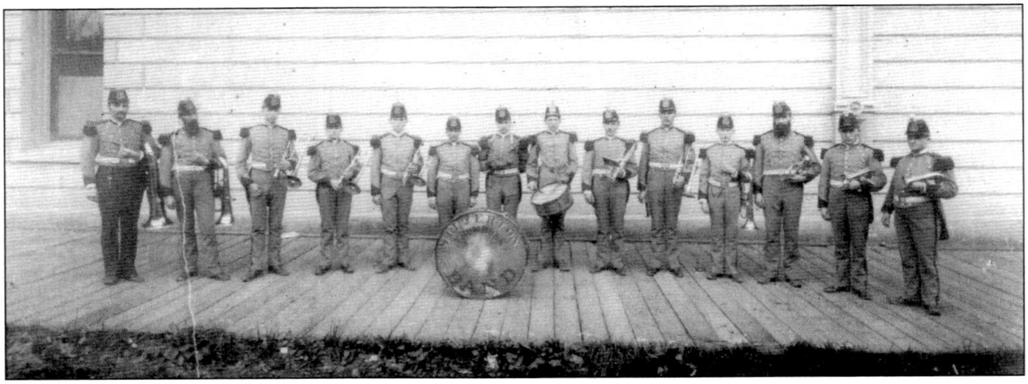

Trombone Band in Portland, August 4, 1886. "[Jake McClaine] wrote to the leader that he wanted to defray all of the expenses of the entire band to Portland the next Saturday night, where they were going to give [President-Elect Grover] Cleveland a big Democratic rally, and have electric lights. Of course, we accepted, as Jake McClaine paid more toward the new instruments and uniforms than any other man in town," said Homer C. Davenport. "Country boy" Homer is on the snare drum. (Courtesy of SCHS.)

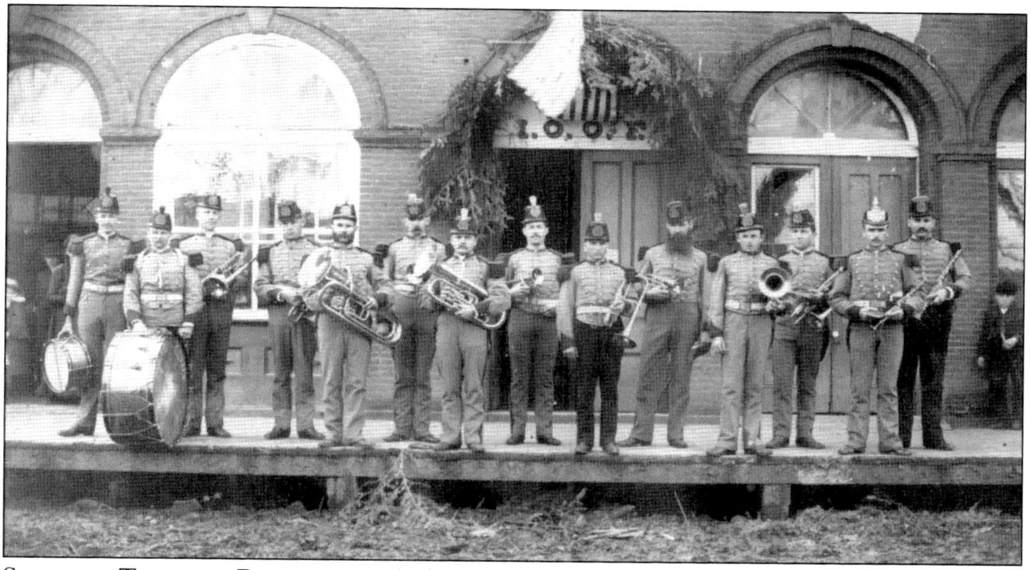

Silverton Trombone Band, 1888. The band is seen on the wooden sidewalk in front of Silverton's first brick building, the Odd Fellows Hall. The building's interior was gutted by fire, however, it was rebuilt within the old brick shell. It was shortened by about three feet when First Street was widened. Homer Davenport and his snare drum are at the far left. Leader Harvey Allen is second from the right. (Courtesy of SCHS.)

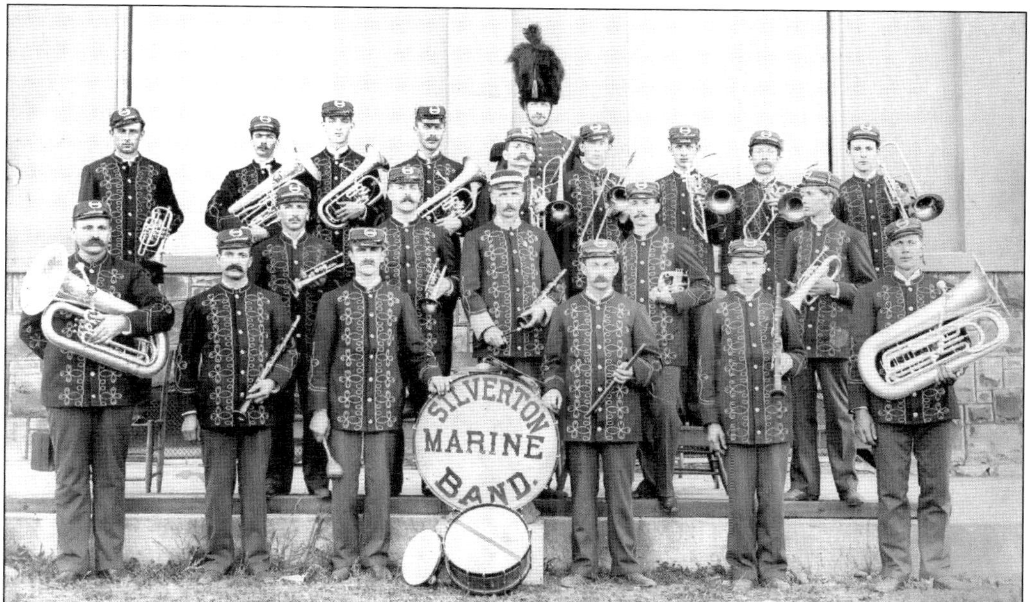

Silverton Marine Band, 1900s. By the turn of the century, "Trombone" was replaced with "Marine" in the band's name. This was no doubt a marketing ploy to ride the coattails of that great USMC Band leader and Victor recording artist, John Philip Sousa. Many of the same members from the older unit are shown, with leader Allen centrally poised over the drums. Gem Theater owner M.G. Cooley is second from the left in the back row with a euphonium. He also taught violin and cornet at the Liberal University during its 1901 session. (Courtesy of SCHS.)

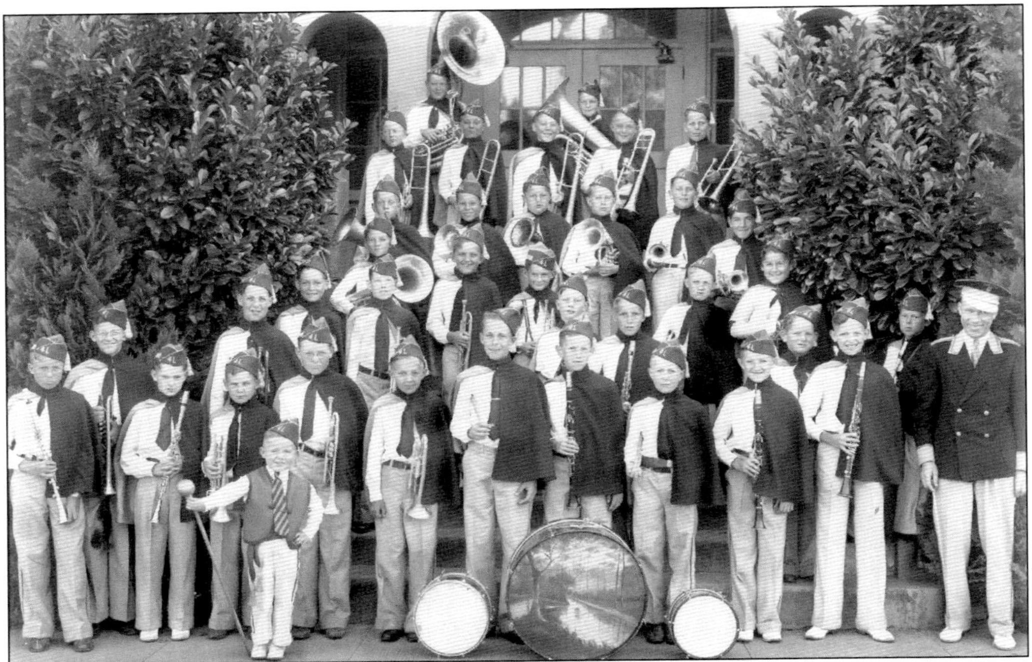

SILVERTON JUNIOR MARCHING BAND, 1930s. This group of musical Cub Scouts is assembled on the steps of the Silverton National Guard Armory. The Oregon National Guard decommissioned the Silverton unit, and the building was leased to the city at minimal cost. It currently is home to Silverton Together, Silverton Area Community Aid, and YMCA service organizations. Likewise, it houses the Silverton City Council Chambers. (Courtesy of SCHS.)

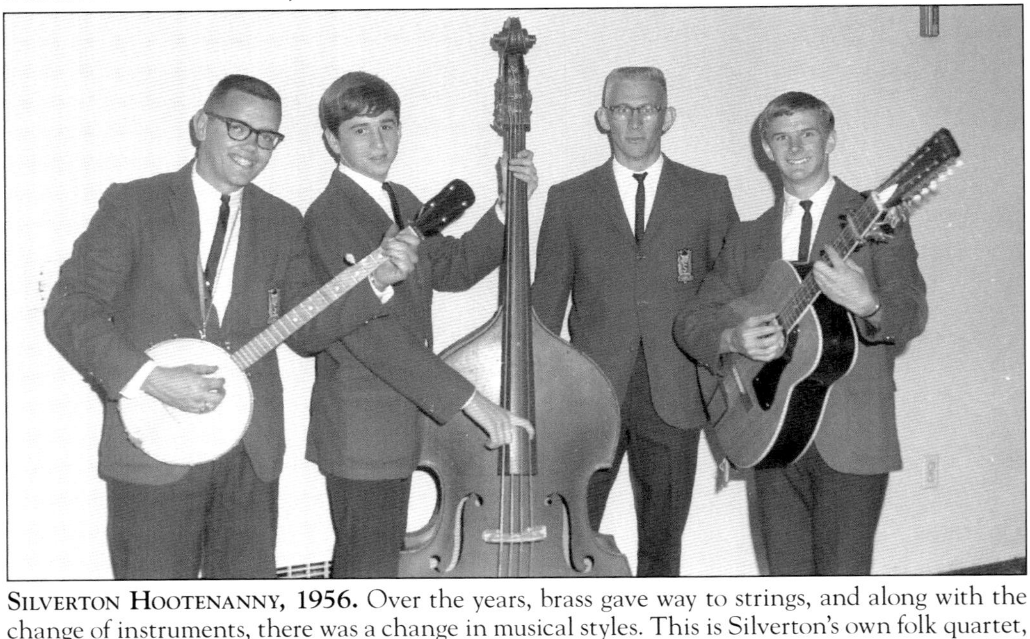

SILVERTON HOOTENANNY, 1956. Over the years, brass gave way to strings, and along with the change of instruments, there was a change in musical styles. This is Silverton's own folk quartet, The Other Ones. Several of the band members are still actively involved in the community. (Bill Hanson photograph; courtesy of Almquist Studios.)

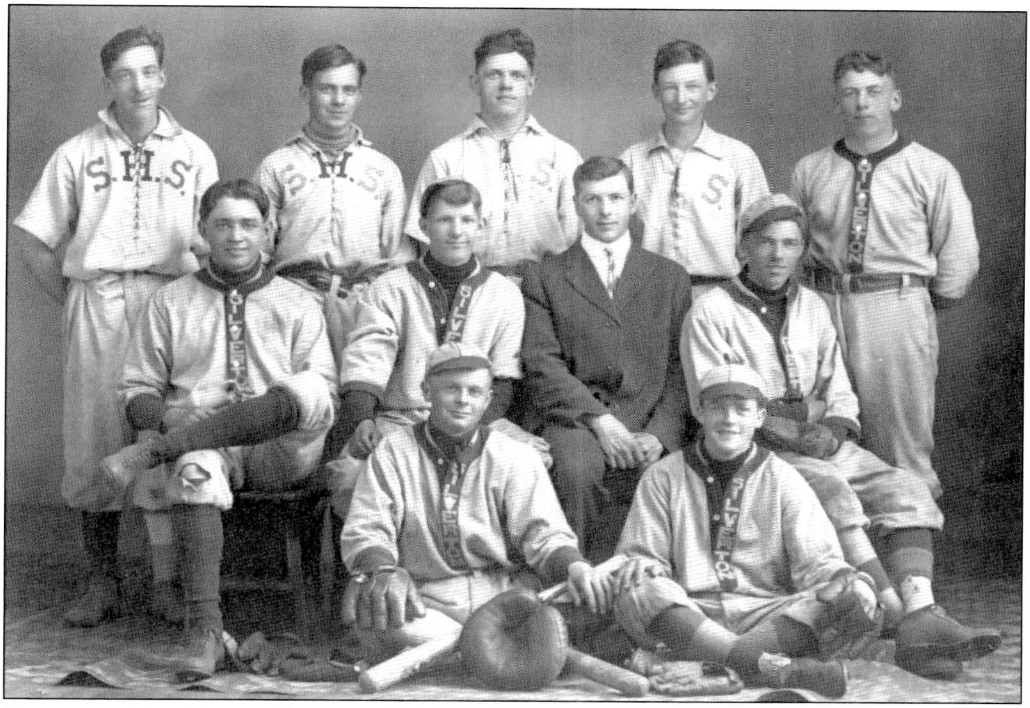

SILVERTON HIGH SCHOOL BASEBALL TEAM, 1909. America's favorite pastime was also Silverton's. Members of the community especially enjoyed baseball at the high school level and later on at the semiprofessional level. Seen here is the 1909 senior varsity lineup. (Courtesy of SCHS.)

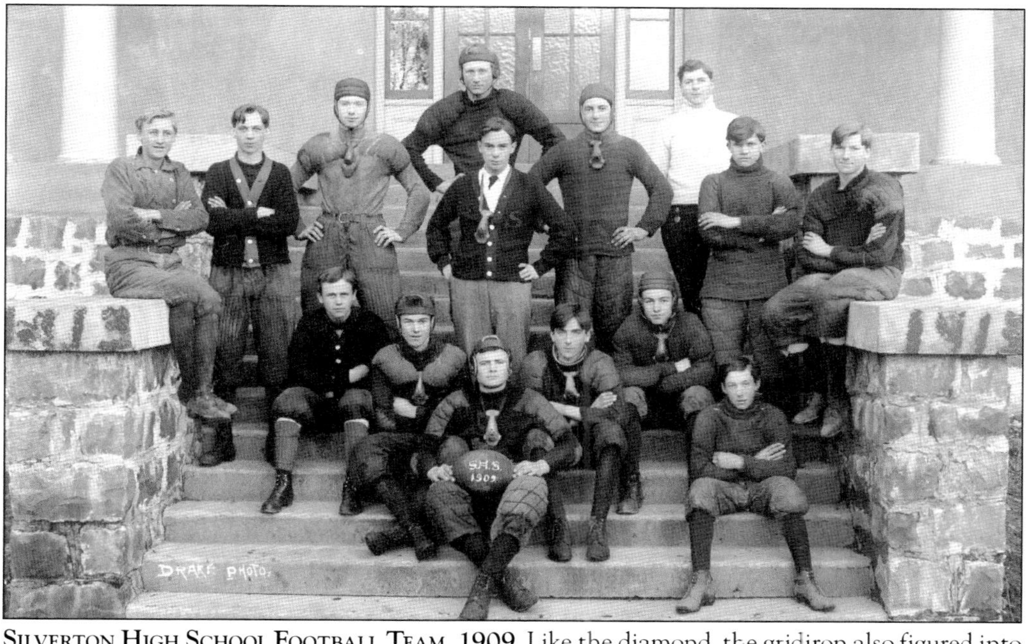

SILVERTON HIGH SCHOOL FOOTBALL TEAM, 1909. Like the diamond, the gridiron also figured into high school fun and games. The unique nose protectors are a novel safety solution that apparently did not stick. (Courtesy of SCHS.)

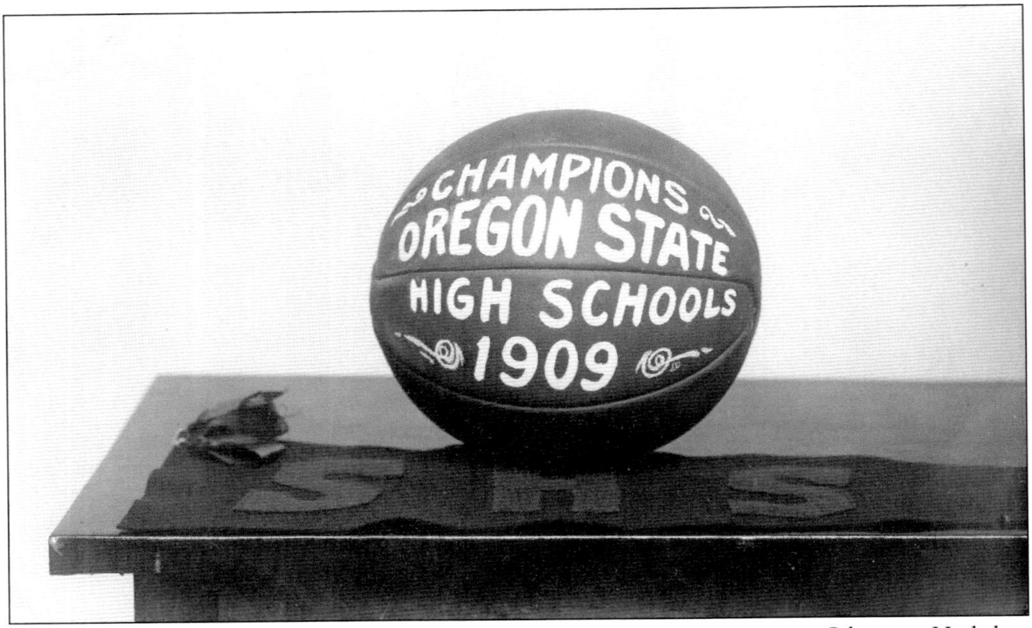

OREGON SCHOOL'S BASKETBALL STATE CHAMPIONS, 1909. For some reason, Silverton High has always produced dynamic basketball teams. In 1909, the team was state champion. (Courtesy of SCHS.)

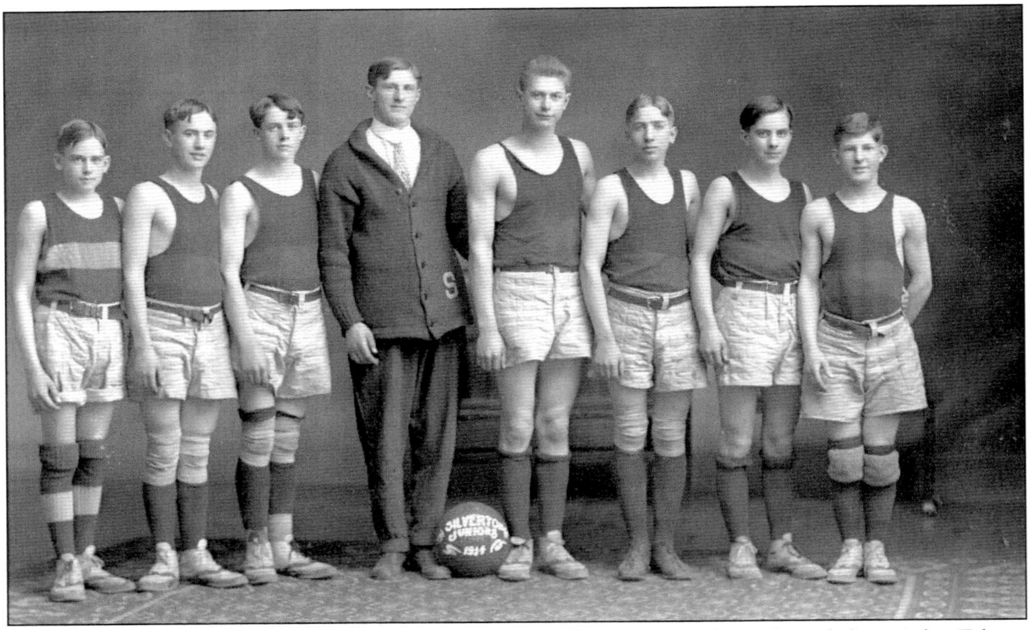

THE SILVERTON JUNIOR VARSITY CAGERS FOR 1914. Those pictured are, from left to right, Edwin Durno; Clarence Sebo; Harvey Carson; Mel Kundert, coach; Oral Palmateer, Otto Alm; Carl Moser; and Willburn Scott. (Courtesy of SCHS.)

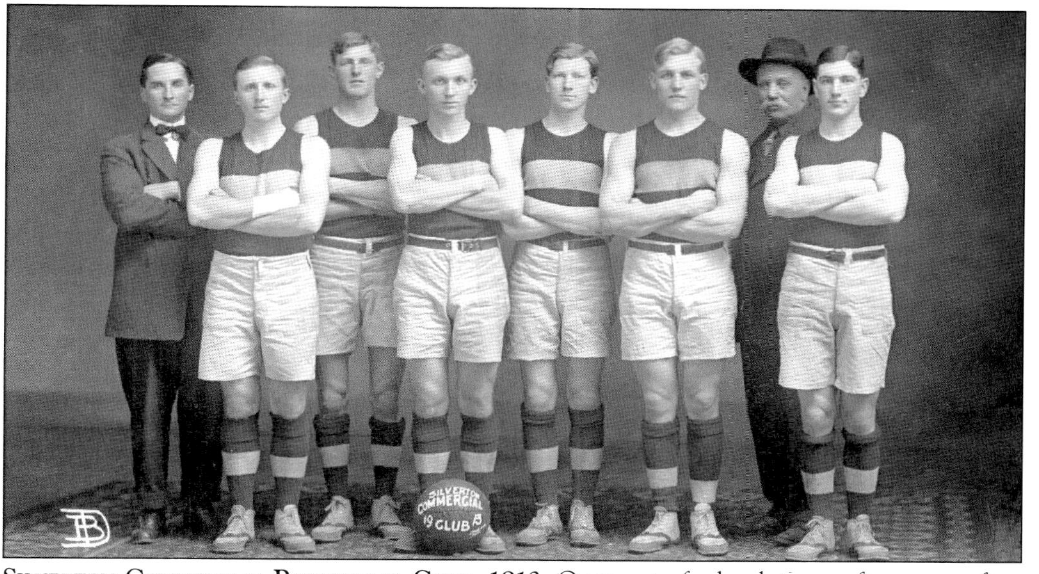

SILVERTON COMMERCIAL BASKETBALL CLUB, 1913. Once out of school, the crafty cagers often joined the various men's leagues. Here is one of the teams. Those pictured are, from left to right, Earl Wood, Chester Wolcott, Melvin Kundert, Vernon Wolcott, Henry Dahl, Carl Voyne, J.K. Mount, and Gifford Smith. (Drake Brothers photograph; courtesy of SCHS.)

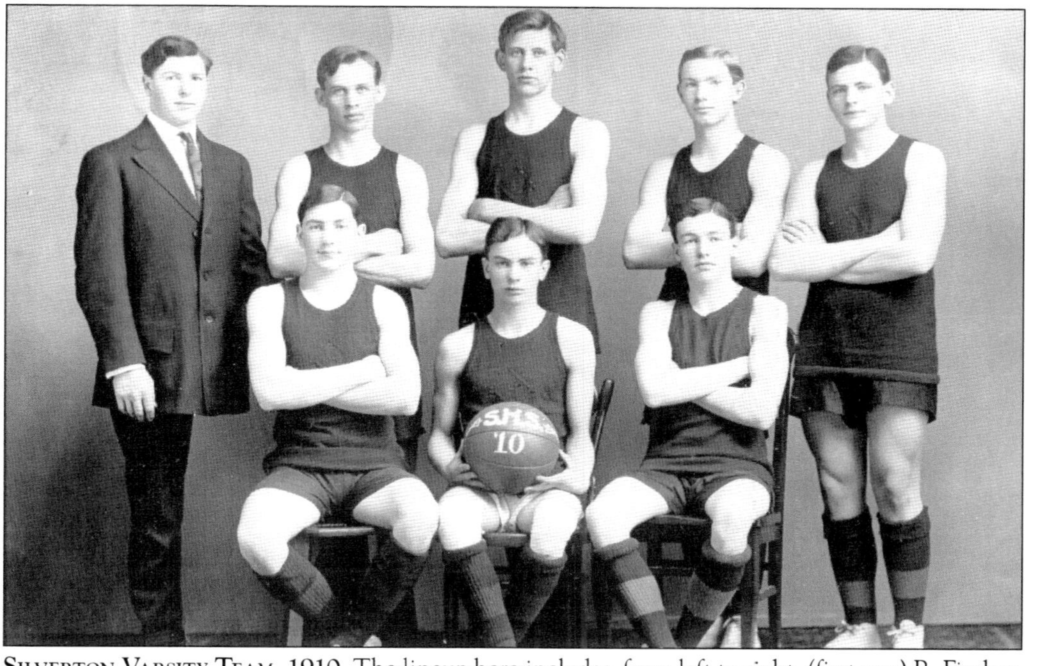

SILVERTON VARSITY TEAM, 1910. The lineup here includes, from left to right (first row) R. Fischer, unidentified, and Ernie Brooks; (second row) manager Wallace Cooley, Lawn Elison, William Steelhammer, Charles Reynolds, and Chester Wolcott. Charlie Reynolds is also pictured on page 78, in the airport section, in front of the various planes he piloted. Wallace Cooley is Rholin Cooley's uncle and kid brother to Gem Theater owner and Marine Band alumni, M.G. Cooley. (Courtesy of SCHS.)

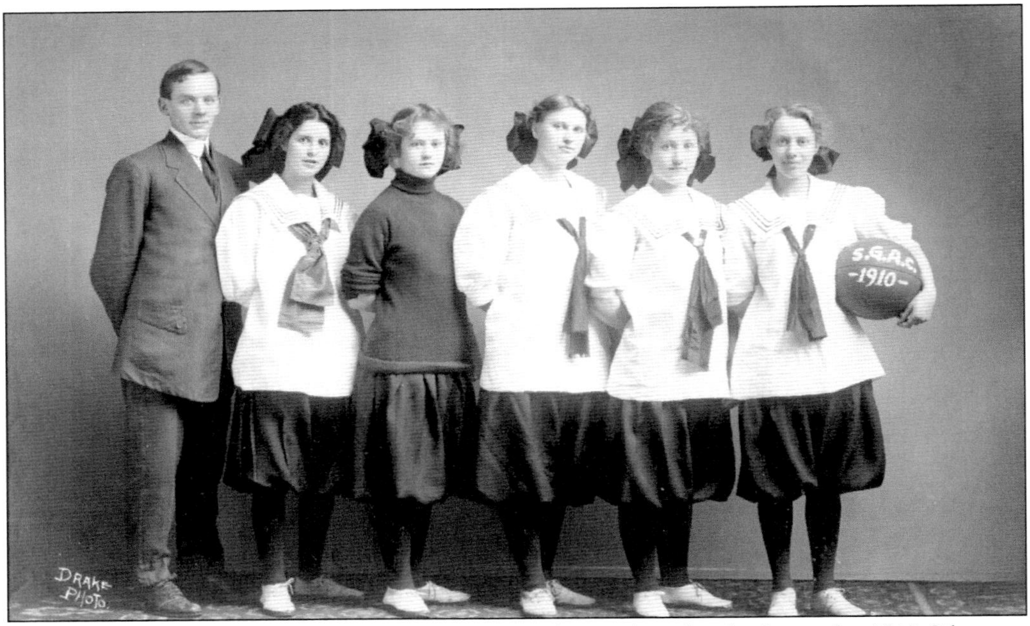

Silverton Girls' Athletic Club, 1910. Not to be outdone by the boys, the 1910 Silverton High School girls' basketball team had more exotic uniforms. Those pictured are, from left to right, coach R. Fischer, Virginia Mascher, Melvina Gjertsen, Olive Jensen, Goldie McGinnis, and Edith Wolfard, captain. (Courtesy of SCHS.)

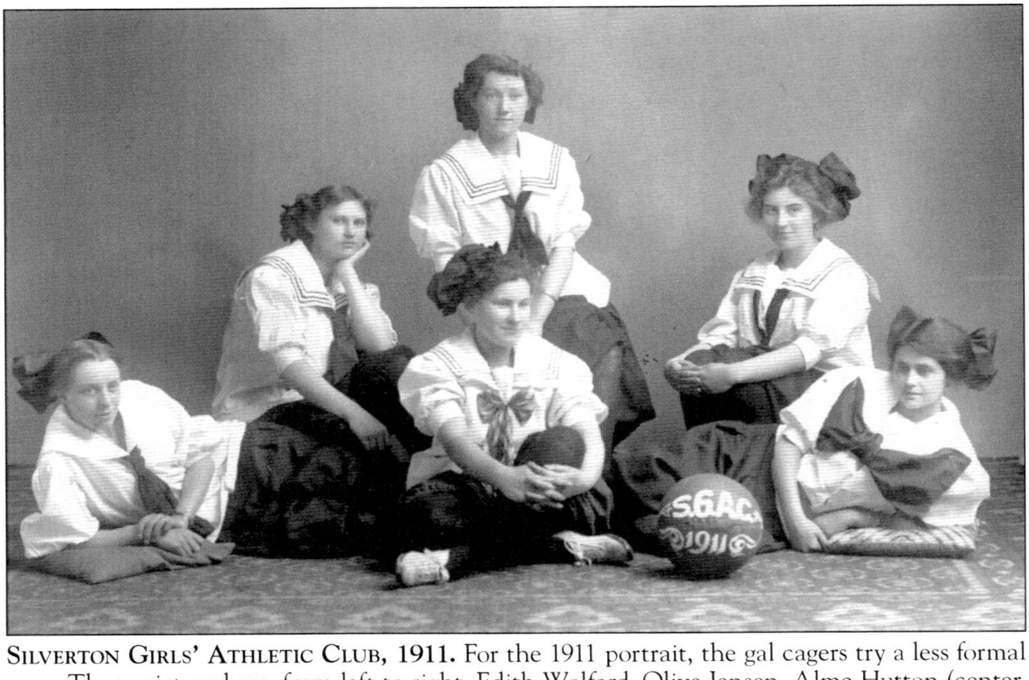

Silverton Girls' Athletic Club, 1911. For the 1911 portrait, the gal cagers try a less formal pose. Those pictured are, from left to right, Edith Wolfard, Olive Jensen, Alma Hutton (center, sitting), Goldie McGinnis, Hattie Nervig, and unidentified. (Courtesy of SCHS.)

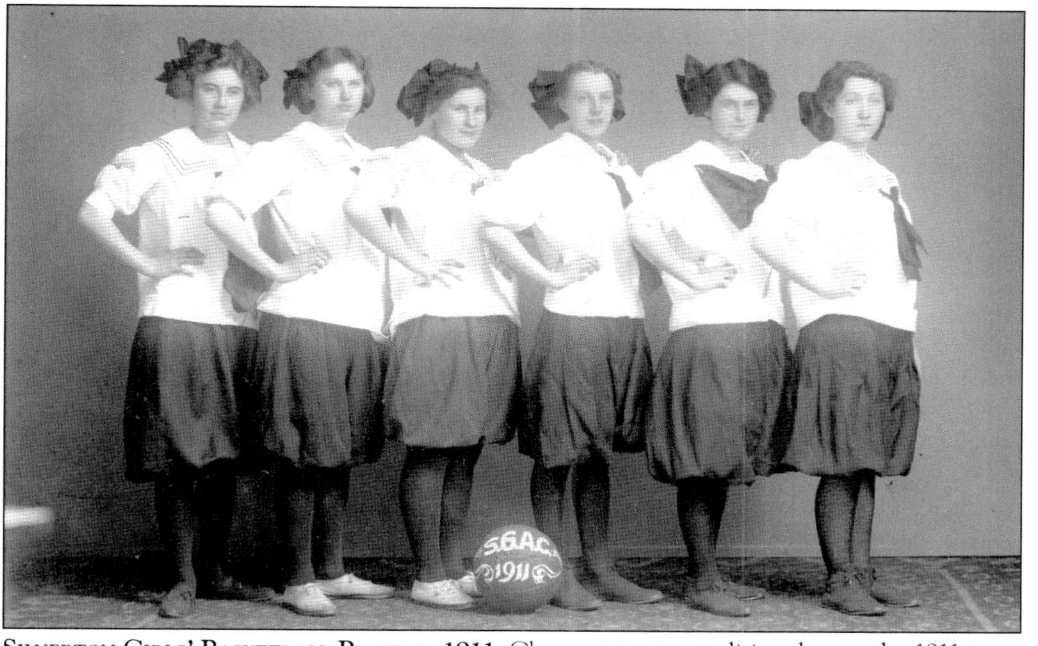

SILVERTON GIRLS' BASKETBALL PLAYERS, 1911. Closer to a more traditional pose, the 1911 team shows off its proper posture. Those pictured are, from left to right, Hattie Nervig, Olive Jensen, Alma Hutton, Edith Wolfard, unidentified, and Goldie McGinnis. (Courtesy of SCHS.)

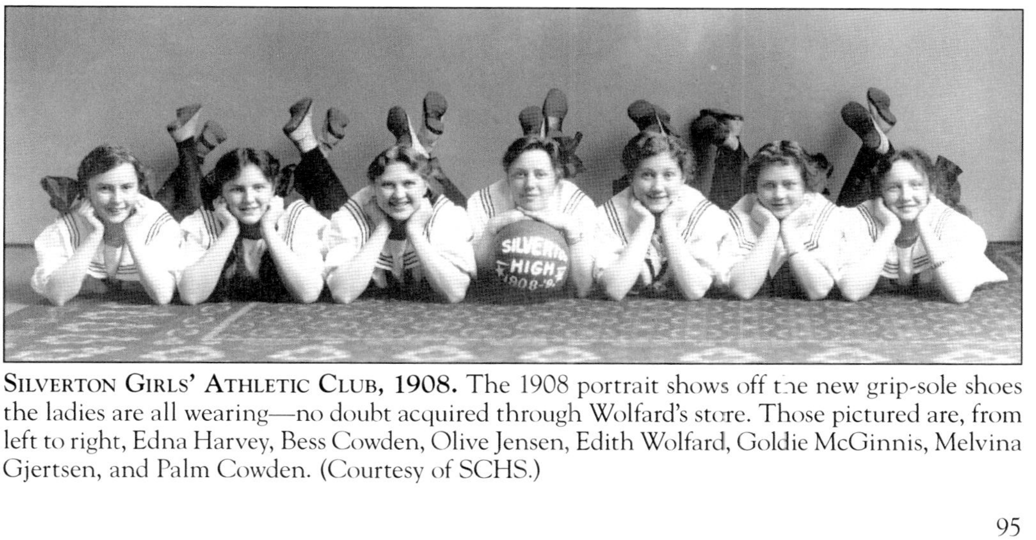

SILVERTON GIRLS' ATHLETIC CLUB, 1908. The 1908 portrait shows off the new grip-sole shoes the ladies are all wearing—no doubt acquired through Wolfard's store. Those pictured are, from left to right, Edna Harvey, Bess Cowden, Olive Jensen, Edith Wolfard, Goldie McGinnis, Melvina Gjertsen, and Palm Cowden. (Courtesy of SCHS.)

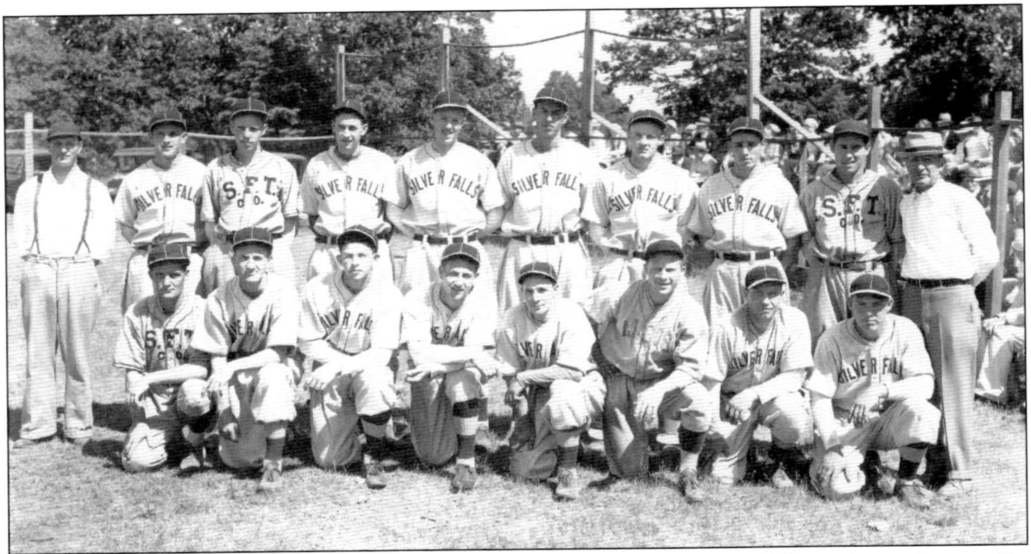

SILVER FALLS TIMBER COMPANY REDSOX, 1936. During the heyday of the industrial sawmills, the Silver Falls Timber Company (SFTC) decided to sponsor a baseball team. Known initially as the Silver Falls Redsox, "ton" was appended to "Silver," and "Falls" was dropped entirely. SFTC employee William "Mack" McGinnis took on the roll of general manager for the team. After retirement, he opened a tavern in town, which is still known as Mac's Place. This shot shows the 1936 team, with Mac on the right and Orlo Thompson on the left. (Courtesy of SCHS.)

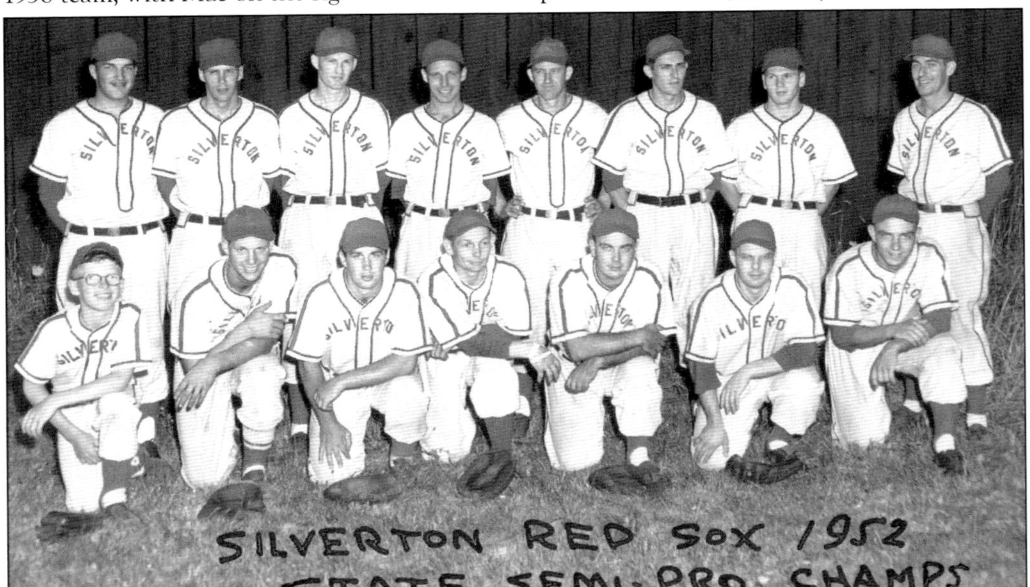

SILVERTON REDSOX—1952 CHAMPIONS. The ball team actually outlived the mill that was sponsoring it. Now a semiprofessional farm team of the Boston Red Sox, the Silverton team took the 1952 Oregon State Championship. Those pictured are, from left to right, (first row) batboy Johnny Skirvin, "Cub" Houck, Roger Dasch, Chris Christianson, Don Hatteberg, Rod Oster, and Irving Roth; (second row) Fred Sandgren, Bud Larson, Dick Gentzkow, Huck Johnson, Ted Kerr, Gene Peterson, Jim Peterson, and manager Wally Flager. (Courtesy of SCHS.)

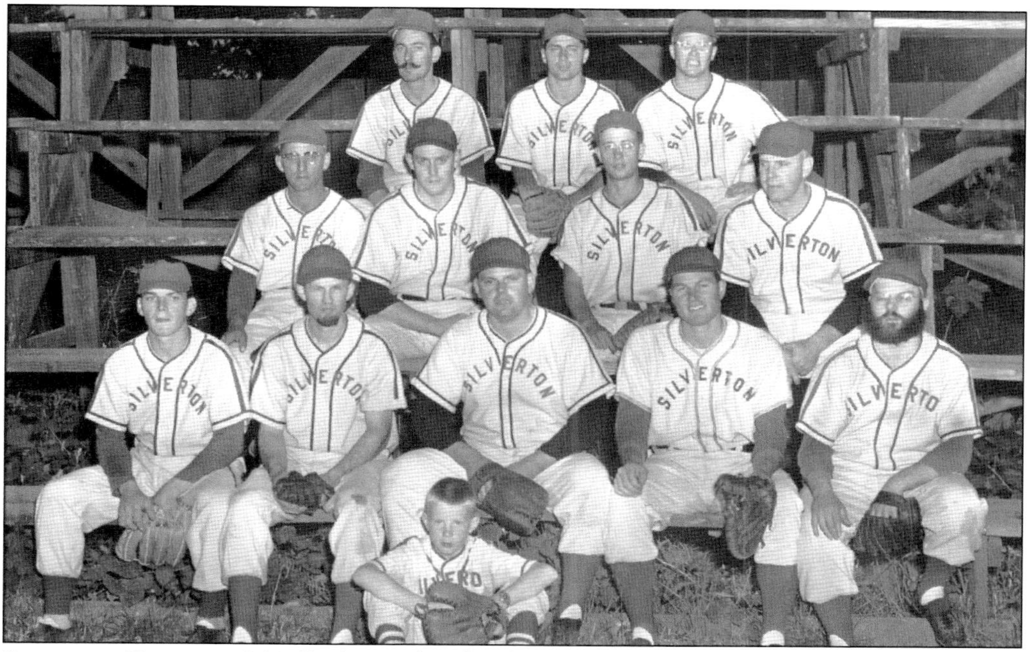

SILVERTON REDSOX, 1954. Back together for the centennial, the lineup includes, from left to right, batboy Bob Henjum (sitting on the ground); (first row) Jim Bowser, Dick Gentzkow, Chuck Sauvain, Harvgey Koepf, and Rod Oster (on loan from the Hassidic semiprofressional team House of David); (second row) unidentified, Don Gensback, Jay Fournier, and Hal Bounbonnais; (third row) manager Wally Flager, Lou Skirvin, and George Connelly. (Carl Hande photograph; courtesy of SCHS.)

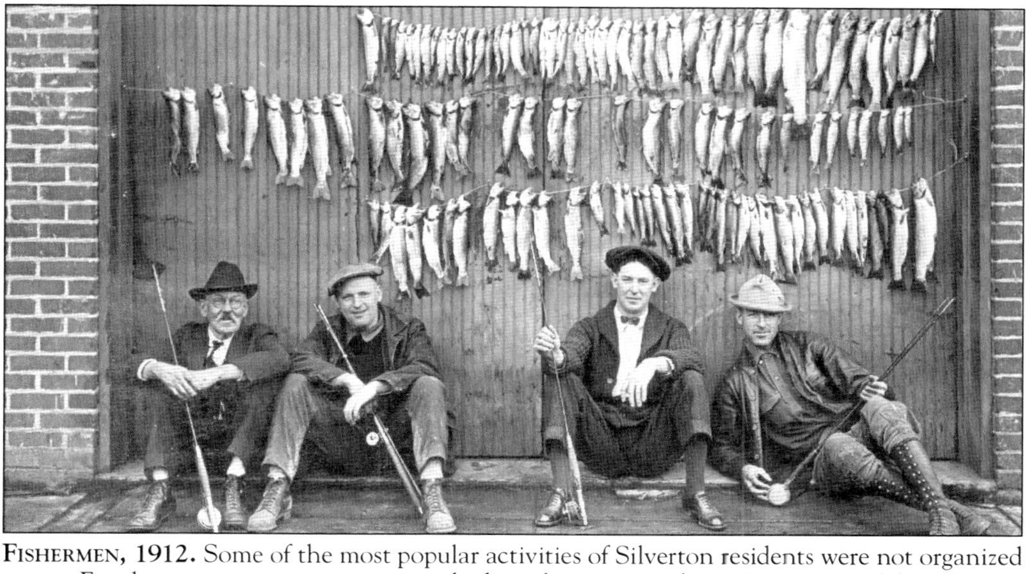

FISHERMEN, 1912. Some of the most popular activities of Silverton residents were not organized sports. For these activities, participants relied on the great outdoors. Hunting and fishing were both common pastimes that had practical and nutritious benefits. Pictured from left to right, Dr. Gunderson, Charlie Johnson, Austin Eastman, and Cal Schlaydor show off a wall of cutthroat trout after a day on the creek. (Courtesy of SCHS.)

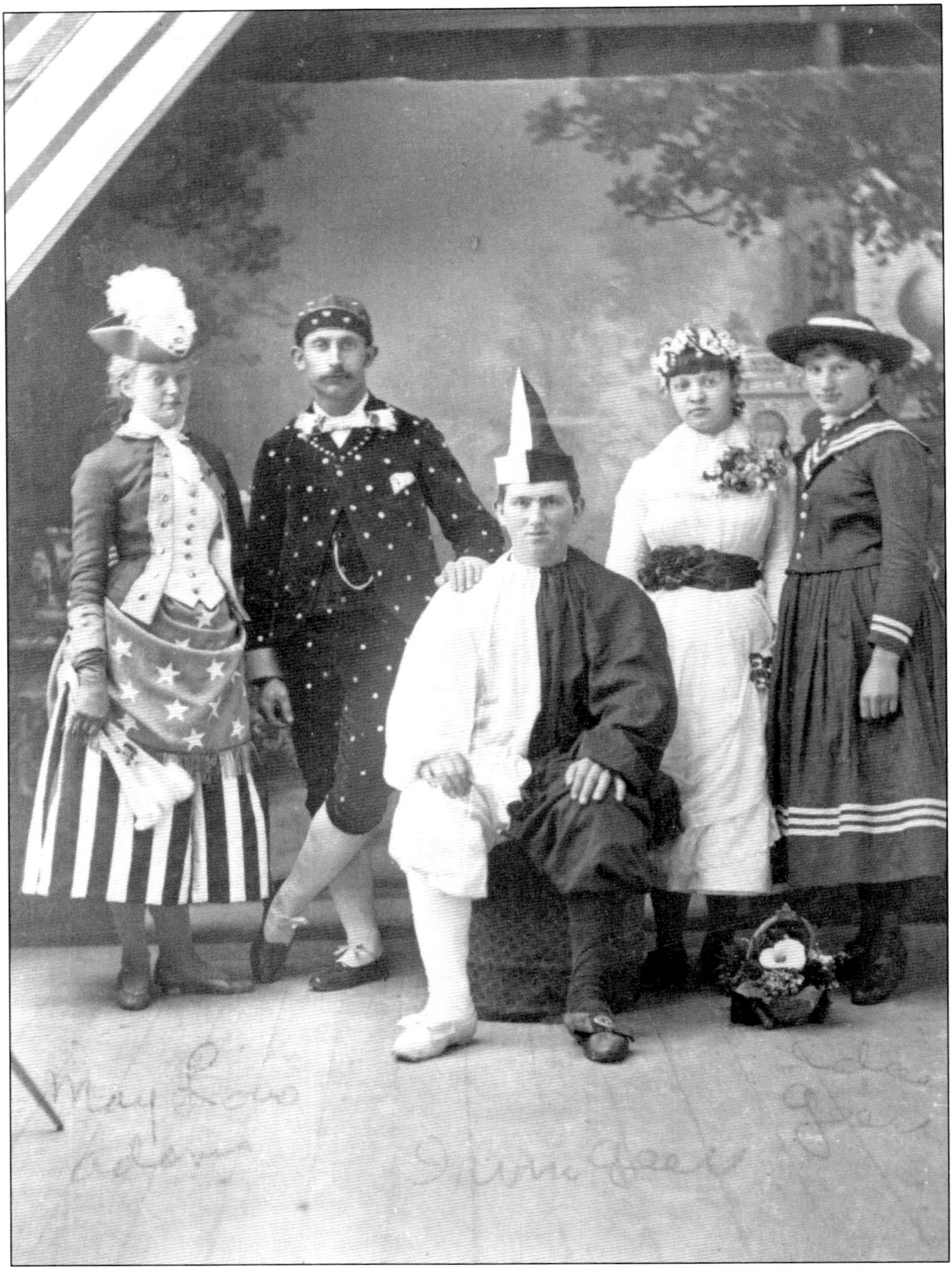

Play at the old Palace Theater, around 1910. With a huge theater available, live performances were popular in the town of Silverton. This is a group of thespians with prominent local names. Those pictured are, from left to right, May Coolidge, Lewis J. Adams, Irwin Geer (seated), unidentified, and Ida Geer. (Courtesy of SCHS.)

Eight

Celebrations and Events

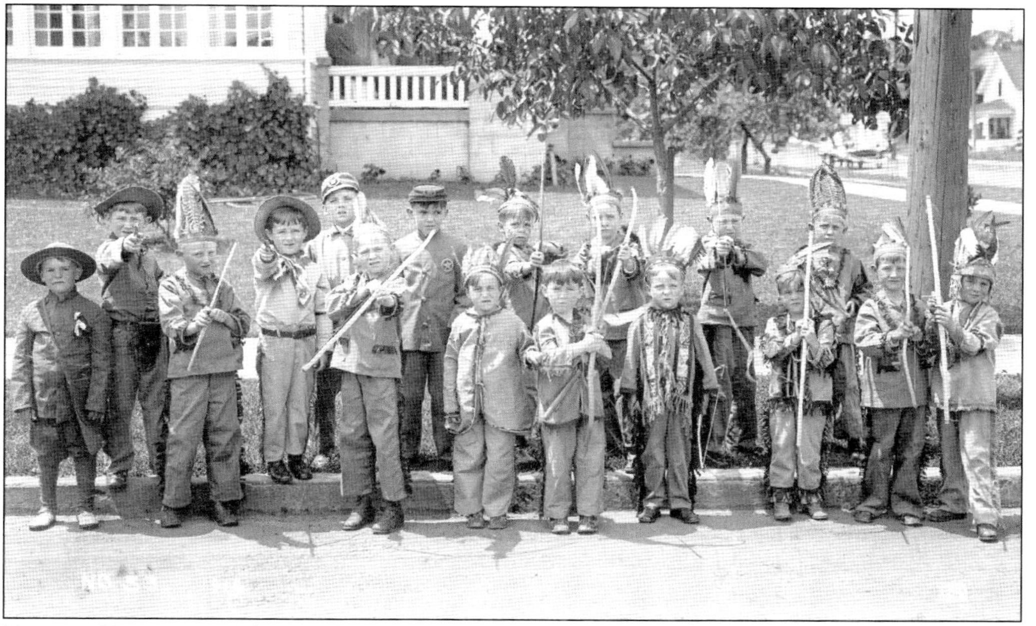

Tribe of Kids, 1914. Silverton loves to celebrate. Silverton celebrates its history, its people, and its pets. The event these young folks are celebrating on the corner of Coolidge and West Main Streets has been lost to time. But then again, who needs a reason to celebrate life? (Courtesy of SCHS.)

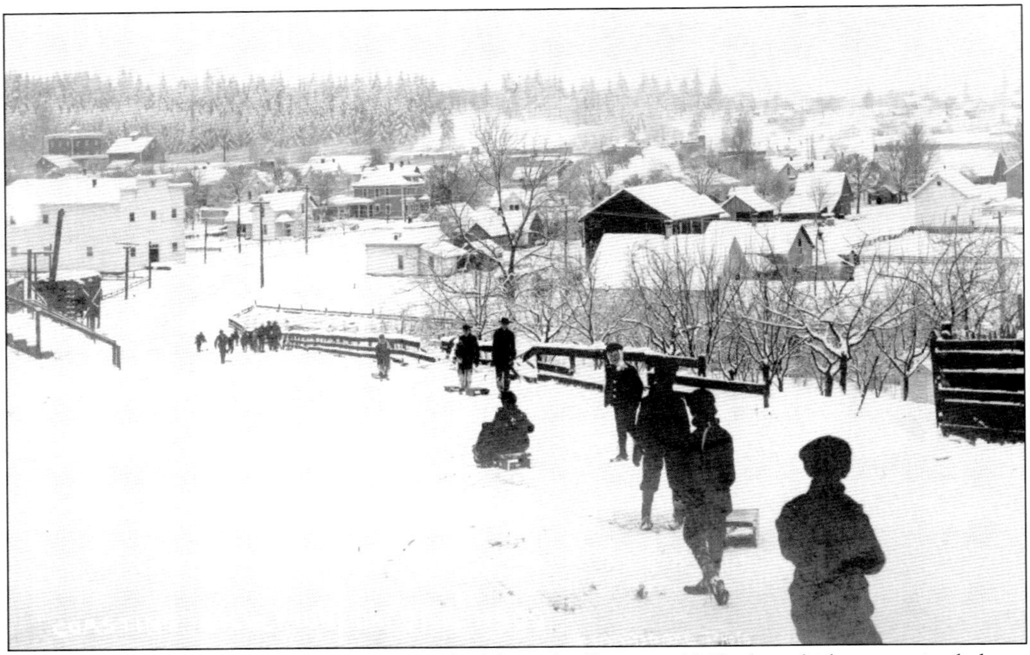

Sledders on Oak Street, 1909. During the blizzard of January 1909, these kids are excited about their snow day. This view is halfway up Oak Street, looking toward town. The American Legion Hall is on the left side of the image at the bottom of the hill. Silverton's 1866 schoolhouse is in the middle of the frame. (Drake Brothers photograph; courtesy of SCHS.)

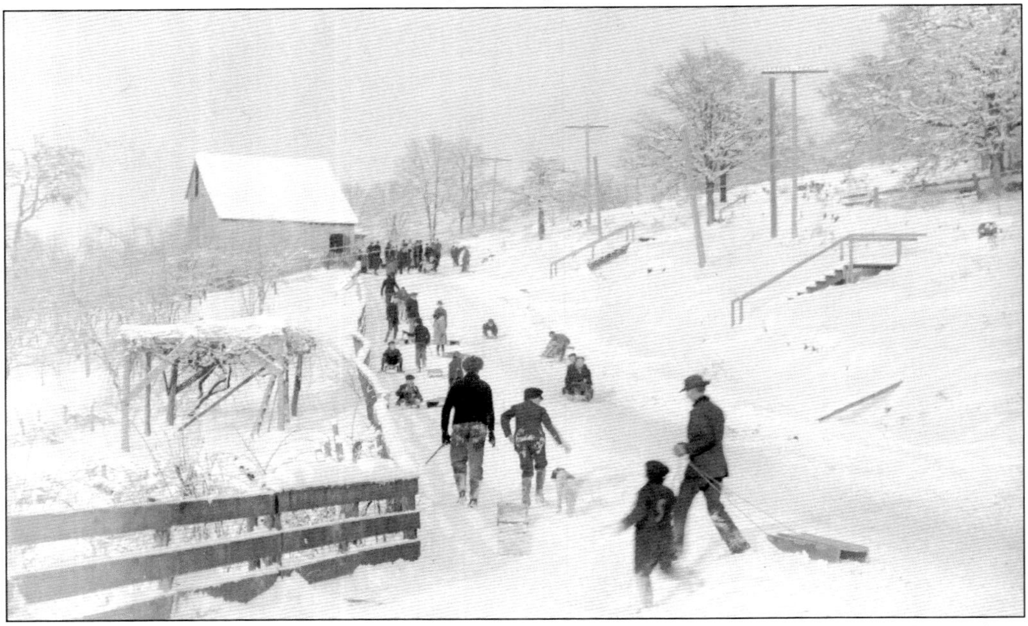

Winter Fun on Oak Street, 1909. Here is another image from the January 1909 blizzard on the same hill as the previous picture. When this photograph was taken, there was hardly a house or tree on Oak Street, however, it is populated with both today. (Drake Brothers photograph; courtesy of SCHS.)

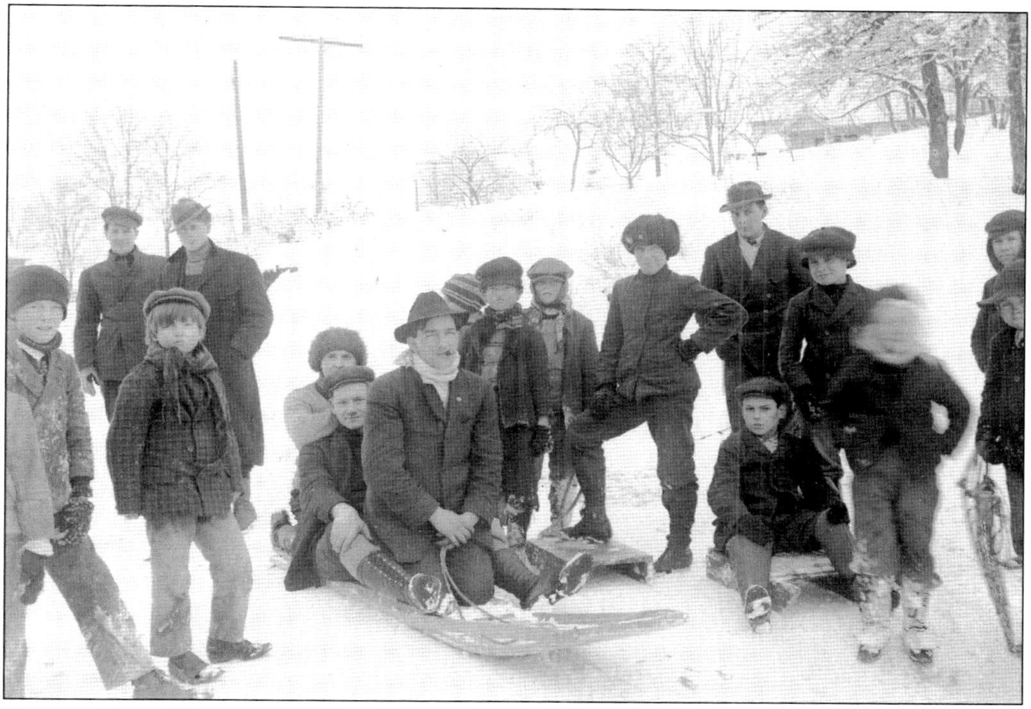

Fans of Cold Weather on Oak Street, 1909. A hearty crew of unidentified sledders poses before sliding down the street. This was apparently before the invention of the Flexible Flier. The common commercial sleds of the era were of the "Rosebud" variety. (Drake Brothers photograph; courtesy of SCHS.)

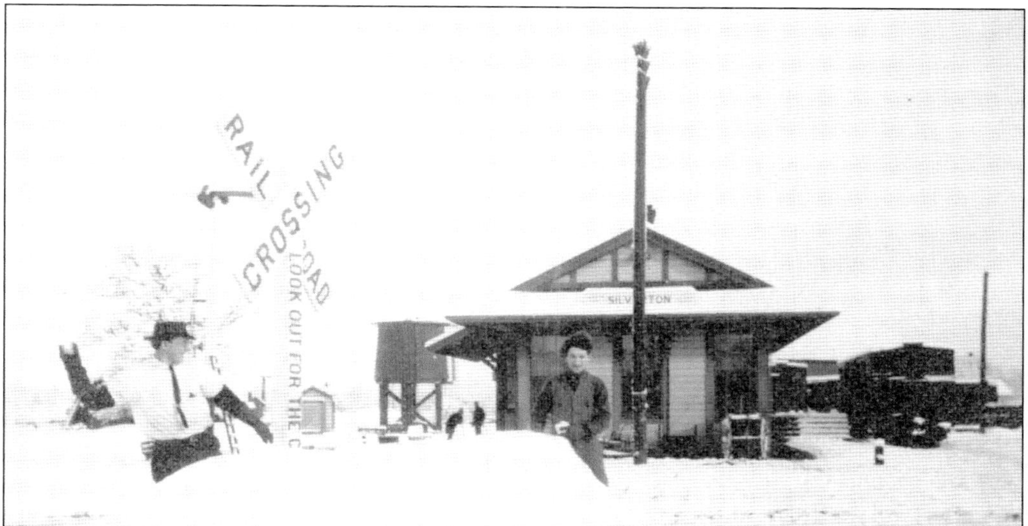

Snowball Fight at the Depot, 1909. Of course, some folks did not get snow days. So, they had to make do and improvise. Here is the start of a snowball fight near the tracks. (Drake Brothers photograph; courtesy of SCHS.)

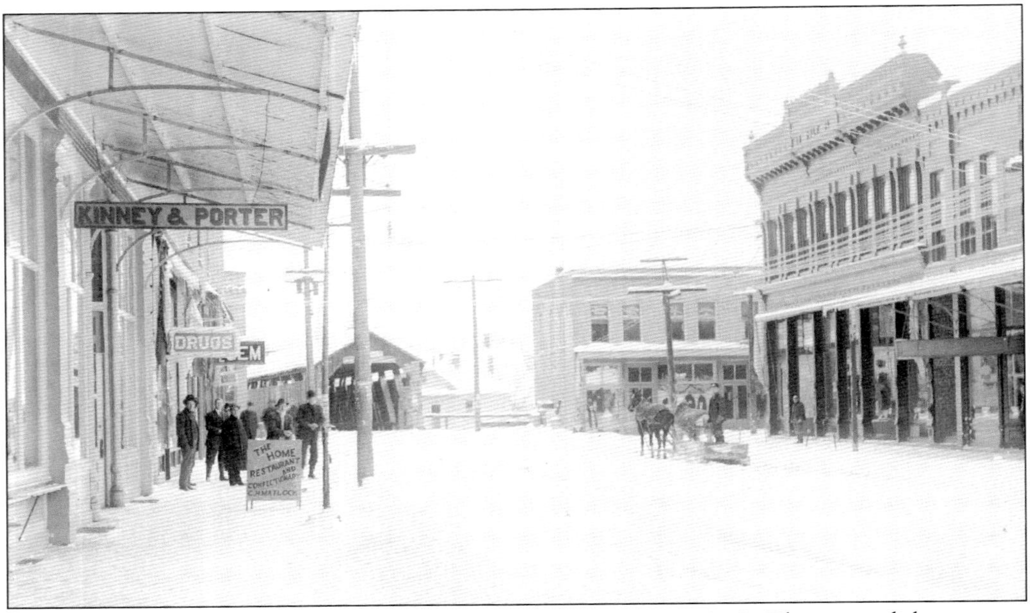

MAIN STREET, LOOKING WEST OVER THE COVERED BRIDGE, 1909. The snow did not seem to effect downtown much. This image, however, offers one of the best views of the old Main Street Covered Bridge. Few images show it, and apparently not a single photograph was taken specifically of bridge. It was as if the people of Silverton had grown ashamed of the old bridge. It was removed and replaced by a modern steel bridge the next year. (Drake Brothers photograph; courtesy of SCHS.)

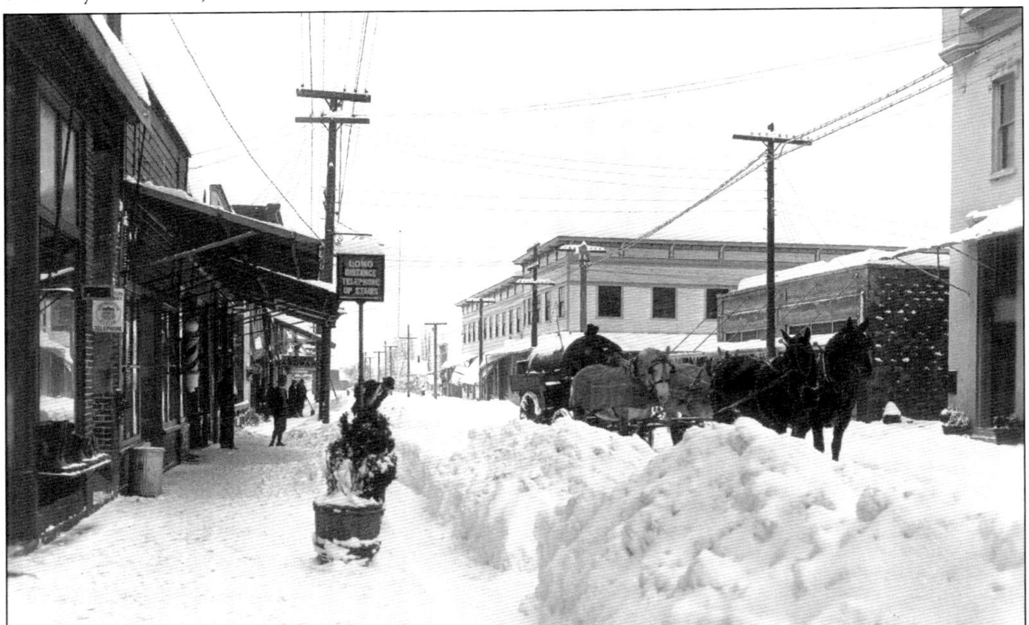

WATER AND MAIN STREETS, LOOKING NORTH, 1914. Five years later, another blizzard occurred in Silverton. This view is looking north on North Water Street. The Palace Theater is seen in the background, behind the wagon. (Drake Brothers photograph; courtesy of SCHS.)

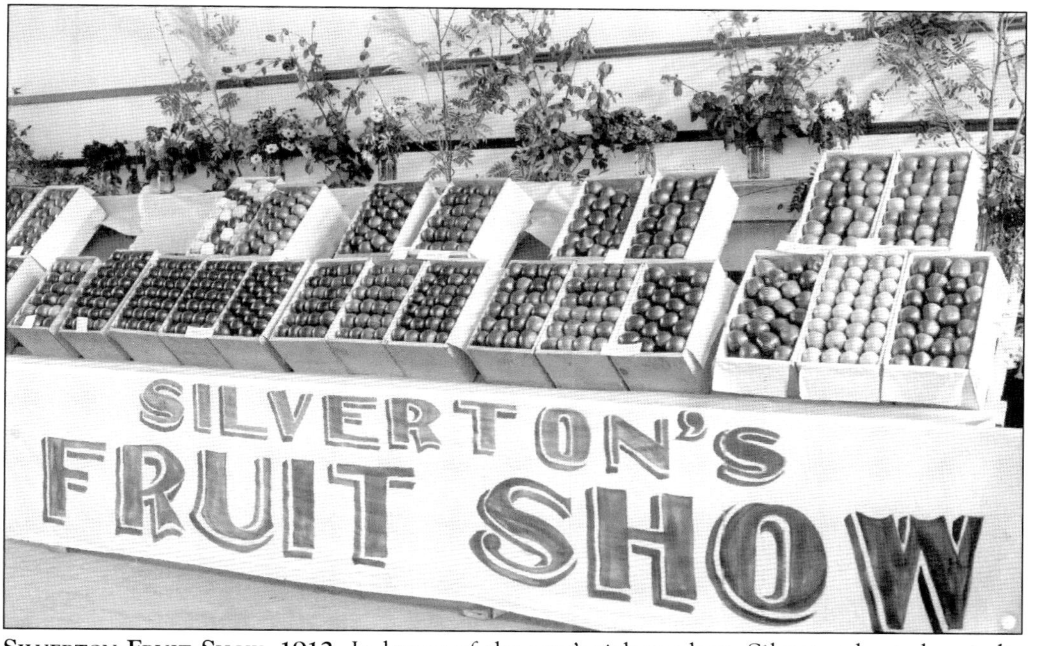

SILVERTON FRUIT SHOW, 1912. In honor of the area's rich produce, Silverton hosted periodic fruit, flower, and produce shows. These produce-focused events were quite common, as were large amounts of local, fresh organic produce. All grocers at the time were, in effect, farmers' markets. (Courtesy of SCHS.)

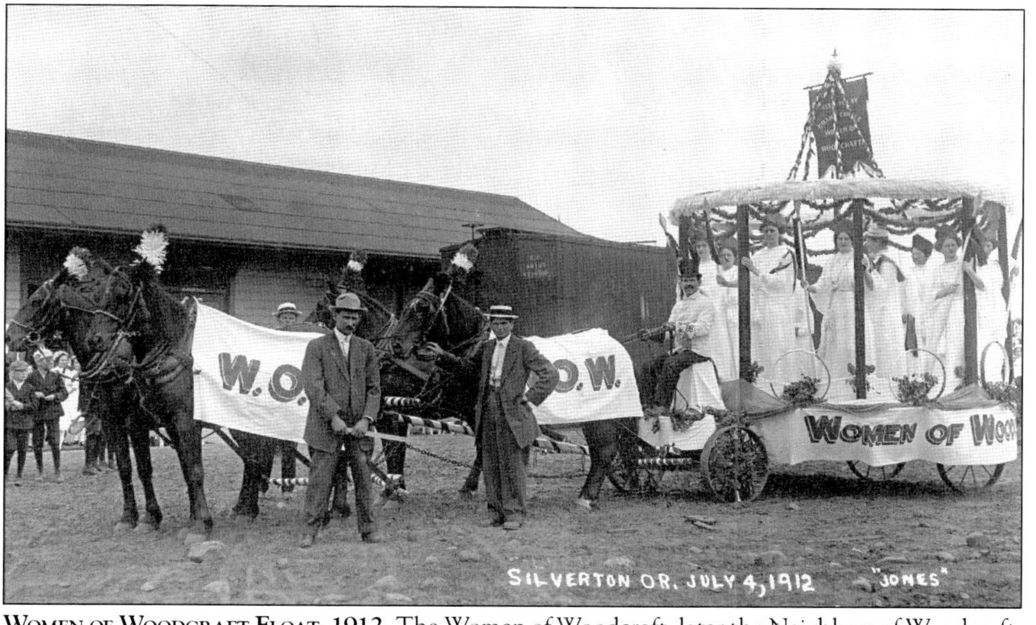

WOMEN OF WOODCRAFT FLOAT, 1912. The Women of Woodcraft, later the Neighbors of Woodcraft, were the women's auxiliary of the Woodmen of the World, which was an early benevolent society of timber workers. The Neighbors of Woodcraft is still active, but now the club is based in Oregon City, Oregon. Members sell life insurance and provide monthly benefits and scholarships to orphans of deceased members, among other functions. (Courtesy of SCHS.)

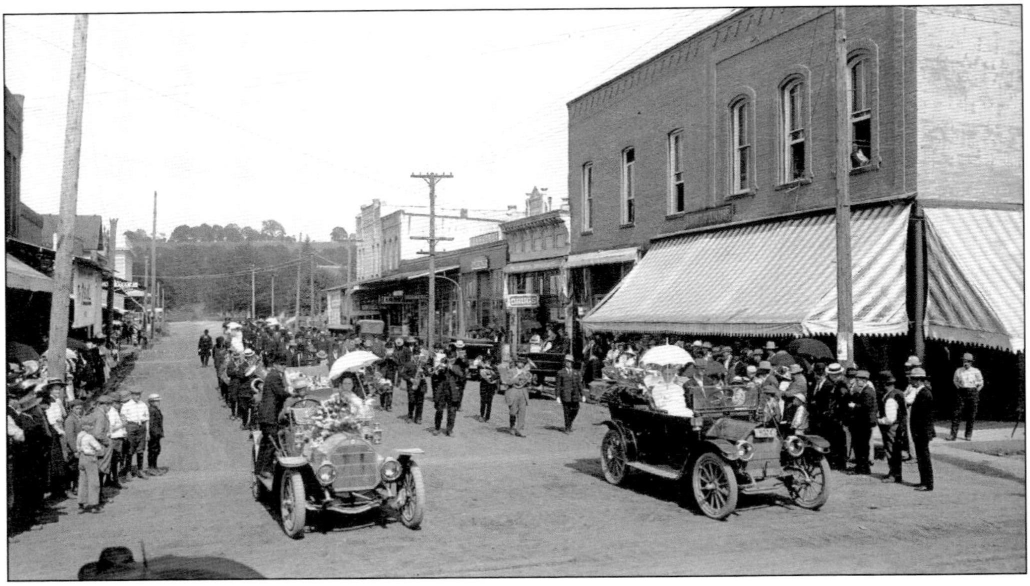

HOMER C. DAVENPORT FUNERAL, 1912. Not all celebrations are intended to be fun. After its most famous citizen, Homer C. Davenport, died of pneumonia, the entire town turned out to celebrate his life and to honor him in death. Several years later, a fitting monument was raised in the Silverton Cemetery by his many friends. His funeral was somewhat controversial at the time, due to the fact that an open bier was used instead of a hearse, and there was a distinct lack of biblical scripture during the service. (Both, courtesy of SCHS.)

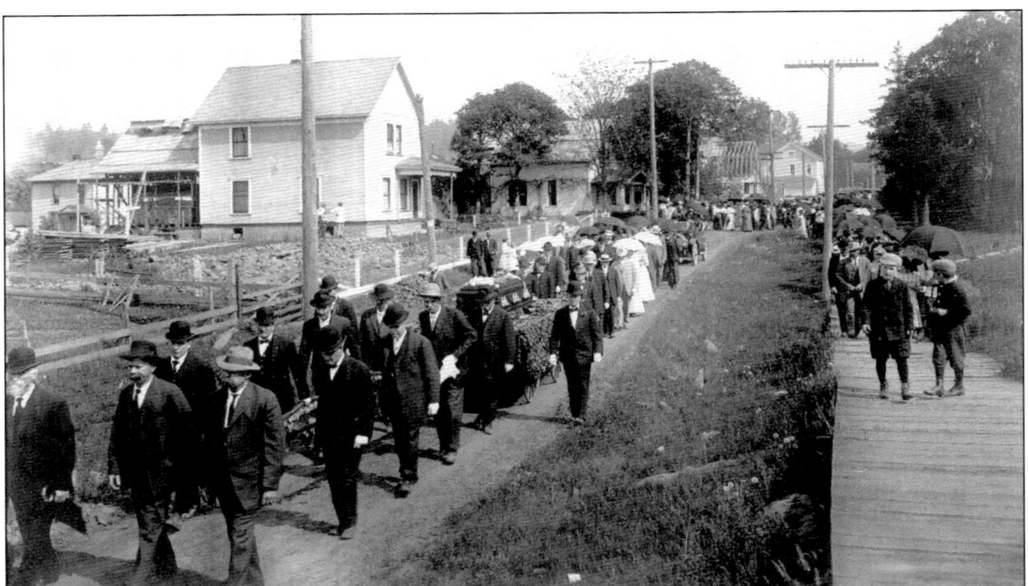

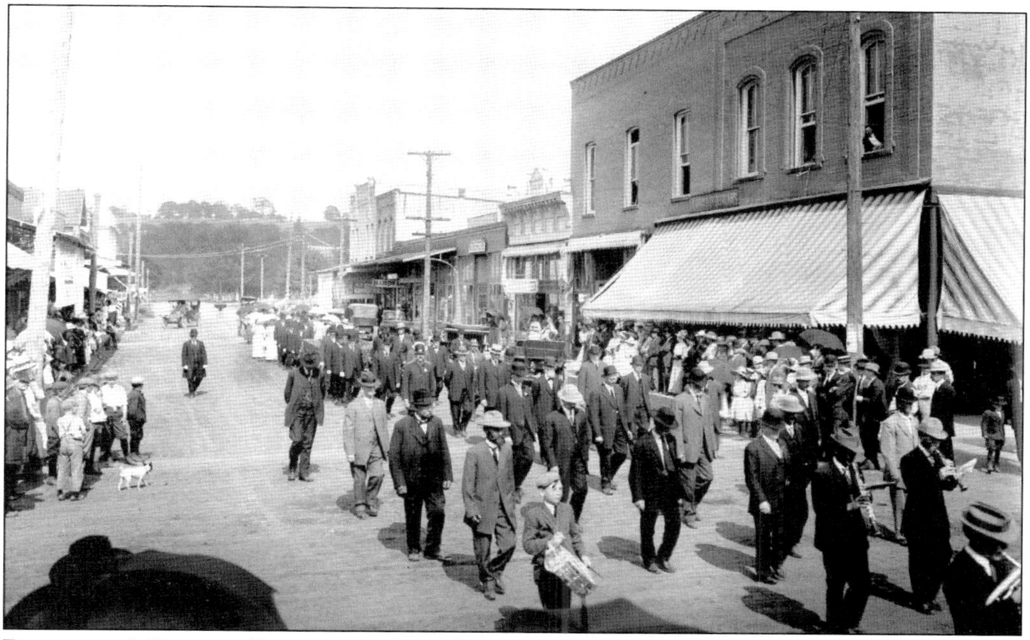

DAVENPORT'S FUNERAL PROCESSION, 1912. Davenport contracted his fatal illness while waiting on the New York docks for the survivors of the *Titanic* to arrive on the RMS *Carpathia*. It would be his last assignment, and he passed away shortly after. Knowing of Homer's deep love for Silverton, his boss and friend, William Randolph Hearst, paid for his body to be shipped home for burial. (Both, courtesy of SCHS.)

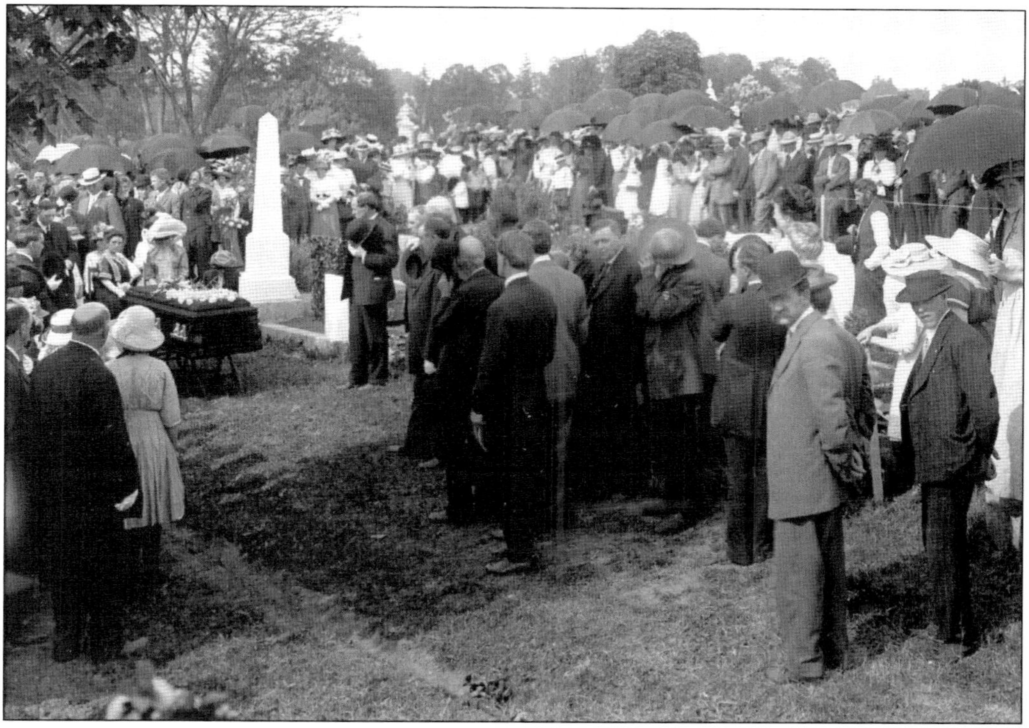

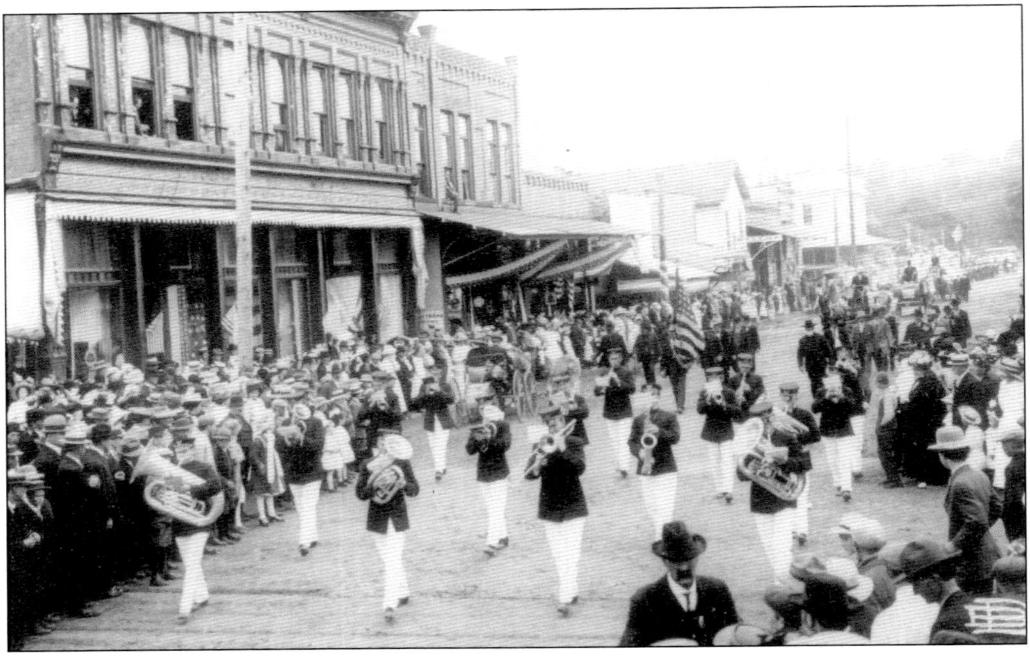

FOURTH OF JULY PARADE, 1914. The big event in town was the annual Fourth of July parade. The Silverton Marine Band, still going strong, gives viewers what they want as they march down Main Street. (Both, courtesy of SCHS.)

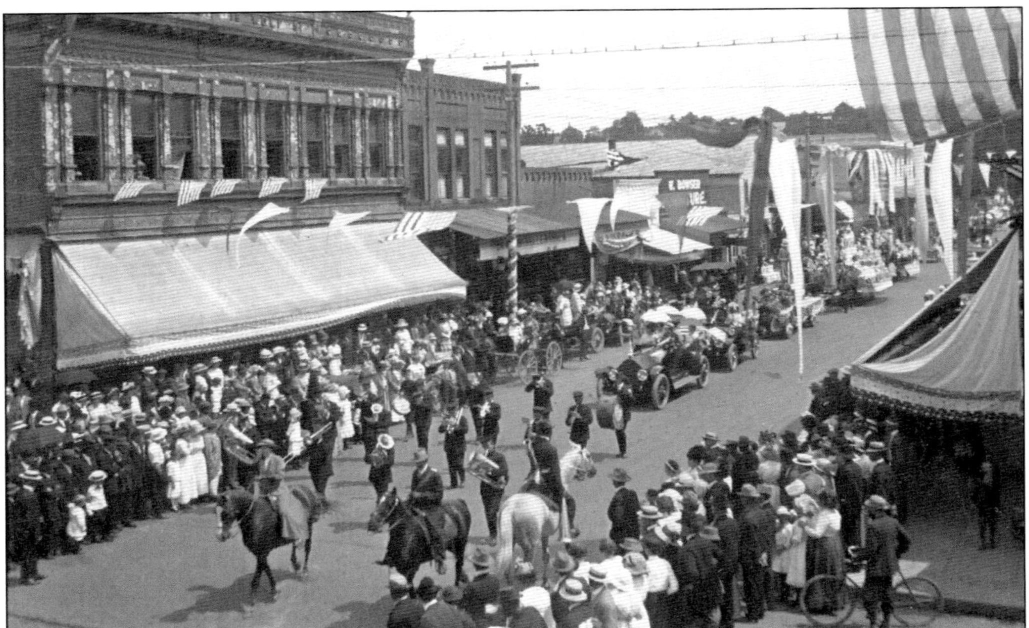

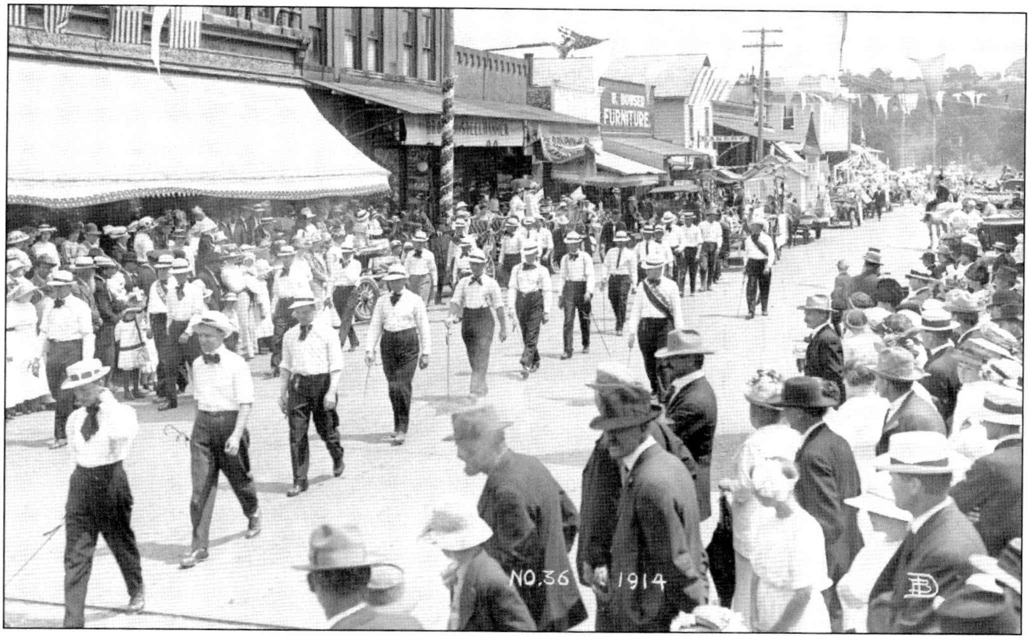

Fourth of July Parade, 1914 and 1915. Here is a line of dapperly dressed men known as the Dandy Dudes in the Fourth of July parade. The next year, the parade committee changed the route (seen below) so that participants walked down North Water Street from the direction of the train station. (Both, courtesy of SCHS.)

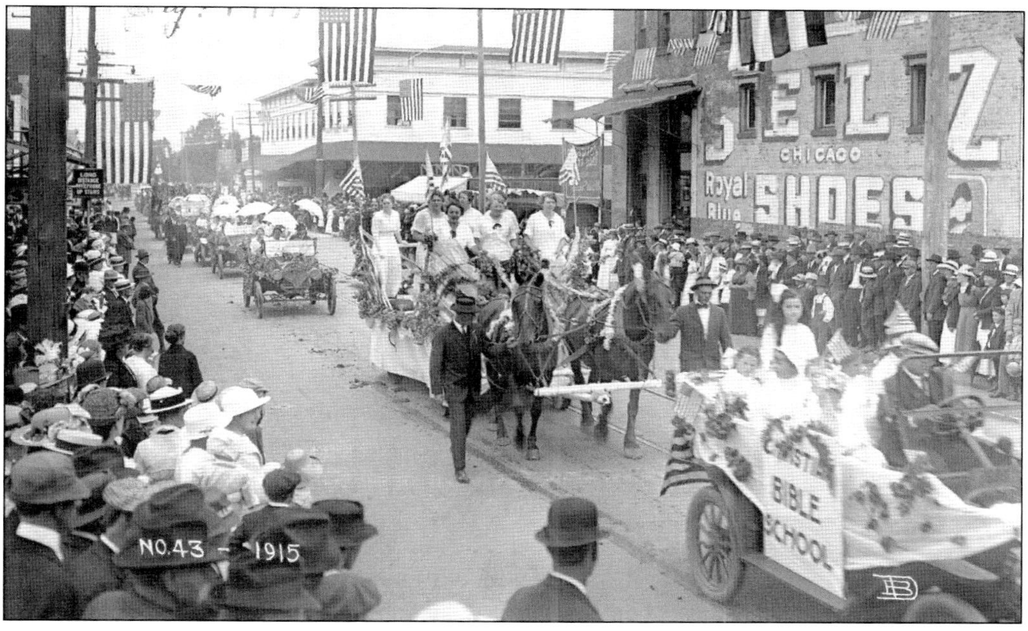

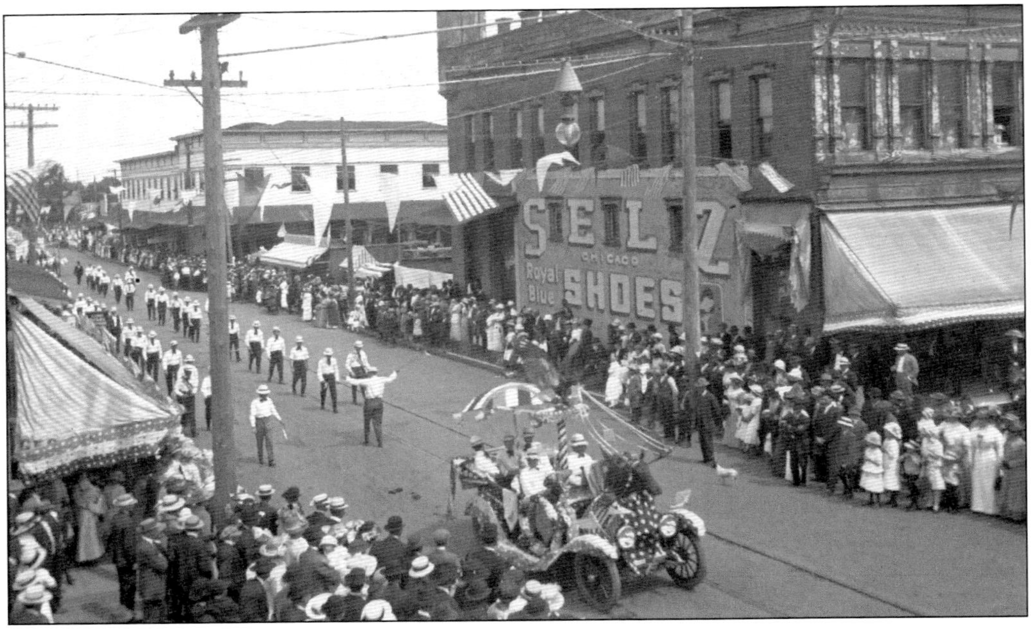

Fourth of July Parade, 1915. Shown above, the Dandy Dudes return, with their leader at the front, marching down Water Street. The new parade route allowed for the inclusion of trains in the parade, as parade marchers could follow the Fischer Flouring Mill rail spur down Water Street toward Mill Street. (Both, courtesy of SCHS.)

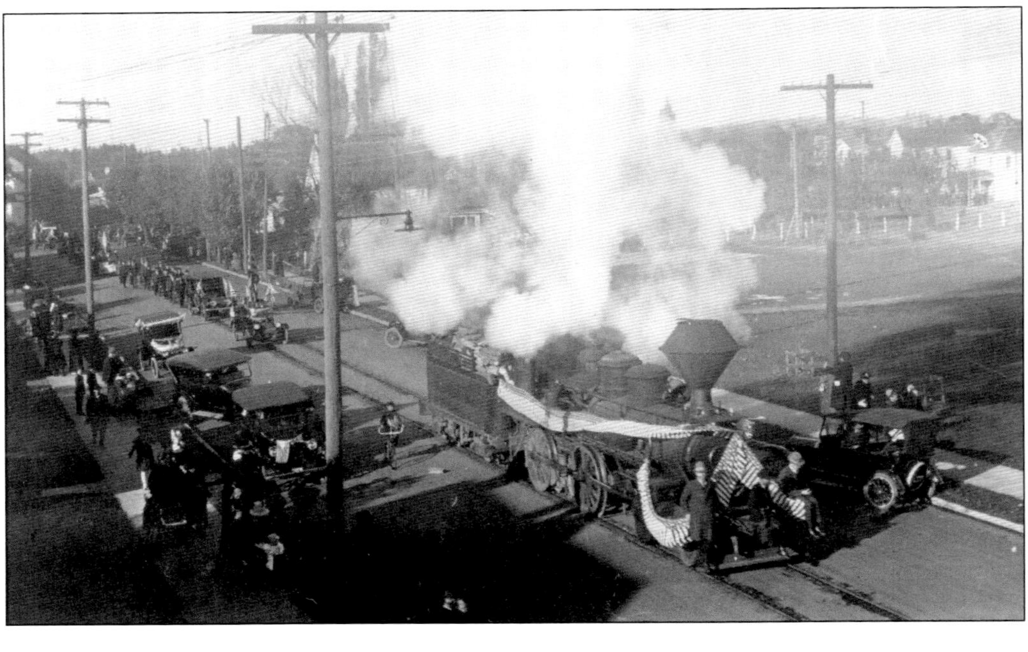

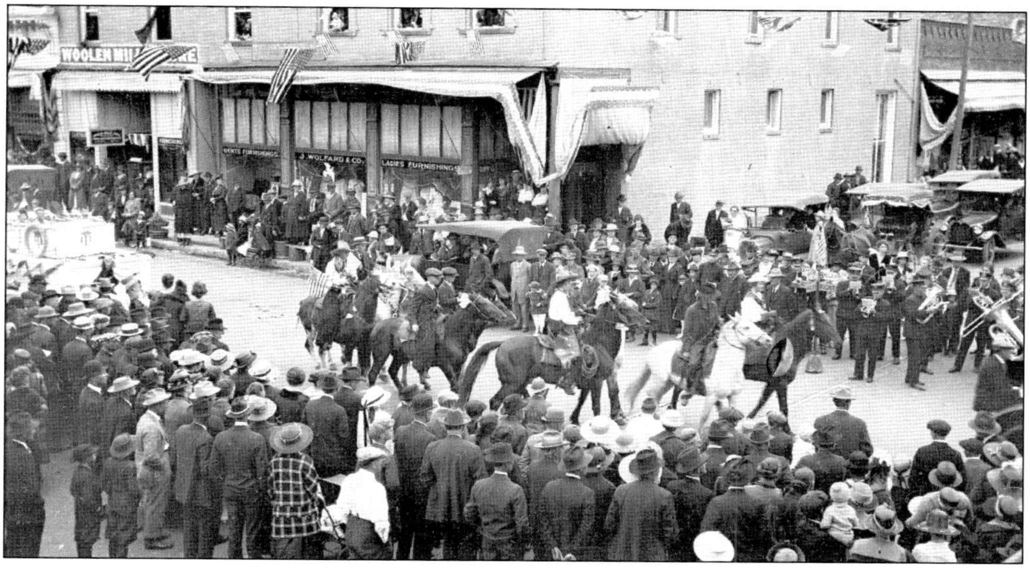

Fourth of July Parade on Main Street, 1918. By 1918, the focus of the parade took on a more militaristic look and feel, given the current events of the time. Possibly marching off to World War I, the image below shows Silverton's National Guard unit. (Both, T.P. Trix Heidenstrom photograph; courtesy of Almquist Studios.)

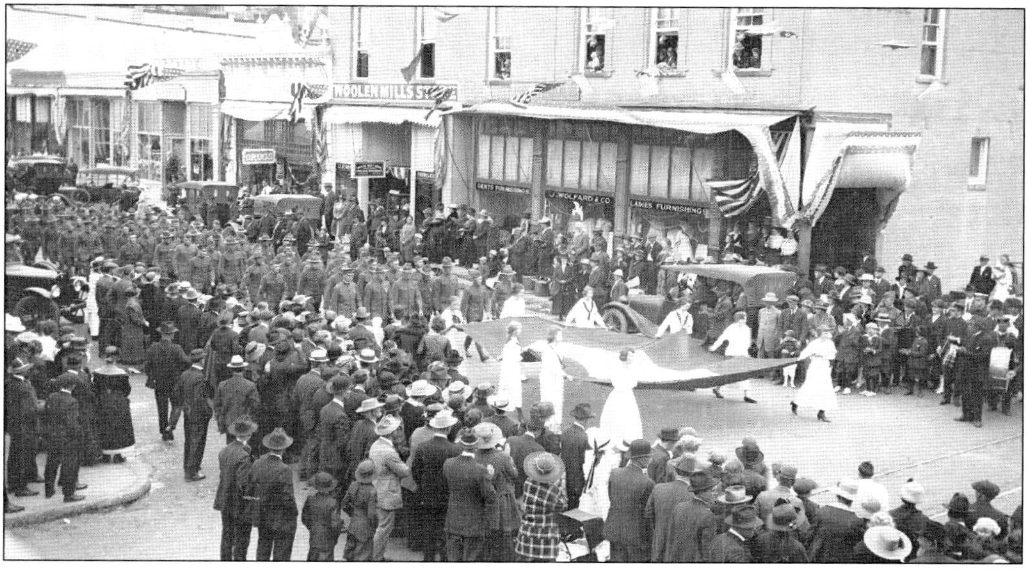

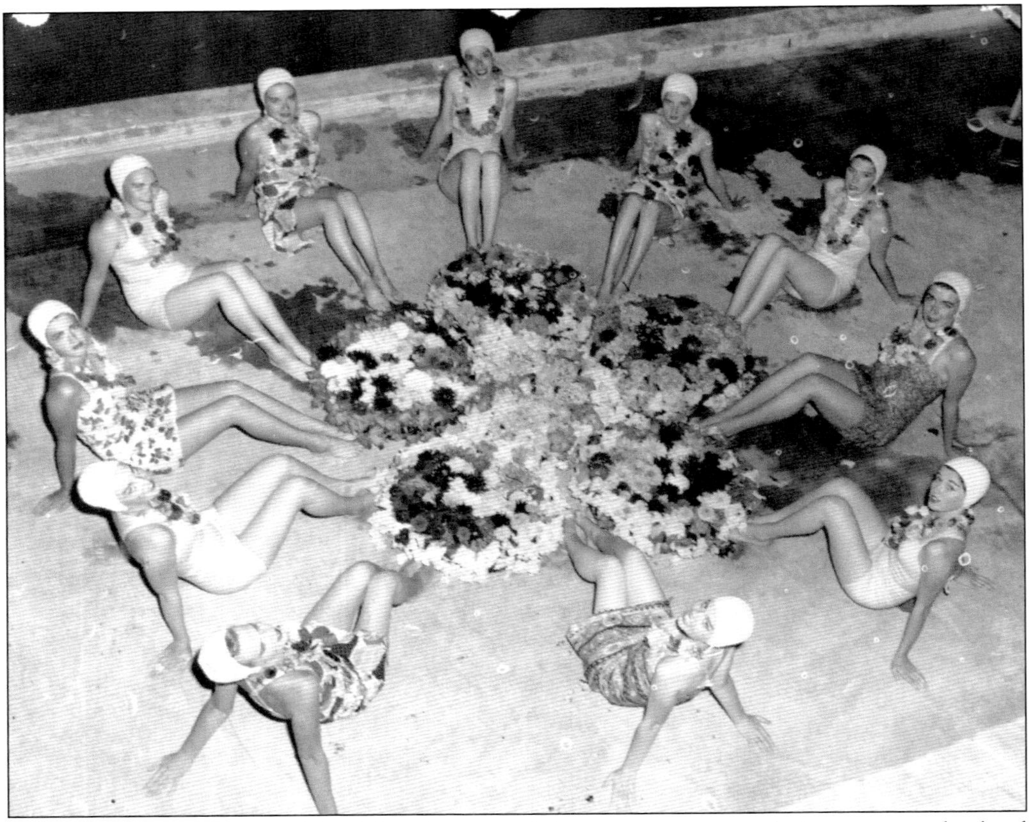

SILVERTON CENTENNIAL, 1954. The Centennial Aquacades practice their moves on dry land before hitting the pool. Jack Fish, of Fish's Bakery, is shown with his Shetland pony cart below. (Both, Bill Hanson photograph; courtesy of SCHS.)

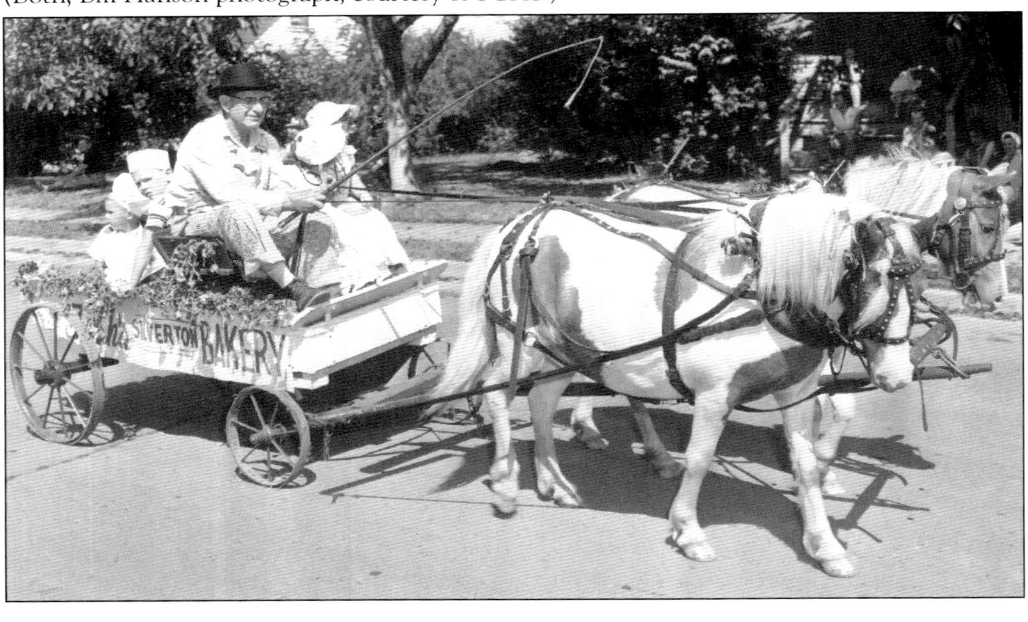

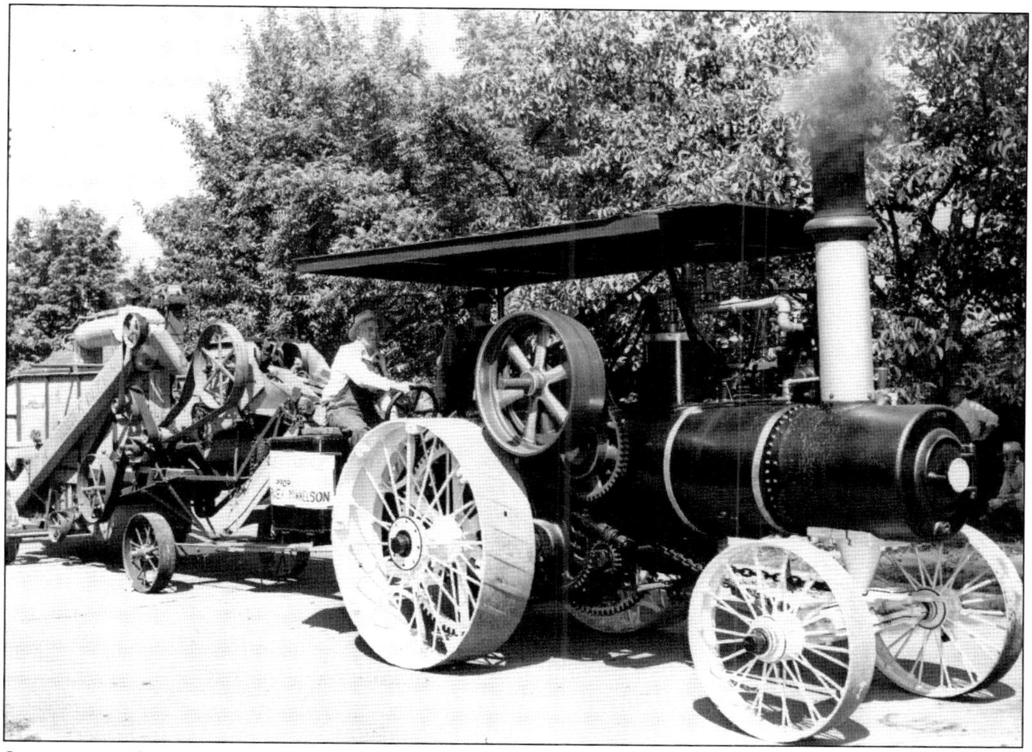

Silverton Centennial Parade Vehicles, 1954. Antique steam engines were common in Silverton parades until the Oregon Legislature passed its Municipal Pressure Vessel Law, effectively outlawing steam-powered vehicles on town streets. The steam "punks" moved west 15 miles for the annual Brooks Steam Up event, which is very successful. Below is the Silverton Lions club's ominous-looking float. (Both, Bill Hanson photograph; courtesy of SCHS.)

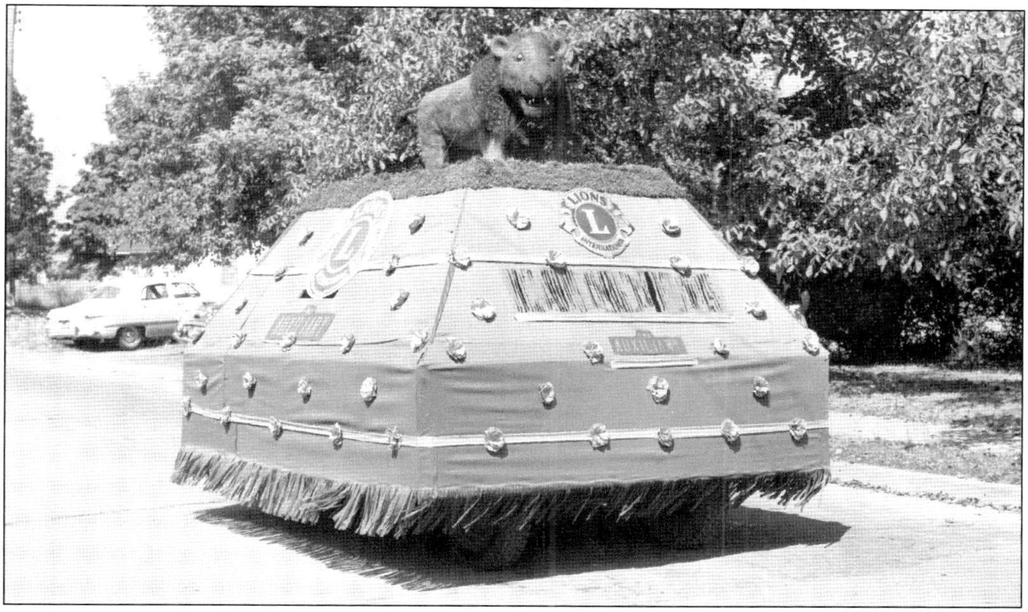

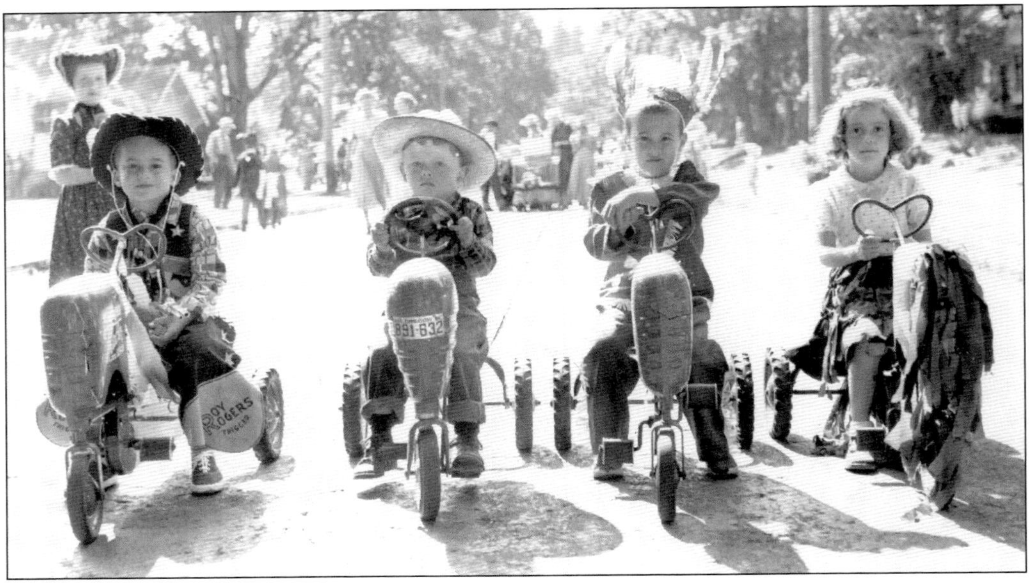

SILVERTON CENTENNIAL PARADE FOR CHILDREN AND PETS, 1954. Ever since the 1930s, Silverton's American Legion Post has hosted a parade for kids and their pets every spring on Memorial Day weekend. The centennial was no different. Above is the pedal tractor patrol, and below is the local baton-twirling team of the Major Minorettes. (Both, Bill Hanson photograph; courtesy of SCHS.)

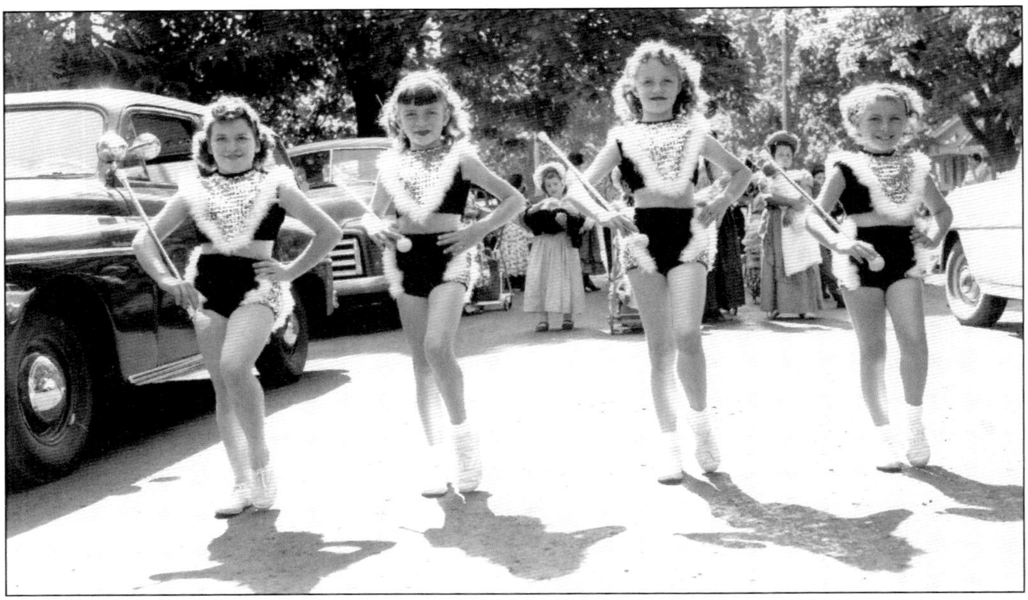

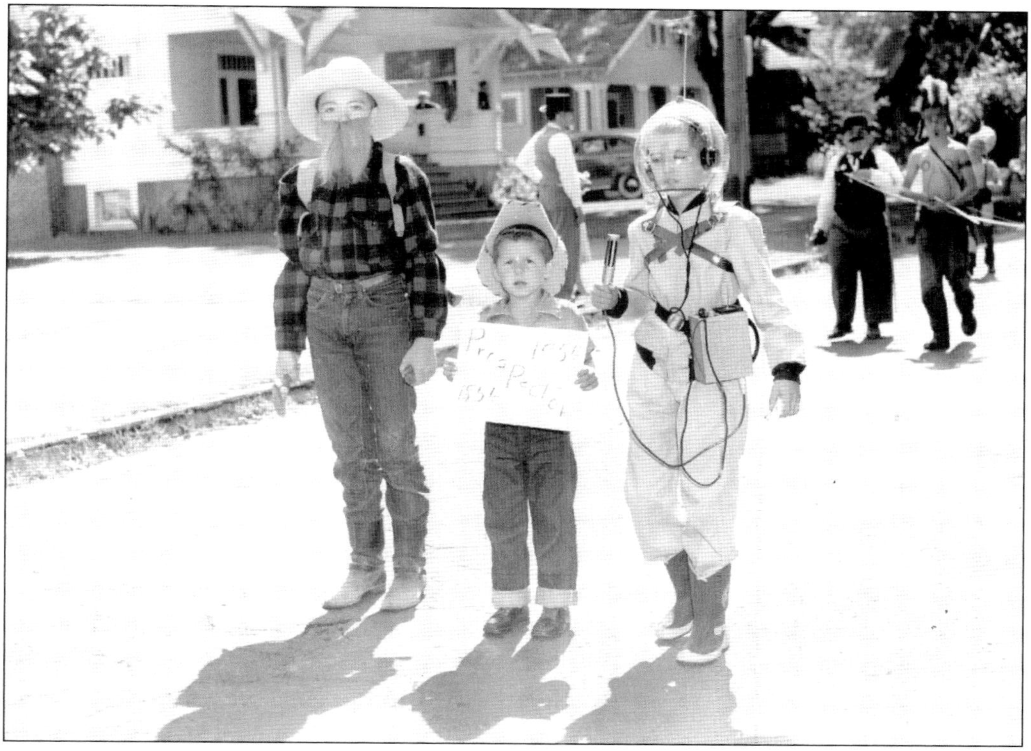

SILVERTON CENTENNIAL PET PARADE, 1954. Above are a historical then-and-now statement about the changing outlook for prospectors and more traditional Pet Paraders. Group themes are often popular, as with the kitties in the wagon below, who seem to be in pioneer garb. A second group sports a nursery rhyme sign honoring dairy products and arachnids. Yes, even pet spiders have been known to join the parade. (Both, Bill Hanson photograph; courtesy of SCHS.)

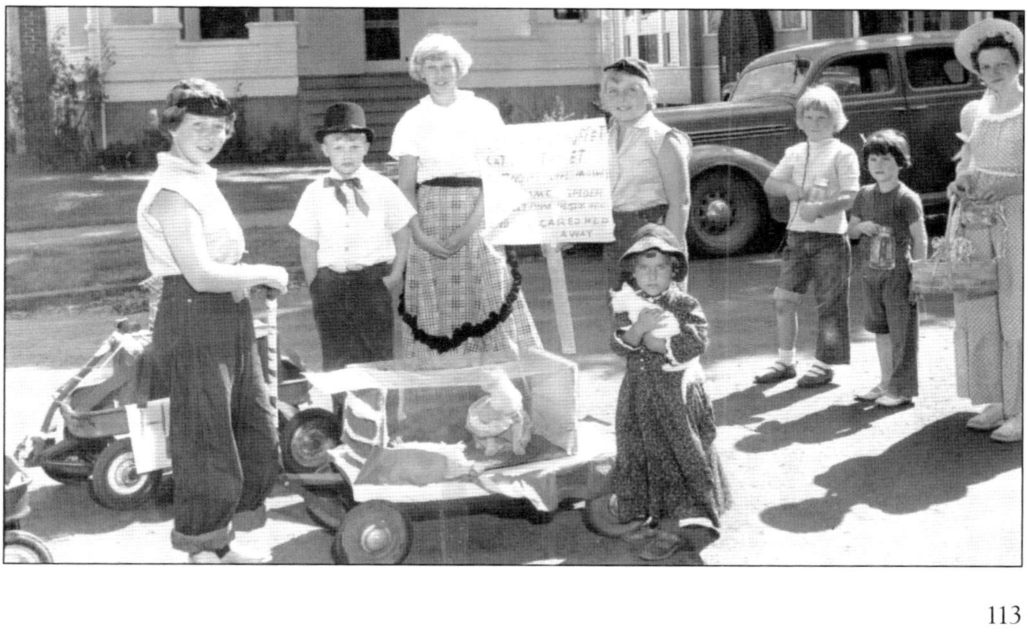

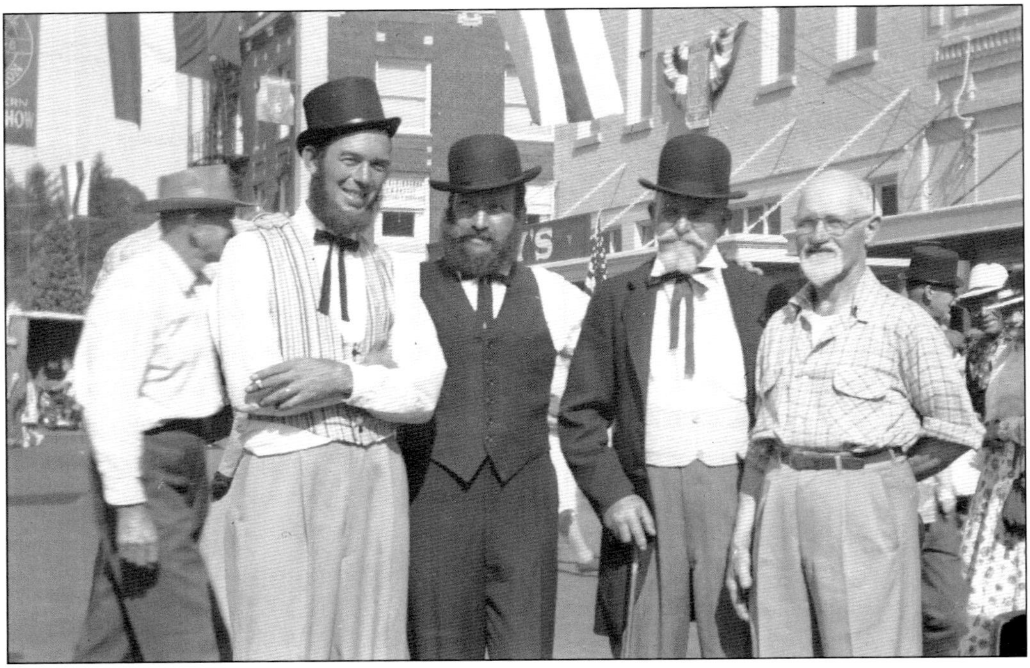

The Men of the Silverton Centennial, 1954. Shown are the centennial coordinators of 1954. These movers and shakers of the centennial pageant are shown in a blocked-off section of Main Street, Silverton's original town square, which was used for the celebration. Shown below is a two-seater Maxwell, which was formally owned by the late Percy Brown, the creator of Silverton's first power station and telephone company. (Above, courtesy of Almquist Studios; below, courtesy of SCHS.)

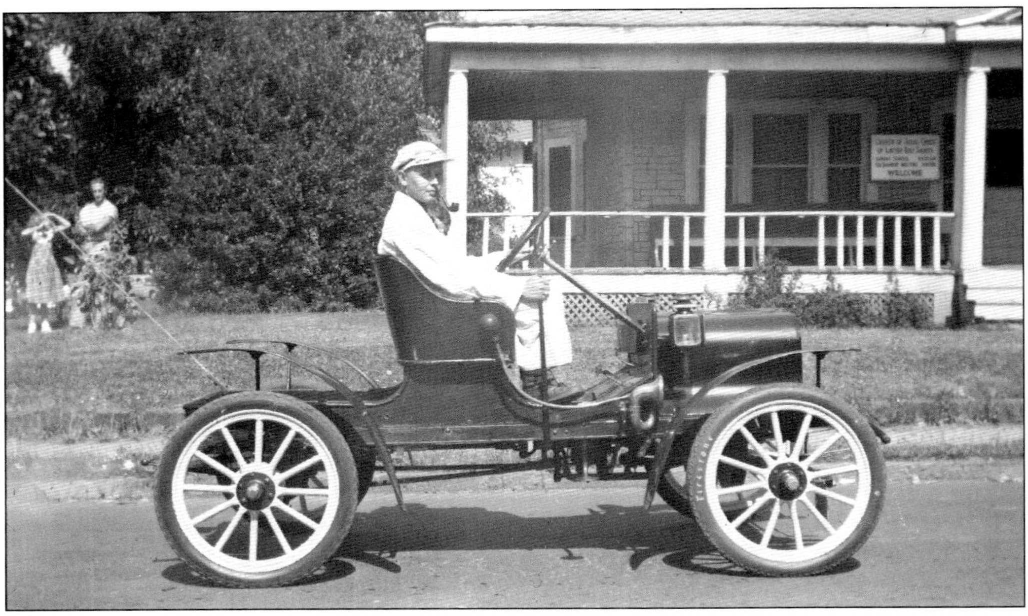

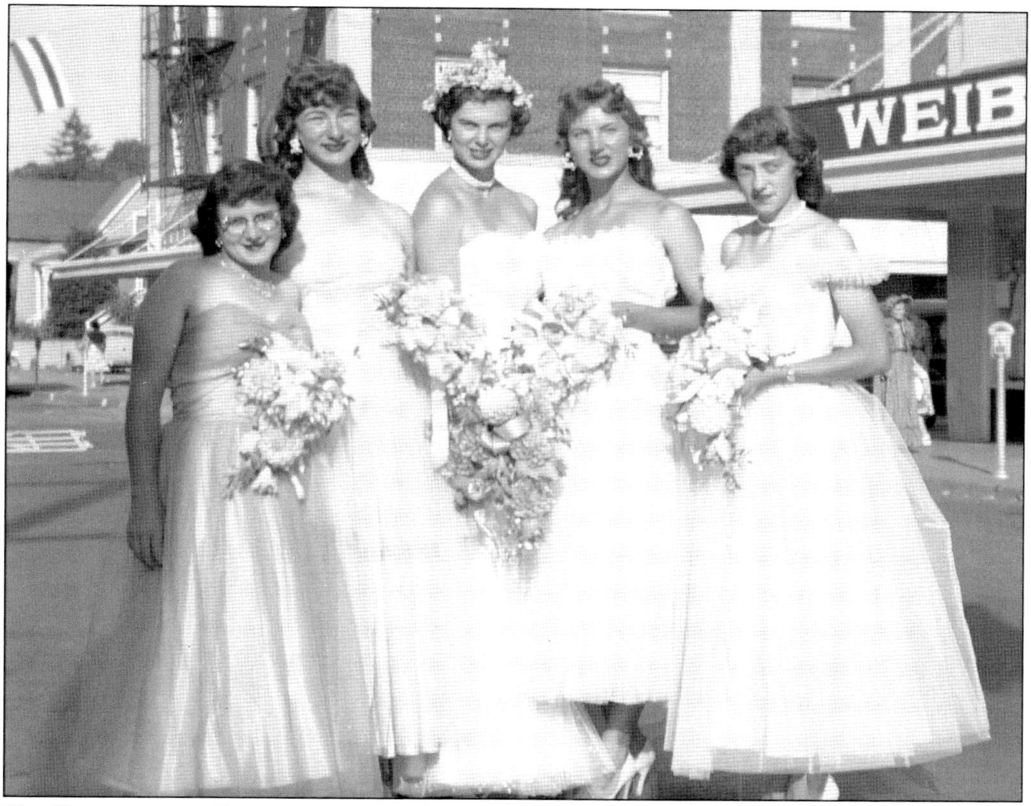

The Beauties and Gentlemen of the Silverton Centennial, 1954. The Silverton centennial court is shown above, and contestants of the Old-Time Whisker Contest are shown below for judging. Whiskers were judged in the following categories: full beards—scrawniest, most elaborate, and funniest; mustaches—Van Dyke (any assortment of mustaches and goatees), reddest, and funniest; and muttonchops—best trained. (Both, Paul Almquist photograph; courtesy of Almquist Studios.)

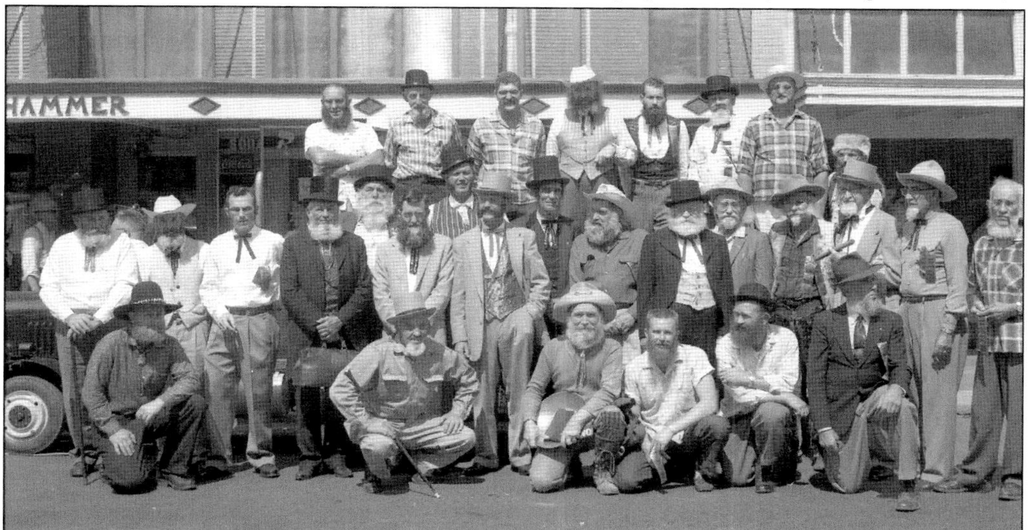

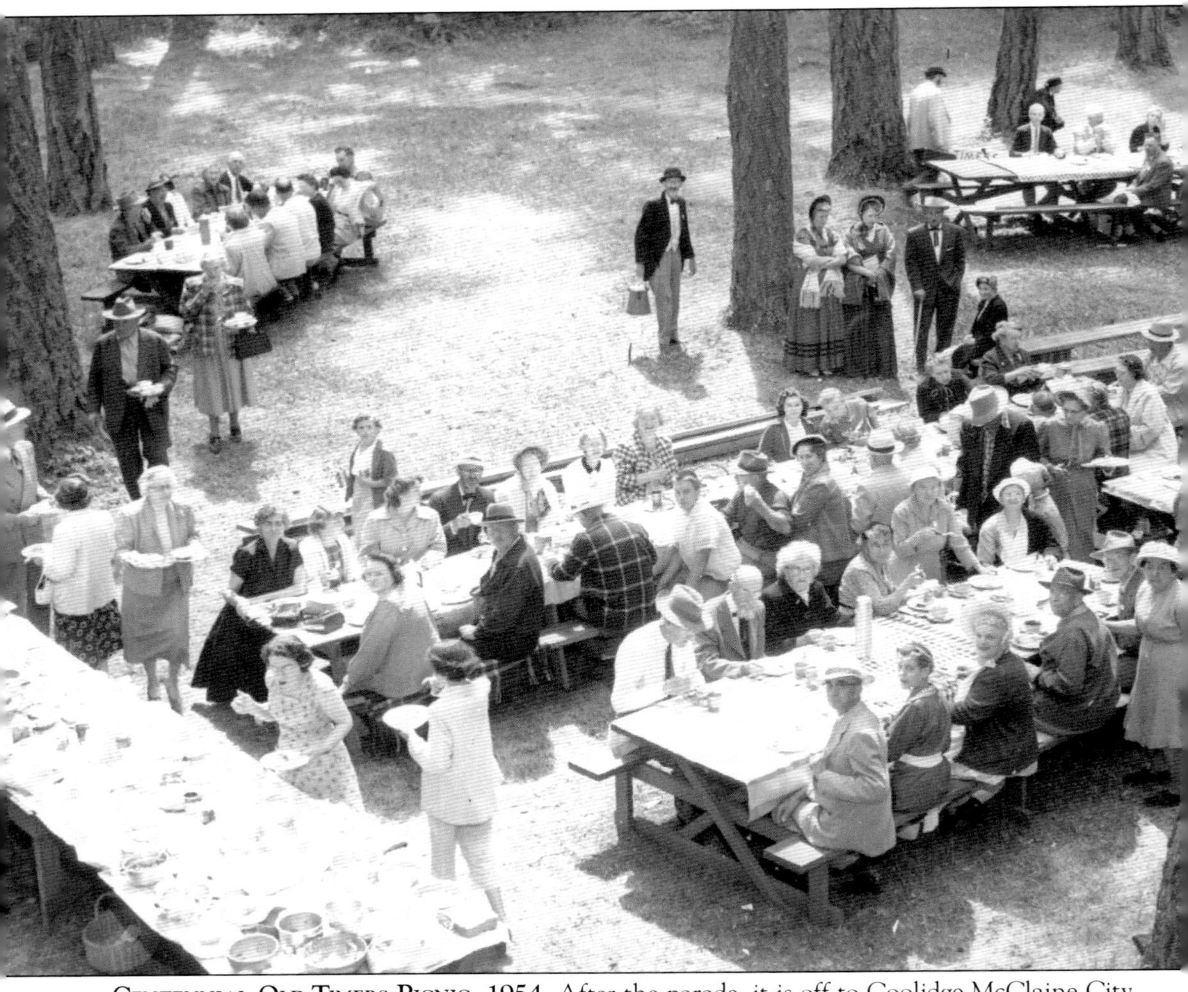

Centennial Old-Timers Picnic, 1954. After the parade, it is off to Coolidge-McClaine City Park for the Old-Timer's Picnic. This first weekend in August has been a traditional summer festival date for many decades. The name has changed over the years, but the celebratory spirit continues. (Courtesy of SCHS.)

Nine

History and the Future

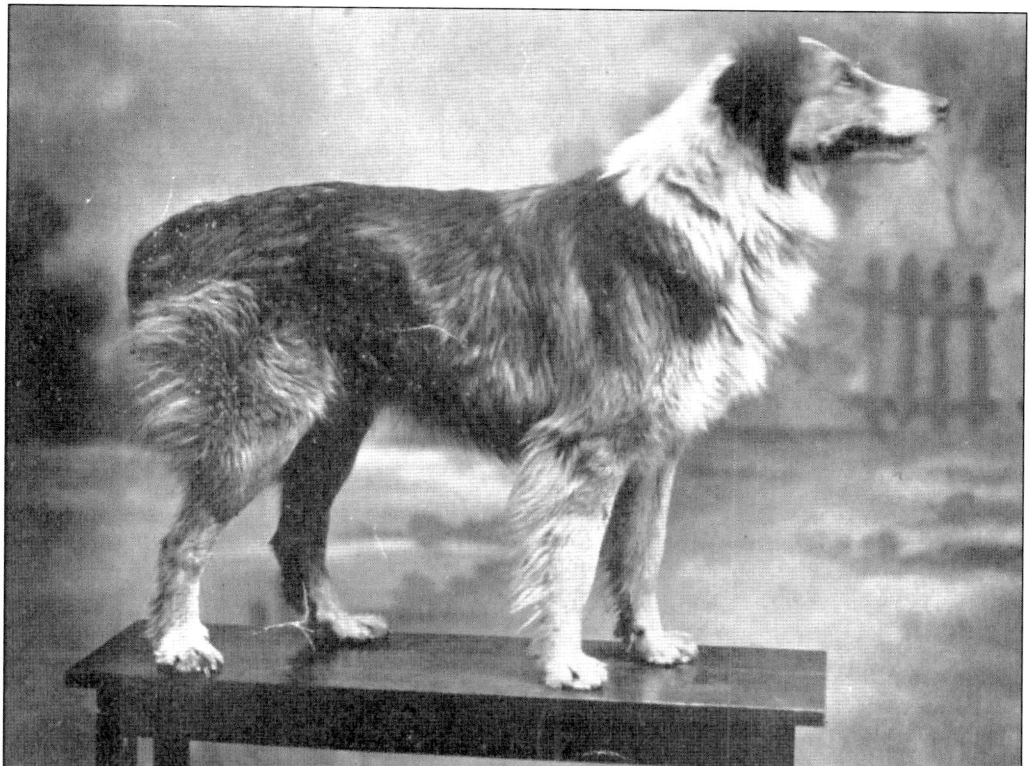

Bobbie the Wonder Dog, 1924. According to Charles Alexander's *Bobbie, a Great Collie*, "Three thousand miles on foot is a mere nothing when you are going home to those you love." Over the years, Silverton characters have included notable animals. Old Bobbie was with his owners in Indiana to visit relatives when he became separated from his family on August 15, 1923. Three days of searching failed to find any trace of the pooch. Six months later, on February 15, 1924, he arrived—hungry, exhausted, and feeble—at the family farm outside Silverton, where he lived out the rest of his days as a pampered canine miracle. Bobbie received a medal from the Oregon Humane Society (OHS) and is buried in the OHS Pet Cemetery. (Courtesy of SCHS.)

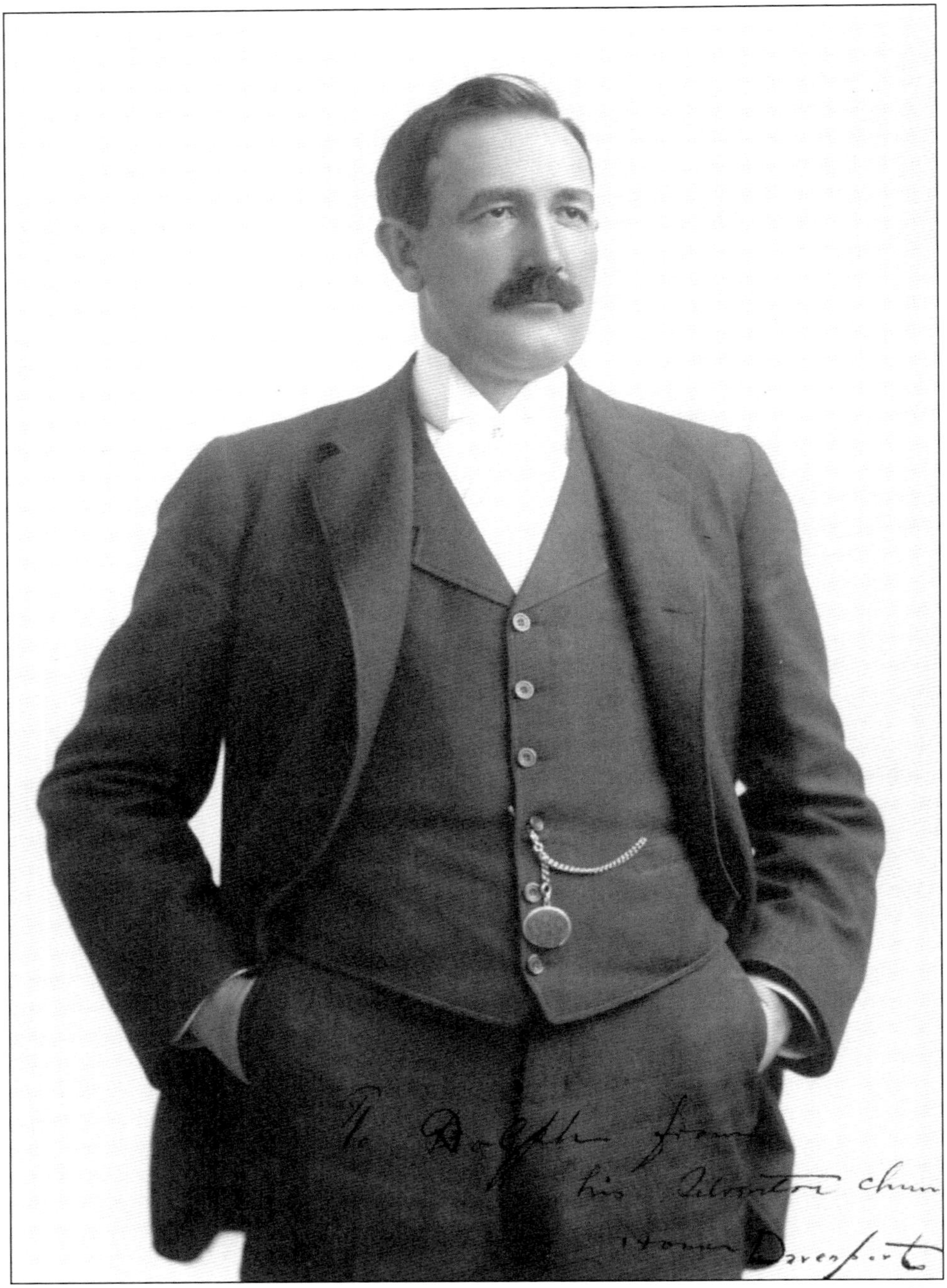

PORTRAIT OF HOMER C. DAVENPORT, 1899. This image was taken when *Hearst* cartoonist Homer C. Davenport was at the top of his game. He was the highest paid political cartoonist and had just published a book of his cartoons the year before. From all accounts, this is the preferred pose he struck during his highly successful lectures. The portrait is signed as follows: "To Dolph, from his Silverton Chum, Homer Davenport, NJ." Adolf was the Silverton merchant Adolf Wolf and father-in-law to Homer's cousin Pearl W. Geer, cofounder of Silverton's Liberal University and Homer's future manager. (Courtesy of the City of Silverton.)

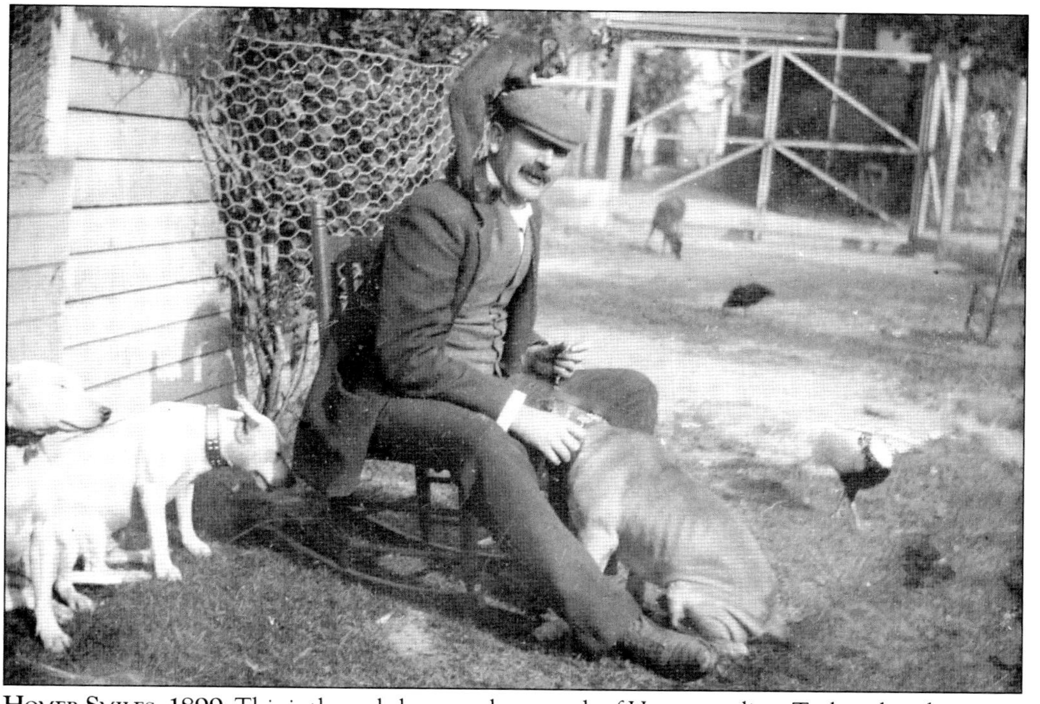

HOMER SMILES, 1899. This is the only known photograph of Homer smiling. Truly in his element at his home in East Orange, New Jersey, here he sits surrounded by his critters. He wears a cap—and his pet monkey, Swinnerton—on his head. The monkey was named for Jimmy Swinnerton, a fellow Hearst cartoonist Homer first met in San Francisco. (Courtesy of the Oregon State Library Photographic Collection.)

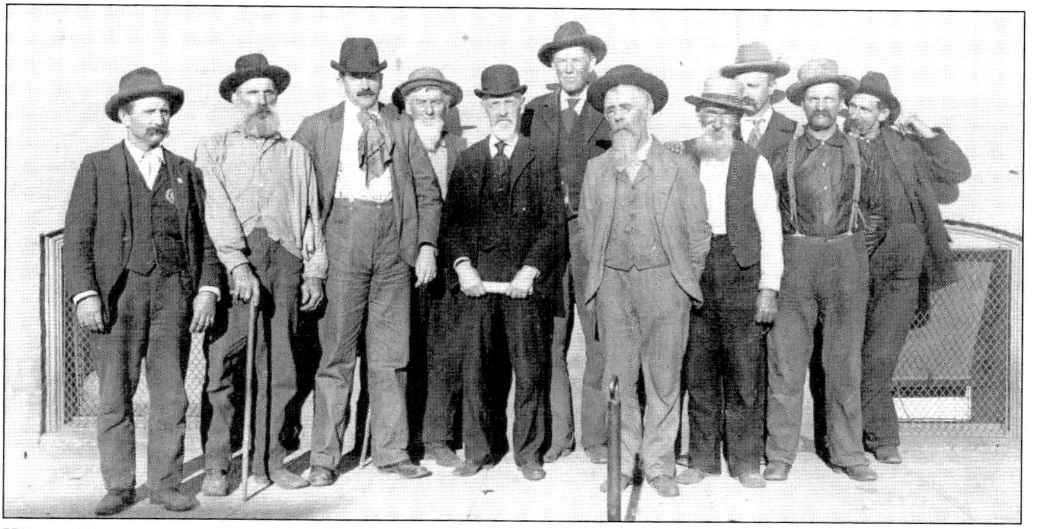

WHEN DAVENPORT COMES TO TOWN, 1905. Taking advantage of the afternoon light, Homer and company line up along side the west end of the Adolf Wolf Building for this portrait. Those pictured are, from left to right, police chief A.J. Simeral, C.C. Eisenhart, Homer Davenport, Captain Phelps, John Davenport, Trenton Hibbard, Joe Davenport, Mr. Fitzgerald, J.G. Smith, Jack Riches, and T.A. Hutton. John and Joe Davenport are Homer's uncles. (Courtesy of SCHS.)

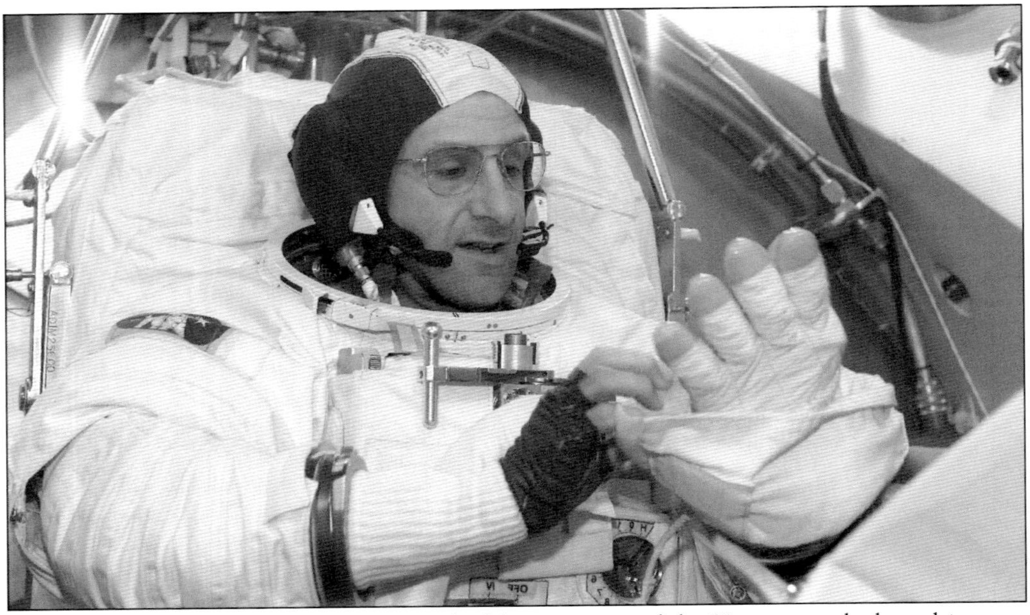

DR. PETTIT SUITS UP, 2002. More recently, Silverton entered the 21st century by launching one of its own into orbit—twice. Native Silvertonian and son to Dr. Virgil Pettit, Dr. Donald Pettit is a chemical engineer by training. The 1973 Silverton Union High School graduate applied several times and was finally accepted to the Astronaut Corps as a mission specialist. Here, he is seen preparing for a mock extravehicular activity prior to launch. (Courtesy of NASA.)

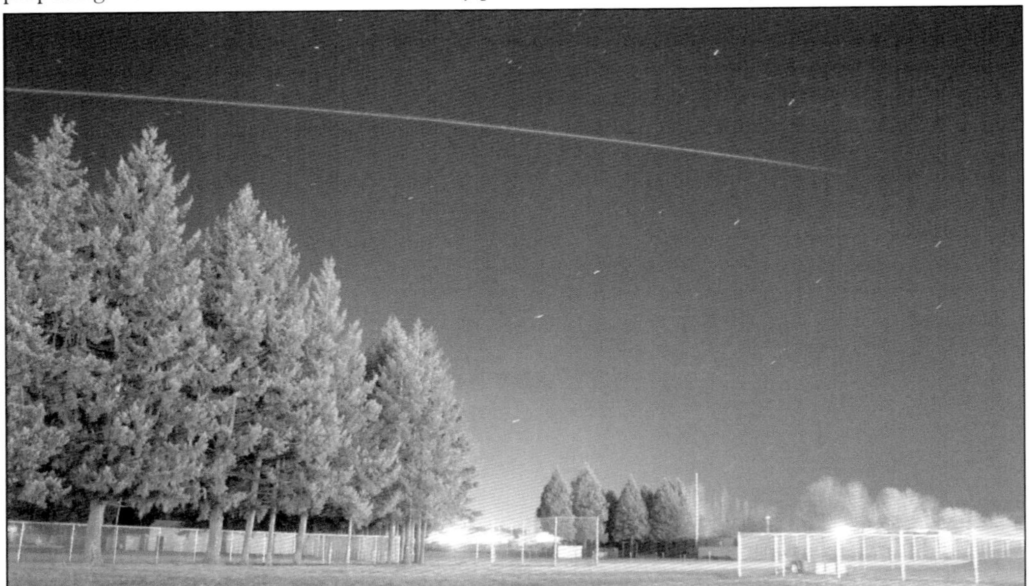

SPACE STATION FROM SILVERTON, 2003. While on the International Space Station for what was going to be a two-month assignment, the space shuttle *Columbia* was lost on reentry. Dr. Pettit and his crewmates were forced to extend their stay to six months, returning to earth under manual control in a Russian *Soyuz*. This is a three-minute time exposure of the International Space Station taken from Silverton Union High School. (Gus Frederick photograph.)

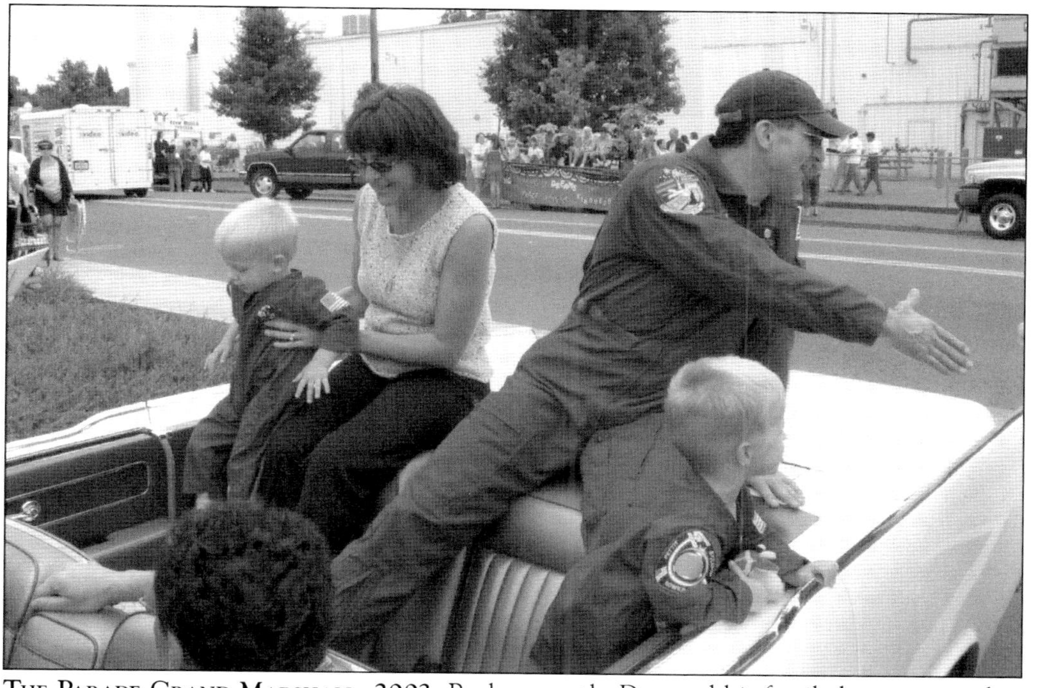

The Parade Grand Marshall, 2003. Back on earth, Don and his family have returned to Silverton for the 30th reunion of the SUHS class of 1973 and the annual Homer Davenport Days parade. Don and Miki Pettit with their twins, Evan and Garrett, wave to the crowds. The old cannery building is in the background. (Gus Frederick photograph.)

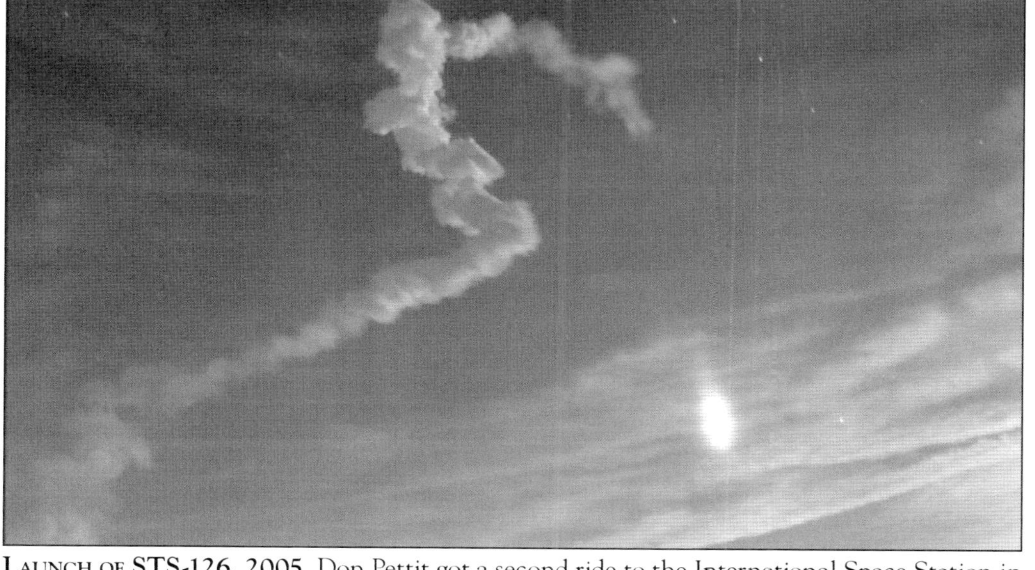

Launch of STS-126, 2005. Don Pettit got a second ride to the International Space Station in 2005 for only a couple of weeks. For this trip, he was part of the crew for the shuttle *Endeavour.* This time exposure was taken during the launch from Kennedy Space Center. It shows the exhaust plume of the solid rocket boosters and a bright line indicating the shuttle's path over the horizon and into orbit. (Gus Frederick photograph.)

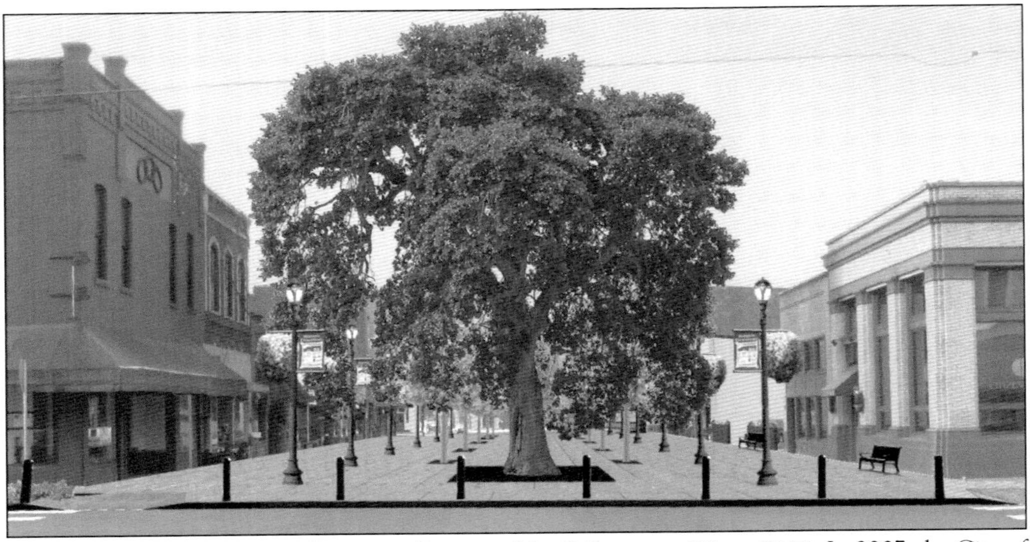

Streetscape Enhancement Project, Concept No. 5, Looking West, 2011. In 2007, the City of Silverton, along with a citizen's advisory group, started looking at ways to improve, enhance, and revitalize Silverton's historical downtown business core. At a town meeting held in the Silverton High School theater, city planner Steve Kay presented five conceptual proposals specifically for the modification of the East Main Street area between Water and First Streets. The fifth concept called for a new pedestrian plaza and the planting of a heritage oak tree. (Courtesy of the City of Silverton.)

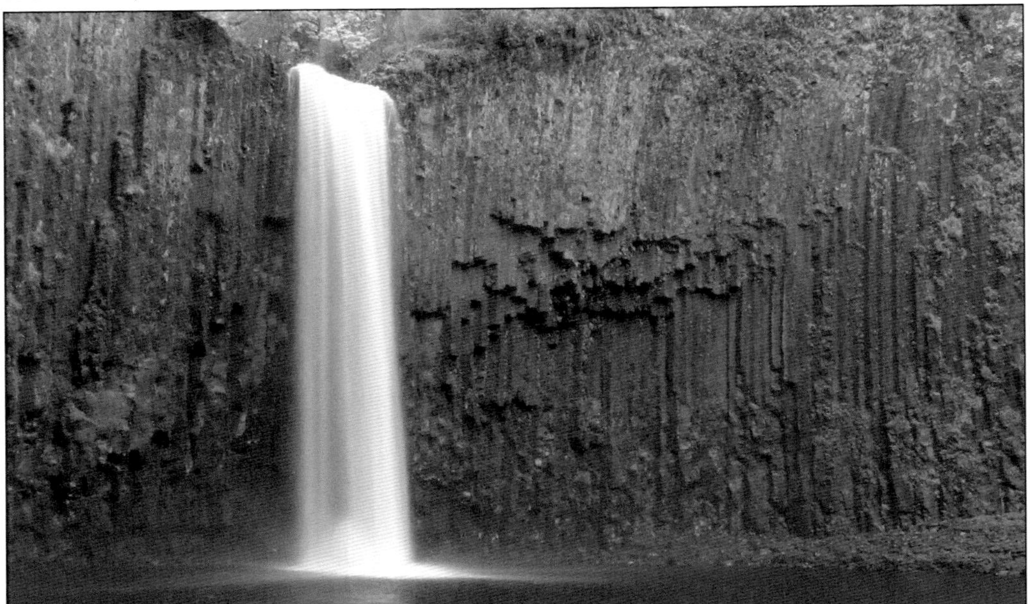

Abiqua Falls, 130 Feet, 2010. The Silverton Country and the town are deeply tied to Abiqua Creek. Over the years, various municipal water schemes have come and gone. Currently, 95 percent of the city's water arrives by way of an elegant aqueduct system, courtesy of gravity and the Abiqua Creek. A dozen or so miles upstream of the city's dam is the majestic Abiqua Falls. Local Silverton daredevil Doug Patton dove off of the falls in 1974. (Gus Frederick photograph.)

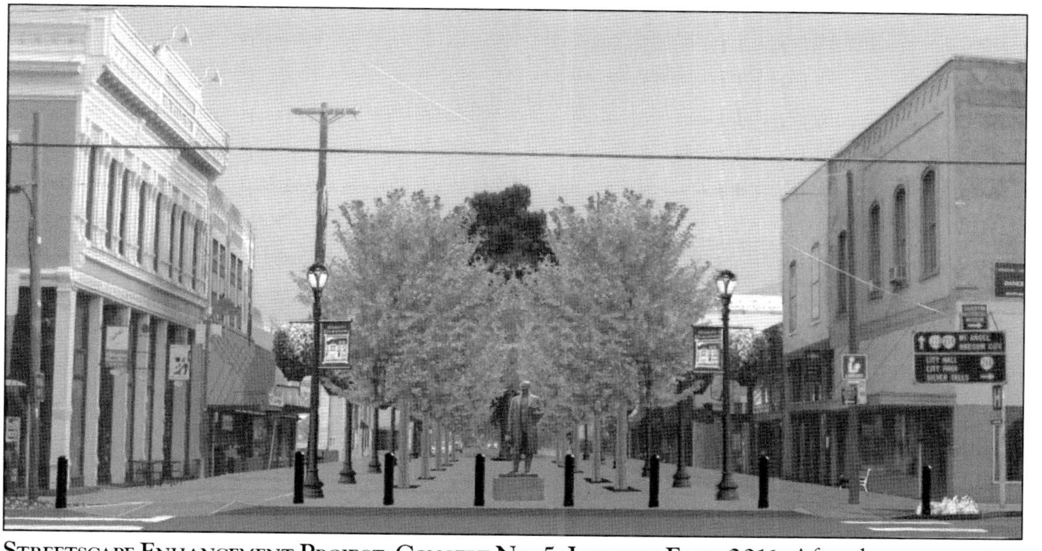

Streetscape Enhancement Project, Concept No. 5, Looking East, 2011. After the presentation, the attendees of the town hall meeting were given a blue sticker to place on their favorite concept. The other four proposals, all variations of vehicular shuffling, lost out to concept No. 5, which did not include vehicles but did include a new oak. In the end, local opposition from a vocal minority killed this project. (Courtesy of the City of Silverton.)

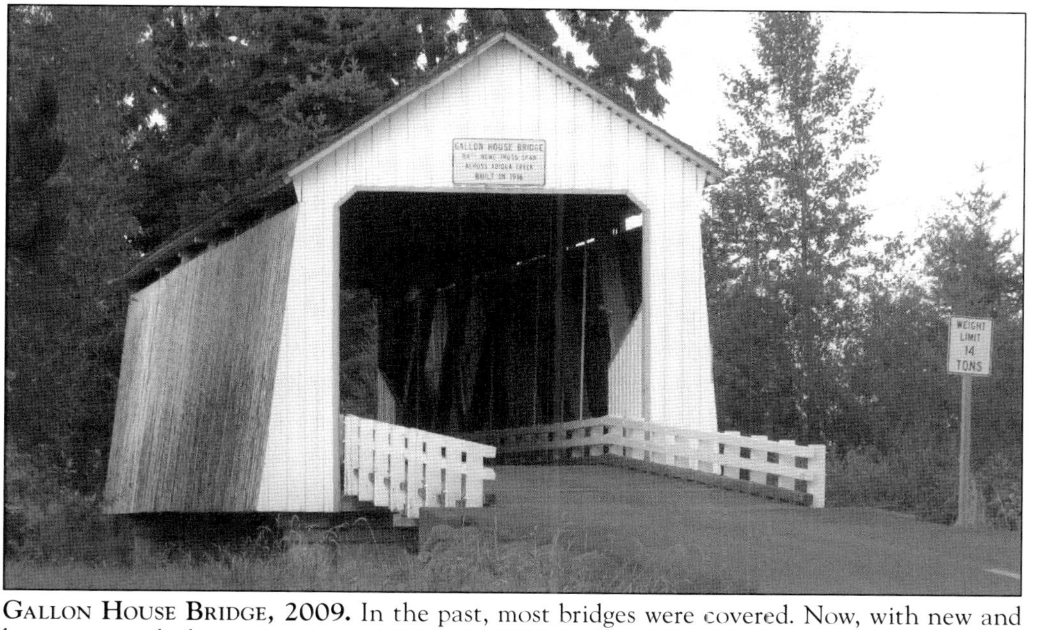

Gallon House Bridge, 2009. In the past, most bridges were covered. Now, with new and better materials, having to protect bridges from the elements is not an issue, and one by one, covered bridges were replaced. Today, the only remaining covered bridge in Marion County is Gallon House, which spans the Abiqua just northwest of town. The name came from the fact that even before Prohibition, Silverton had passed local ordinances against the sale of alcohol. Mount Angel had no such laws, so imbibers met halfway in a hands-across-the-water show of intercommunity cooperation. Then Prohibition happened, and all booze was out, even in Mount Angel. But the name stuck, and the bridge survived. (Gus Frederick photograph.)

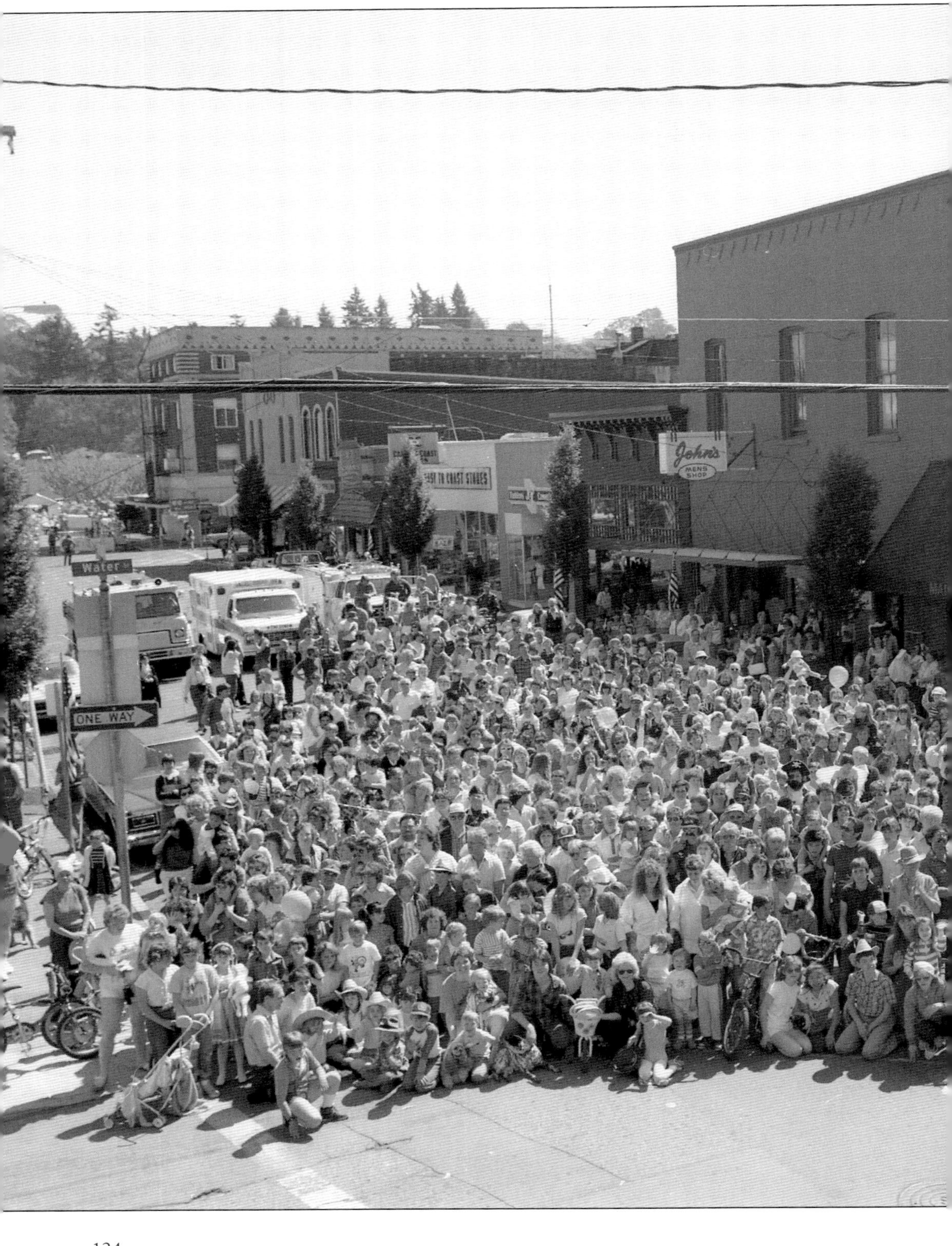
Water
ONE WAY
John's
MENS SHOP
COAST TO COAST STORES

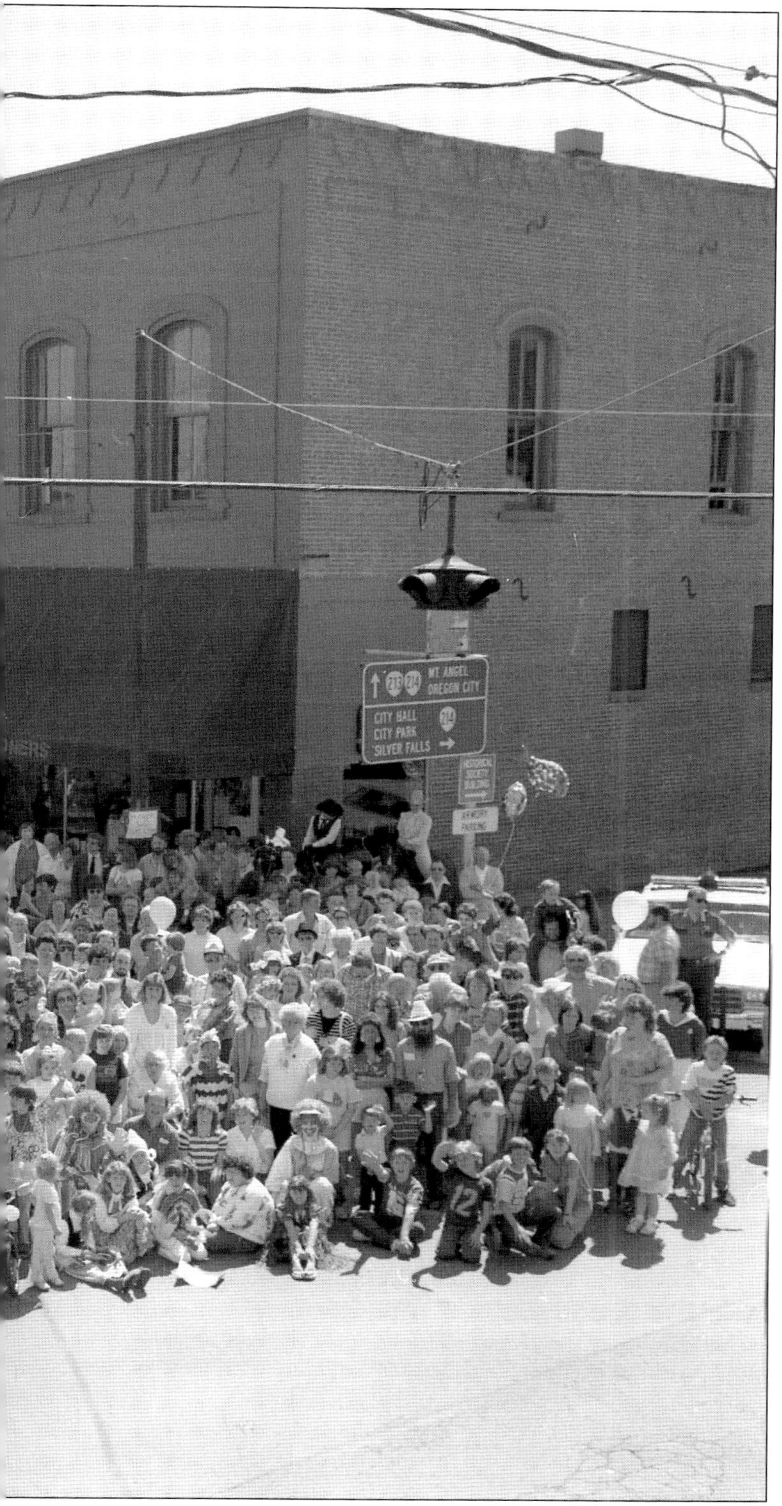

SILVERTON FAMILY PORTRAIT, 1986. A fitting final shot is this family portrait of Silverton, which was taken after the 1986 Pet Parade. Curt Almquist placed himself on the roof of the same building that his grandfather T.P. Trix Heidenstrom used to take shots of the 1918 Fourth of July parade on page 109. This scene was repeated several years later across the creek in Town Square Park. However, the early morning timing of the event limited the numbers. East Main Street, between Water and First Streets, is the town's "living room." Throughout any given year, the street is periodically blocked off from traffic so that the people can come and go without fear of being hit or run over. The task at hand is to pass the town and its stories down to the future generations as intact as possible. And a true Town Square Park should be in the center of town, with an oak tree in the living room. As Homer Davenport wrote over 100 years ago, "The tree seemed to be a center around which we could build." Truer words have never been written. (Curtis Almquist photograph; courtesy of Almquist Studios.)

BIBLIOGRAPHY

Alexander, Charles. *Bobbie, a Great Collie*. New York: Dodd, Mead and Company, 1926.

Davenport, Homer C. A *Country Boy*. New York City: G.W. Dillingham Company, 1910.

Down, Robert H. A *History of the Silverton Country*. Portland, OR: Berncliff, 1926.

Frederick, Gus. *Cartoons by Davenport: Annotated Re-issue*. Silverton, OR: Heron Graphics, 2006.

Hande, Jack. *Silverton Stories from the 1920s, 1930s, and 1940s*. Vol. 1. Silverton, OR: Hande Hus Publishing Company, 2003.

Hande, Jack. *Silverton Stories from the 1920s, 1930s, and 1940s*. Vol. 2. Silverton, OR: Hande Hus Publishing Company, 2005.

McEachern, Philip Duncan. *Silverton: Morphology of an Oregon Town*. Eugene, OR: self-published, 1989.

Wade, Murray. *Oregon Magazine–Silverton*. Salem, OR: November, 1921.

Wade, Murray. *Oregon Magazine–Silverton*. Salem, OR: December, 1929.

Index

Abiqua Falls, 122
Air show, 79
Ames Hardware, 69
Bobbie the Wonder Dog, 117
Byberg, Jonas J., 38
Cooley's Gardens, 39–43
Coolidge-McClaine Bank, 57, 58
Coolidge-McClaine City Park, 25
Covered bridge, 102, 123
Crandall Coon Price, Polly, 9
Davenport, Homer C., 104, 105, 118, 119
Downtown business core, 55
Eastman Brothers Factory, 37
Eugene Field School, 15, 52
Fischer Flouring Mill, 27–29
Fourth of July Parade, 106–109
Gallon House Bridge, 123
Geer, Pearl W., 50
Halladay, Bessie, 80
Hops pickers, 30, 31
International Space Station, 120, 121
Kolstad Cannery, 44, 76
Liberal University of Oregon, 50
Mammoth bones, 10
Mark Twain Junior High, 54
Mascher, Minnie, 48, 49
McClaine, Uncle Jake, 14, 25, 88
Old oak tree, 12, 13
Opera house, 68
Opera house fire, 71
Other Ones quartet, The, 90
Pavement, 22, 23
Pet Parade, 113
Pettit, Dr. Donald, 120, 121
Power plant, 20, 21
Silver Falls Timber Company, 34–36
Silverton Airport, 78–81
Silverton Centennial, 110–112
Silverton Centennial Aquacades, 110
Silverton Chamber of Commerce, 46
Silverton City Hall, 17
Silverton High School, 48, 49, 93–95
Silverton Lumber Company, 35
Silverton Marine Band, 89
Silverton Redsox, 96, 97
Silverton Rotary Club, 46
Silverton train station, 76, 77
Silverton Trombone Band, 88, 89
Space shuttle *Endeavour*, 121
Stayton Cannery, 45, 46
St. Pauls Catholic Church and School, 51
Utility poles, 18
Water well, 19
Wolf Building, 64
Wolfard's store, 65
Women of Woodcraft, 103